CURATING
CHURCH

Jacob D. Myers

CURATING CHURCH

Strategies for Innovative Worship

Abingdon Press™
Nashville

CURATING CHURCH:
Strategies for Innovative Worship

Copyright © 2018 by Abingdon Press

This book is printed on acid-free paper.

Library of Congress Cataloging-in-Publication Data has been requested.

ISBN 978-1-5018-3248-2

Scripture unless otherwise noted is from the Common English Bible. Copyright © 2011 by the Common English Bible. All rights reserved. Used by permission. www.CommonEnglishBible.com.

18 19 20 21 22 23 24 25 26 27—10 9 8 7 6 5 4 3 2 1

MANUFACTURED IN THE UNITED STATES OF AMERICA

to rechurch
(in memoriam)

"For a breathless moment in time,
a little group of diverse peoples
was caught up in a dream as old as life
and as new as a hope that just emerges
on the horizon of becoming [human]."

—Howard Thurman, *With Head and Heart*

Contents

Contents

Acknowledgments

There are so many to thank for their support and encouragement through the writing of this book. First and always, I wish to thank my incredible wife, Abby, and my amazing daughter, Taylor, for the joy they bring to my life. Truly, my cup overflows because of their love and kindness.

I also want to thank my editor at Abingdon Press, Constance Stella. Thank you for taking a risk on a freshly minted professor and for nurturing this project toward completion. This book literally would not have been possible without your support.

I am blessed to work with and among scholars and practitioners who sharpen my thinking. Thanks to Trey Lyon, Gerald Liu, Brandon Maxwell, Belinda McCafferty, Marietjie Pauw, Mindy McGarrah Sharp, and Richard Voelz, who each provided great feedback and insights on chapters of this book. *Curating Church* is better because of your wisdom and gentle correction.

I am thankful for the support of President Leanne Van Dyk and Dean Christine Roy Yoder for providing me an academic workload conducive to the life of the mind. As always, I am indebted to the amazing staff of the John Bulow Campbell Library at Columbia Theological Seminary for the community of scholarly inquiry they support. In particular, I am grateful for the work of Erica Durham and Mary Martha Riviere for tracking down articles and art exhibition tomes.

This book is dedicated to the men, women, and others who made up the beautiful, quirky, messy community of rechurch. You have taught me so much about how to be a minister and how to be in fellowship. There are far too many folks I wish to name than space allows, but there are several who deserve an extra portion of gratitude:

To Michael Tutterow, for going all-in on this risky—even dangerous—vision and for your grace, perseverance, and pastoral leadership through difficulties that you did not deserve;

To my fellow "junior ministers" (Matt Rich, Andy Smith, and Shelley Woodruff), for your creativity, your sarcasm, and your friendship;

To the rechurch band (Matt Norman, Lane Andrews, Paul Wallace, Elizabeth Wallace, Patrick McGuire, Keith Pierce, and Cayden Norman), and I especially want to thank our leader, Wes Hunter, for your easygoing spirit, incredible musical talent and vision, and for tolerating my mandolin playing;

To those who sacrificed so much time and energy to make rechurch happen—both in the spotlight and behind the scenes. In particular, I wish to thank Dale Doud, Abby Myers, Carolyn Meaders, Gwen Cottrell, Randall Hampton, Cecil Cannon, Ann Cannon†, Alexis Hunter, Lori Dunn Mayfield, Ric Mayfield, Michelle Norman, Abby Cook, Chip Yeager, Suzy Brister, Jim Wallace†, Hellen Wallace, Vicki Tutterow, Chuck Williams, Scott Pyron, Debra Pyron, Mandy Moses, Martinez Scorza, Sarah Scorza, and Cheryl Casper. Without your creativity, ingenuity, and composure under pressure, rechurch could not have become the blessing it was to so many.

Marti Andrews Cooke and Belinda McCafferty also deserve an extra portion of gratitude for making rechurch a space where children could worship God alongside adults and for keeping this dreamer's feet on the ground when my stratospheric visions were impossible.

Preface

Art is not an escape from life, but rather an introduction to it.

—*John Cage*[1]

My seminary prepared me wonderfully for the church of the 1950s. Though I received a robust and rigorous theological education, I entered ministry disillusioned by the disparity between my knowledge of things divine and my ignorance of contemporary ways of thinking and being.

After seminary, I began to serve in a borough of Atlanta called Little Five Points. There I attempted to plant a church in conscious conversation with postmodernity. My early years in ministry taught me many things, foremost among which was how ill-equipped I was to engage a culture that was foreign to me. I picked the name *Trinitas* for my fledgling community—and you do not need to know much about hipsters or homeless people to guess how little they use Latin.

Trinitas emerged through trial and error. I hosted weekly "theology on tap" conversations in a local pub, curated alternative worship experiences in a coffee shop/bakery that was not open on Sunday nights, and forged relationships through a weekly Texas Hold 'Em poker game at the Vortex (a bar whose façade is a giant skull).

The focus of my ministry was engagement. I wanted to understand how the gospel might make sense in such a radically post-Christian context. As my ministry unfolded, another concern emerged: How might we engage with postmodern cultures without abandoning so much of the church's

---

1. Richard Kostelanetz, *Conversing with Cage* (New York: Limelight Editions, 1991), 211.

theological richness? Thus, an ancillary aspect of my ministry was that of conservation through attempts at recontextualization, casting the church's figures and theologies in fresh light. I discovered that many of the folks I grew to love in Little Five Points had endured horrific injustices by the church. I found myself—through countless conversations over a frothy pint or a steaming mug—attending to these horrors and seeking forgiveness on the church's behalf.

Through the ministries of worship, preaching, spiritual formation, and of course, church planting, I began to witness transformation. This was not a transformation as I might have previously defined it based on the Southern Baptist vocabulary I'd inherited. The transformation I observed was a transformation *in* culture. It did not mean a radical reorientation or abandonment of the cultural patterns that make Little Five Points what it is; rather, I witnessed transformation taking shape in small ways: a willingness to talk about God amid suffering; an openness to community not based on objectification or abuse; a heightened sensitivity to the divine in the world around them; a welcoming of otherness.

Though much has happened in my life since my time in Little Five Points came to an end, the questions and concerns that shaped my ministry there continue to inform my teaching and research. As a professor of homiletics at Columbia Theological Seminary, I seek to equip my students to engage cultures with a "prophetic imagination," to borrow my colleague emeritus's parlance.[2] This book presents the best of my thinking to date at the intersection of culture and ministry. As I wrote this book, I imagined people called of God to proclaim the good news of Jesus Christ and the possibility of new life made possible through God's love and justice. But none of us minister in a vacuum. Ministry takes place *in* culture. Thus, I hope that this book will provide both a theoretical and practical framework for curating church in cultures.

---

2. See Walter Brueggemann, *The Prophetic Imagination*, 2nd ed. (Minneapolis: Fortress, 2001).

Curating Church: A Vision for Ministry

*Curating is caring for the culture, above all by enabling its artistic
or creative transformers to pursue their work. This facilitation is done, preferably,
with empathy and insight, effectively, and with some style.*

—*Terry Smith*[1]

Art refracts life. Art draws from the world even as it reflects the world back to itself with shocking, sometimes frightening, clarity. The supreme power of art—its "magic power," as Herbert Marcuse calls it—is art's capacity to make us discontent with the world of our experience.[2] By offering a vision of how the world exists and how it *could* be, art's power to subvert, to rupture, everyday experience calls for a response.

Many have argued that pastors and church leaders are artists.[3] Such models for ministry have failed to win me over. For starters, I've never been any

---

1. Terry Smith, *Thinking Contemporary Curating* (New York: Independent Curators International, 2012), 3.

2. Herbert Marcuse, *One-Dimensional Man: Studies in the Ideology of Advanced Industrial Society*, 2nd ed. (London: Routledge, 1991), 65.

3. For instance, see Bruce Ellis Benson, *Liturgy as a Way of Life: Embodying the Arts in Christian Worship* (Grand Rapids, MI: Baker Academic, 2013); Eugene L. Lowry, *The Homiletical Beat: Why All Sermons Are Narrative* (Nashville: Abingdon, 2012); Kirk Byron Jones, *The Jazz of Preaching: How to Preach with Great Freedom and Joy* (Nashville: Abingdon, 2010); Constantine R. Campbell, *Outreach and the Artist: Sharing the Gospel with the Arts* (Grand Rapids, MI: Zondervan, 2013); Albert Rouet, *Liturgy and the Arts*, trans. Paul Philibert (Collegeville, MN:

good at art. I can't draw or paint or sculpt. I have little musical talent—and I am under no delusion that just because I know where to put my fingers on a guitar's frets to form a G-chord that that makes me a musician.

Aptitude aside, I cannot stand the pressure of it all. Ready. Set. ART! Art is a verb. Standing before an easel, brush in hand, I freeze. It's as if the white nothingness of the canvas bleeds into my soul, drowning me in my own creativity.

But I have always appreciated the works of others. I enjoy standing in a gallery or sitting in a concert hall, soaking it all in. I love to quaff from the artistic goblets of others. Such moments of aesthetic pleasure fill me up. Most of the time I have no clue what the artist intends by his, her, or their creation. And I don't much care. What I love about art is what it does to *me*, how it sets my mind—my very spirit—on a path I could not have otherwise envisioned. Art helps me. Art challenges me. Art makes me see the world differently.

Over the past twenty years, I have followed God's call to care for "the least and the lost," to proclaim the gospel, to serve Christ's church. If I have accomplished anything sufficient to the calling God has placed upon my life, it is due to my ability to filter and organize the work of others who've come before me in such a way that those under my care have glimpsed the gospel afresh. What I came to realize is that there is a name for people like this: *curators*.

Curation: Meaning and History

Nobody knows who curated the first art exhibition, but this practice is as old as recorded history. Myths, rituals, and cultural customs are acts of curation—filtering, preserving, and combining materials of social significance to shape a people's sense of identity and purpose.

At its most primitive core, curation is the art of selection. But the *process* of selection, by which one chose *this* lithograph or *those* vases or *these* stories among a host of others, says a lot about how we think and how we

Liturgical Press, 1997); John S. McClure, *Mashup Religion: Pop Music and Theological Invention* (Waco, TX: Baylor University Press, 2011); Trygve David Johnson, *The Preacher as Liturgical Artist: Metaphor, Identity, and the Vicarious Humanity of Christ* (Eugene, OR: Cascade Books, 2014); and Manuel Luz, *Imagine That: Discovering Your Unique Role as a Christian Artist* (Chicago: Moody Publishers, 2009).

understand the world (of God). To put it technically, curation both reflects prior epistemological commitments *and* it constitutes a method of producing knowledge. More about this later.

The word *curation*, much like examples of curation, has taken many forms throughout history. Etymologically, the word is ambiguous. The Latin noun *cura*, and its verbal form, *curare*, means both "cure" and "care." This double-meaning is not insignificant.

In ancient Rome, *curatores* were civil servants who took care of a city's infrastructure (e.g., aqueducts, bathhouses, sewers). Pontius Pilate, for instance, is designated by the first-century Roman historian Tacitus as the *procurator* of Judea, an administrative posting in which he was charged *to take care of* a province (i.e., to collect imperial taxes and manage the military).

In Medieval times, the word took on more metaphysical dimensions. The *curatus* was a priest, so named for his work of providing care for the souls of a parish and administering the "cure" of the gospel. In 590 CE, Pope Gregory the Great penned a work entitled *De Cura Pastorali*, or *Pastoral Care*. This pamphlet became a bestseller (to put it anachronistically) when the Byzantine Emperor Maurice mandated the work's distribution to every bishop within the Empire. Gregory's words transformed the function of the parish priest or bishop to that of a spiritual father charged to care for the souls of his parishioners, much as the *abba*, or ascetic elder, cares for his monks.[4]

It was not until the eighteenth century that the *curator* emerged as the one charged with taking care of a museum's collection. Art historians find a rare point of unanimity in describing the sociopolitical significance of the first museums in Europe. National galleries like the Louvre and the British Museum, both of which were established in 1753, were "handmaidens of imperialism," depicting the political masters to their respective publics as "custodians of world culture, rescuers of what had been ignorantly neglected or even threatened with destruction in the countries of origin."[5] God save the Queen!

Art exhibitions also started to emerge beyond the auspices of state-sanctioned museums, and the function of the curator expanded. The most

---

4. See George E. Demacopoulos's helpful introduction in *St. Gregory the Great: The Book of Pastoral Rule, Popular Patristics*, vol. 34 (Yonkers, NY: St. Vladimir's Seminary Press, 2007).

5. Karsten Schubert, *The Curator's Egg: The Evolution of the Museum Concept from the French Revolution to the Present Day*, 3rd ed. (London: Ridinghouse, 2008), 23.

famous example of this is the *Salon de Paris*, which was commissioned in the late-seventeenth century by the French Academy of Fine Arts. Originally restricted to members of the Royal Academy of Painting and Sculpture and thereby reflecting an aesthetic elitism, for more than a century the *Salon* was deemed the most prestigious annual or biannual art event in the world.

In 1748, the Academy established a jury to curate the exhibition, further elevating the *Salon's* prominence. However, in 1863 the *Salon* jury rejected around three thousand paintings (including works by Manet, Cezanne, and Pissarro!). The public outcry led Emperor Napoleon III to allow an alternative venue to exhibit these rejections. This show became known as the *Salon des Refusés*, (*Exhibition of Rejects*). This event led to the proliferation of exhibitions that were organized by artists and curators beyond the auspices of the State and Academy.

When most of us hear the word *curator* today, we think of one who works in a museum or art gallery, preparing exhibits for public consumption. In many ways, this carries forward the democratic ideals of the Enlightenment, whereby the museum is seen to function as an "egalitarian enabler," blurring the borders between the elite and the general populace.

Only in the 1960s did the curator become conceivable apart from formal institutions. Groundbreakers like Harald Szeemann in Europe and Walter Hopps in the United States fashioned art installations that challenged the institutional framework of art, revolutionizing the curator's role. Without the need to satisfy a museum's board of directors and wealthy patrons, curators were free to conceive exhibitions that challenged and subverted sociopolitical and economic norms. It's easier to speak boldly and truthfully when you aren't afraid of losing your job—a truth that pastors and church leaders know only too well.

Curation and Culture

Curation is homeomorphic to culture. Curation evinces cultures as a continuous stretching and bending of infinitely diverse manifestations of human sociality into new shapes. These new shapes are made of the same substance as the cultures themselves. In other words, curators can claim no Archimedean point of privilege apart from culture. Drawing upon Kathryn Tanner's work in her magisterial text *Theories of Culture*, I take "culture" to signify a universal, irreducibly diverse, differentiating, conventional, contingent, and world-defining element of human society.[6]

And yet, like a *Möbius strip* (a twisted band forming a closed loop with only one surface or side), curation produces variations out of our cultural topographies that can shift (or twist) the epistemological ground upon which we stand. By this I mean that curation operates within the same Euclidean space as culture itself; it is inseparable from culture. And yet, at the same time, curation transforms culture—reinforcing, challenging, and pruning the materials and concepts that will in turn reinforce, challenge, and prune future cultural artifacts. Movement is inherent to this process: we may end where we started, but we will not do so without being changed in the process. Likewise, curation transforms the curator as much as it transforms the audience.

Curation is also temporally significant. It tethers us to the past because our education and life experiences shape what we value and deem worthy of conservation. To put it another way, our aesthetic choices today arise out of our prior encultured learning about what counts as beautiful, none of which are value-neutral.[7] Curation orients us to the future, as well. The very act

6. Kathryn Tanner, *Theories of Culture: A New Agenda for Theology* (Minneapolis: Augsburg Fortress, 1997), 25–29. Tanner's emphasis on the porosity and the constantly shifting characteristics of culture instruct the work of cultural curation: "Interconnections among cultural elements . . . are never so fixed that they cannot be broken apart and rearranged in the ongoing course of cultural process" (56).

7. There is a difference between our processes of sense perception and the categories we employ to make sense of our perceptions. This difference is named in the hiatus between *aesthesis* and *aesthetics*. Both are Greek terms, and Western ways of thinking in the wake of our inherited Greek-philosophical heritage have tended to subsume the former into the latter. In other words, *aesthesis* has been made to ride shotgun for *aesthetics*. *Aesthesis* signifies an elementary awareness of sensory stimulation. This word points to our experience of smell, sight, and hearing. *Aesthetics*, on the other hand, takes our processes of perception a step further. *Aesthetics* aims to classify our sense perceptions, helping us to differentiate the fragrant from the acrid, the beautiful from the ugly, the melodious from the cacophonous. In recent years, decolonial interventions between aesthetics/aesthesis have impacted conversations taking place in the art world. In brief, decolonial aesthetics/aesthesis attempts to free art from the epistemic and sensory fetters of Western imperialism that persist long after the colonial project has fallen apart. See Walter D. Mignolo, *The Darker Side of Western Modernity: Global Futures, Decolonial Options* (Durham, NC: Duke University Press, 2011). See also Mignolo's essays: "Coloniality of Power and De-Colonial Thinking," *Culture Studies* 21, no. 2/3 (2007): 155–67 and "Delinking: The Rhetoric of Modernity, the Logic of Coloniality and the Grammar of De-coloniality," *Culture Studies* 21, no. 2/3 (2007): 449–515. For a helpful overview of

of conservation is teleological—and maybe even eschatological—in that it projects us into the future, drawing from the past and the present to help us imagine the world otherwise. There is an intentionality to curation that displays our concern for the future.

Hans Ulrich Obrist, one of the most prominent art curators in the world today, argues convincingly that the emergence of curation as an enterprise unto itself arises directly out of contemporary cultural phenomena. He writes, "The current vogue for the idea of curating stems from a feature of modern life that is impossible to ignore: the proliferation and reproduction of ideas, raw data, processed information, images, disciplinary knowledge and material products that we are witnessing today." He goes on to note the effects of the Internet on the production and dissemination of cultures and the pro-liferation of cheaply produced objects. The result, Obrist argues, "has been a shift in the ratio of importance between making new objects and choosing from what is already there."[8] We could do worse than to suggest that curation has arisen out of contemporary cultures as a mode of engaging with those cultures meaningfully.

Contemporary Artistic Curation

By its most common understanding in popular conversation, curation is about the present. There is a *nowness* to curation that keeps a finger on the pulse of culture and aims to synch with that rhythm. I learned this firsthand when I worked as a youth pastor in the early 2000s. I recall leading a multi-week series for my youth group on sacred and secular music. The goal, I hasten to add, was not to condemn secular music and convince all my youth to listen to DC Talk; rather, I wanted them to develop a more sophisticated musical awareness sharpened by theology.

I graduated from high school in 1997, just two or so years before I was to lead this Sunday night series. I selected some of my favorite bands from when

this movement, see Rubén Gaztambide-Fernández, "Decolonial options and Artistic/Aesthetic Entanglements: An Interview with Walter Mignolo," *Decolonization: Indigeneity, Education & Society* 3, no. 1 (2014): 196–212.

8.   Hans Ulrich Obrist with Asad Raza, *Ways of Curating* (New York: Farrar, Straus and Giroux, 2014), 24.

I was in high school: Nirvana, Stone Temple Pilots, and Pearl Jam, along with artists from different genres whom I knew but never particularly enjoyed. The series was an absolute bust!

My youth had never heard of many of these bands. They recognized songs by Green Day and the Red Hot Chili Peppers because these bands had continued to produce hits. Moreover, there were marked cultural differences between my Jacksonville, Florida, and their Henrietta, North Carolina. These differences shaped our musical sensibilities. By week three, they were leading the conversation, teaching me what constituted "popular" music in their context. The point of this story is to underscore the temporal and spatial flux that sustains curation. Our filters wear out quickly, and they travel poorly; indeed, facing our daily multimedia barrage, these filters require changing almost daily.

The verb "to curate," and its gerund form, "curating," emerged in the 1980s. The verbalization of curation has radically expanded the term's semantic range. In our day, people curate all kinds of things: menus at gastropubs; clothing at boutiques; knitted scarves on Etsy; trends on BuzzFeed; and even Pokémon cards on Scratch, which is an event-driven programming language allowing users to create and publish material online. A recent *New York Times* article traces the evolution of the verb "to curate," noting how its mere mention evokes a sense of authority, adding value to that which is curated.[9]

An exemplar of this curatorial impulse is Lin-Manuel Miranda. The writer/director/ performer of *Hamilton* fame curates Spotify lists frequently and shares them with his fans. Some are about relationships or breakups. Others focus on social justice issues (immigration, racism, etc.). Through his curatorial efforts, Miranda doesn't merely reflect culture; he shapes culture. What is more, Miranda is rather adamant that we should listen to his mixes in order, as he takes great pains to curate the rise and fall of his Spotify lists.[10] We need not strain to recognize these parallels with the energies we pastors and church leaders expend on our weekly liturgies.

---

9.   Alex Williams, "On the Tip of Creative Tongues," *The New York Times*, October 2, 2009, http://www.nytimes.com/2009/10/04/fashion/04curate.html?_r=0.

10.   I am indebted to my friend and pastor, Trey Lyon, for directing me to Miranda's Spotify curations.

Not all embrace this phenomenon. Art critic David Balzer's neologism "curationism"—a word with overt pejorative reference to creationism— critiques the curatorial impulse, which, since the mid-1990s, has come to dominate Western thought and practice. One of the major takeaways of Balzer's book is the self-reflexivity inherent in curation. He notes that we curate "in relation to ourselves," meaning, that curation holds enormous sway over how we understand ourselves in relation to our world of experience.[11] Such self-reflexivity also undergirds the work of pastoral ministry, where our theological and sociopolitical proclivities shape what we do and say in worship.

The self-reflexive element of contemporary art curation is articulated most poignantly by Paul O'Neill in an essay entitled "The Co-dependent Curator," published in *Art Monthly*. He writes,

> We are becoming so self-reflexive that exhibitions often end up as nothing more or less than art exhibitions curated by curators curating curators, curating artists, curating artworks, curating exhibitions (all of which can be rearranged in the order of your choosing). The principle is so dependent on the double negation of self that a responsible proposition and the negation of its negation mean one and the same thing.[12]

Curating liturgies, homilies, and spiritual formation venues are just as self-reflexive for pastors and church leaders and can sometimes fall under O'Neill's critique. It is not the case that we first understand the world and then proclaim this understanding in worship; rather, in the processes of developing liturgies and writing sermons we come to understand the world otherwise, and this new (self-)understanding in turn shapes future sermons and liturgies.

Curation is also a buzzword in the world of business. Companies work to curate "retail experiences," by which retailers add a specialized aura of knowledge and experience alongside their products. Consider the specialty grocer Trader Joe's. When you go to Trader Joe's, you have selections to make, but all possible selections have already been filtered, chosen according to brand specifications that make the Trader Joe's experience what it is. That's curation.

---

11. David Balzer, *Curationism: How Curating Took Over the Art World and Everything Else* (Toronto: Coach House Books, 2014), 16.

12. Paul O'Neill, "The Co-dependent Curator," *Art Monthly* no. 291 (Nov. 2005): 9.

In his book *Curation Nation*, documentary filmmaker and curator Steven Rosenbaum boils down curation to two essential elements: organization and value.

Central to curation is the task of organizing. Curators rightly bear the name when they possess sufficient knowledge about a discipline or product to organize—to sift, filter, collate, and present—elements that constitute that product or discipline. This task transcends mere aggregation. Rosenbaum writes that "aggregation without curation is just a big pile of stuff that seems related but lacks qualitative organization."[13] This is why humans are able to curate, while computers can merely aggregate.

Curation also adds value to products, services, and disciplines. For instance, imagine you desire to purchase a new television but are unsure what one is best for you. Like most of us, you'll likely start with a Google search. When you search for "best television," Google returns 544,000,000 websites. True story. Instead of clicking every single link, you'll want to consult the experts at consumerreports.com, who specialize in testing and thereby valuing products like televisions. As reliable experts, their opinion adds value to the products they review.

Or let's say you want to take your family to Barcelona for Spring Break (I highly recommend Restaurant Montiel in the Born district of Barcelona, by the way). When you enter the key words "travel" + "Barcelona," you only have to sift through 97,700,000 results. In response to the staggering amount of information available to us with a few keystrokes, curatorial services have emerged to lend value to certain products and services. Don't read through millions of websites. Check out tripadvisor.com as you plan your Iberian adventure.

Rachel Held Evans is a wonderful example of an online curator. In the mid-2000s, she started a blog to share her opinions about God, faith, the church, and doubt, earning her a reputation for incisive commentary and wit. Whenever Evans tweets about an event, "likes" an organization on Facebook, or blogs about an issue, she is at once organizing and adding value to said event, organization, or issue; she's curating. In recent years, Evans has openly

---

13. Steven Rosenbaum, *Curation Nation: How to Win in a World Where Consumers are Creators* (New York: McGraw-Hill, 2011), 4.

embraced this label. For instance, in the "Why Christian" event that she organized with Nadia Bolz-Weber in 2015, Evans and Bolz-Weber describe their
role as co-curators.[14]

As a final example, consider NASA. NASA has developed the Astromaterials Acquisition and Curation Office, which is responsible for the curation
of extraterrestrial samples from NASA's past missions. Their purpose includes
"the documentation, preservation, preparation, and distribution of samples
from the Moon, asteroids, comets, the solar wind, and the planet Mars."[15]
One of the side benefits of this website is that it enables astro-geeks to glean
informed knowledge, trusting in the NASA reputation more than that random dude in Gaffney, South Carolina, who lives in his mom's basement and
runs a blog spouting alien conspiracy theories.

In sum, curation has never meant just one thing. Rather than trying to
constrain its semantic range, in this book I'll be aiming at the fullness of all
that curation can mean for the life and work of the church. At base, the dynamic and generative tension at the heart of curation, between care and cure,
is pragmatically helpful, if not theologically poignant.

A Theological Case for Curation

Thus far, my argument has been largely pragmatic: curation *already* aligns
with much ministerial work, even as it adds greater precision to the tasks
of ministry. Look at the way curator Mari Carmen Ramírez describes the
expectations and function of the contemporary art curator: "The *centrality*
accorded to contemporary art curators in the new system is evident in the
multiplicity of extra-artistic roles and the diversity of performative areas that
have come to define our current practice." This could just as easily pertain to
contemporary expectations of pastors. Ramírez continues, "As we all know,
curators now have to function as aestheticians, art historians, and educators,
as well as cultural diplomats, politicians, community organizers, and fund
raisers, among many other roles."[16] If your experiences in pastoral ministry

14. See https://whychristian.net/schedule/.

15. "Astromaterials Acquisition & Curation Office," National Aeronautics and Space Administration, http://curator.jsc.nasa.gov/.

16. Mari-Carmen Ramírez, "Panel Statements and Discussion," in *Curating Now: Imagi-*

have been anything like mine, you feel pulled in so many directions that they might as well call you Rev. Gumby.

Curation and Christian ministry overlap in many ways. Both are borne by cultures and both constitute cultures by the way they take shape. Moreover, curation ramifies from the twin tasks of *care* and *cure*. This ought to resonate with our church work. We administrate. We provide care. We proclaim God's Word as a "cure" for modern malaise and social evils. Thus, curation is not merely pragmatic but theologically significant for church ministry.

Curators and ministers are also charged with the *production* of meaning. We structure spaces for call and response. The church, the *ekklesia*, has no independent existence apart from its *being called* of God in Jesus Christ to participate in God's mission of reconciliation, liberation, and restoration. The church is constituted by God. But it is comprised of people, each of whom has been *called out* (*ek-klesia*) of culture—though never *apart* from culture—to provide care and cure for the world God loves.

Because curation is oriented toward care and cure, toward stewardship and transformation, curation facilitates the church's reason for being and guides its ways of operating. Some artists are also curators, but not all curators are artists. Indeed, with Robert Storr, Hans Ulrich Obrist, and others, I don't believe that curators and artists are necessarily the same thing. So, too, for ministers: some ministers are artists, but that does not make the work of ministry coterminous with art. In the same way, it is theologically dubious to collapse the "work" of ministry into the *opus Dei*, the work of God.

My operating assumption in this book—in all my books, as a matter of fact—is that the church is called to participate in God's mission in the world, which is summed up in the words of Jesus: "I came so that they could have life—indeed, so that they could live life to the fullest" (John 10:10b). Thus, no separation is defensible between ecclesial and political life. To insist otherwise is to make a mockery of Jesus's work and witness, which led to his execution under the auspices of both the religious and political authorities of his day.[17]

---

native Practice, Public Responsibility, ed. Paula Marincola and Robert Storr (Philadelphia: Philadelphia Exhibitions Initiative, 2002), 26.

17. I discuss this point at length in my book *Making Love with Scripture: Why the Bible Doesn't Mean How You Think It Means* (Minneapolis: Fortress, 2015).

Churches are porous, taking on the ways of thinking, speaking, and being from their local—and increasingly global—cultures. Central to the task of ministry, therefore, we must understand our local, regional, and global cultures and *engage* with them. At the same time, and since churches are called to share in God's work of incarnational rejuvenation (Rev 21:5), curation offers us a framework for ministries that *conserve* what is life-giving in our ecclesial traditions and that seek to *transform* our cultures in and beyond the church in partnership with the Holy Spirit.

This book arises out of my driving conviction that churches are "called out" (*ekklesia*) to *engage* at the overlapping and interpenetrating sites of ecclesial and secular cultures, to *conserve* and thereby extend what is best in our ecclesial cultures for all the world to see, and to *transform* our myriad and constantly shifting cultures until our earthly kingdoms reflect God's kin(g) dom of love and justice. This theological conviction structures a pastoral intention: I aim to help ministers and church leaders conduct the work of engagement, conservation, and transformation in creative and effective ways. To this end, my book is divided into three sections or *galleries*.

In Gallery I, I share my own work as a liturgical curator. I worked for five years in Atlanta, Georgia, to curate liturgical spaces for engagement, conservation, and transformation—first in Little Five Points and later in Buckhead. In this Gallery, I present four liturgies offered for and enacted by real churchgoers. In addition to describing the liturgies themselves and discussing the logistics that went into these worship gatherings, I also share the pastoral/ theological visions that gave rise to each worship experience. Lastly, I offer my reflections about these liturgies in light of my education and growth over the intervening years. My aim here is to offer examples of theological and liturgical curation in action so that you might learn from both our mistakes and successes and attempt such liturgies that are fitting for your own cultural and ecclesial contexts.

In Gallery II, I describe five diverse art installations in critical conversation with each exhibition's curatorial vision. I present these as models for understanding how contemporary art curators think so that we might expand our curatorial imaginations. I also include commentary from art critics, whose job it is to reflect upon how well the curator's vision was achieved in and through the exhibition. Lastly, I reflect on these disparate art events through the lens of a practical theologian, asking what liturgical takeaways we might receive for our own work of ministerial curation. In curating these exhibitions of curation, I offer examples that strive to engage with diverse constituencies and that also seek very different ends.

In Gallery III, I present what I am calling "curating possibilities," which are at once possibilities for curation and curating fresh approaches to issues of contemporary ecclesial and cultural significance. Here, I offer no template; rather, I aim to offer sufficient content that may be added to the process-oriented guidance on offer in Galleries I and II. My intention here is to empower you to gather your own liturgical teams to engage such matters with an eye to *care* and to *cure* in these polarizing times we are facing. I offer suggestions based on my research and experience. These three "curating possibilities" on offer in Gallery III could catalyze your work toward a three-part liturgical series, or they might lay the groundwork for three different series.

My hope and prayer is that this book will aid you and the communities entrusted to your care to imagine your work together according to the motif of curation. Such can facilitate the work of ministry, equipping you to engage more meaningfully with your contemporary cultural realities and move toward authentic transformation in ways that do not shut down but open up conversation and interpersonal engagement. In any case, I have done my curatorial work, and now I invite you to make this textual exhibition your own.

Curating Church: Lessons from a Misfit Liturgical Community

> *The how of selecting the artworks and other materials and of mounting the exhibition as an arena of experience is as crucial as what it is for and why it is consequential.*
>
> —*Terry Smith*[1]

Eight hundred and thirty-three days. That's how long we were blessed to sustain a liturgical experiment we called rechurch. It was a time of discovery, creativity, headaches, surprises, and joy. From November 4, 2007 until February 14, 2010, a community of worship and grace thrived. Looking back, I marvel at how rechurch grew into a space where it was okay to take big risks. I laugh at how comfortable we became with failure. It was and remains one of the most meaningful, life-giving worship communities in which I've ever participated. *Requiescat in pace.*

In this Gallery, I wish to articulate for you as accurately as I'm able the rechurch milieu. But in some ways, this is a misnomer: rechurch was never a *thing* that one could capture in a sentence or two. We never allowed it to retain a *proper* name—hence its lowercased spelling. Its evanescence and its resistance to taking itself too seriously were intrinsic to its DNA. Our motto,

---

1. Terry Smith, *Thinking Contemporary Curating* (New York: Independent Curators International, 2012), 5.

New Ideas Welcome, was also a kind of mission statement. Thus, rechurch was always becoming something *else*, something more than it was, and that's why so many people loved it . . . and feared it.

Background

As I mentioned in the Preface, the theological, liturgical, and aesthetic beginnings of rechurch started in an altogether different environment. Like most major cities, Atlanta plays host to a variety of people. Different folks congregate into disparate communities that take on their own look and feel. The Little Five Points neighborhood and the Buckhead neighborhood are about as different from each other as you could imagine.

Little Five Points is known for its eclectic, countercultural flare. Its current cultural panache took shape during the Vietnam War, when droves of hippies flocked to the recently impoverished neighborhood. Its economic condition was partly due to white flight and partly to a proposed interstate route right through the heart of the borough. This construction plan never materialized, but it nevertheless altered the borough's destiny. Many of those hippies are now doctors, professors, and lawyers and still live in the neighborhood in renovated Victorian homes.

Except for a Starbucks that managed to creep in (despite months of vitriol and protests from its neighbors), Little Five Points has managed to resist commercialization. It is home to two indie bookstores, three indie record stores, several high-end thrift stores, a natural food store, and numerous locally owned and operated restaurants and pubs.

Having worked in Little Five Points for several years to form the Trinitas community, I was then invited to join the staff of Wieuca Road Baptist Church (WRBC) as the Coordinator of Missional Community and Alternative Worship. My charge was simple: to help WRBC forge meaningful connections with its neighbors in Buckhead and beyond and to create a worship venue that would facilitate WRBC's new missional trajectory.

Buckhead is one of the most posh and affluent neighborhoods in Atlanta, and WRBC is situated right at its jugular. Located at the corner of Wieuca Road and Peachtree Road, which is Atlanta's most well-known artery, WRBC is surrounded by skyscrapers and high-end retailers like Tiffany & Co., Saks

Fifth Avenue, Nordstrom, and Giorgio Armani. The church is right across the street from Phipps Plaza, the swankiest mall in Atlanta, and less than a mile from Lenox Mall. If Atlantean neoliberal capitalism were a hurricane, WRBC rested in its eye.

My prejudices aside, I jumped right in to my new call at WRBC. I started by chatting up folks at the coffee shops, pubs, and restaurants near the church and quickly discovered that many of my assumptions about the kind of people who lived in Buckhead were false. Even as lots of its inhabitants were upper-middle class, working in business, medicine, and law, many were also school teachers and accountants and cooks. What is more, I learned that even as the aesthetics and architecture of Buckhead were vastly different from those in Little Five Points, many of its inhabitants shared an epistemological sensibility that was quite similar. In other words, even as the Buckhead and Little Five Points residents *looked* different, they *thought* in similar ways.

WRBC was once a flagship church in the Southern Baptist Convention. Then the church had boasted a membership of over five thousand people. Unfortunately, because of demographic and cultural shifts—exacerbated by decades of in-fighting—the congregation had dwindled to under one thousand when I joined the staff in 2006. To make the church more appealing to an increasingly diverse community, they had started a contemporary worship service called "the Corner," which was apt considering the church's physical location. During an interim period without a senior pastor, the WRBC leadership elected to combine the traditional and contemporary services. The Corner's existence had contributed to the conflict at the church—some were opposed to even the idea of contemporary worship; others loved it.

With the hiring of Michael Tutterow as WRBC's fourth senior pastor, energy mounted for relaunching the Corner. Michael had gained notoriety through his tenure as the lead pastor of Winter Park Baptist Church in Wilmington, North Carolina, where he brought healing and solidarity to a church that had divided itself over worship styles. Michael had been able to help Winter Park Baptist embrace its identity as one church with two modes of worship expression. He seemed like the perfect person to restore WRBC to health and wholeness.

When I joined the pastoral staff at WRBC, I hosted a series of listening sessions with those worshipers who had attended the Corner and were still grieving its demise. Through these conversations, I discovered a marked difference between the assumptions, hopes, and ways of thinking expressed by the Corner's participants and the folks with whom I was chatting outside of the church. I realized that even as relaunching the Corner would make many of these WRBC members happy, it would sustain the cultural, epistemological, and theological disparities between WRBC and its neighbors.

I made my case to Michael that WRBC ought not attempt to recreate the Corner for three reasons. First, Michael and I shared a theological proclivity toward missional approaches to ministry, and thus we didn't wish merely to create another service; we wanted to nurture a *gathering*. The distinction between a service and a gathering transcends semantics: we wished to cultivate a worship environment where participants were given greater agency. A worship *service* connotes something that is done *to* or *for* consumers. (You go to a service station to have work done on your car; you call a taxi service to have someone drive you somewhere.) You are rendered passive. A worship *gathering* signifies differently. It signals a coming together that subverts a consumer mindset that commodifies the gospel. A gathering situates the worshiper with others in a way that transcends Sunday morning. We wanted to give this nascent community space to thrive in the world and not just in an ecclesial incubator.

The second reason was pragmatic. There was no way that we could compete in the attractional ministry game with Andy Stanley's Buckhead Church just a few miles down the road. Rather than working to market this new gathering as a sleek, sexy, worship machine, I thought it more prudent to nurture an alternative space that stressed face-to-face communal engagement and congregational empowerment.

Thirdly, I believed that the liturgical theology of contemporary worship was antithetical to a ministry approach aiming to foster authentic relationships with the kinds of people I was meeting in the Buckhead pubs and coffee shops. I am not the first to observe that contemporary worship maintains the assumptions and infrastructure of traditional worship. The differences are largely aesthetic: replace pews with chairs; replace the organ with an electric guitar and drum kit; replace the choir with a praise band; replace suits and dresses with khakis and polo shirts. The shape of the liturgy is every bit as uniform and predictable between these styles of worship.

Alternative worship—we preferred the label *experiential worship*—does not aim to fit biblical texts and worship elements into a set structure. Rather, experiential worship, as we would come to embody it, asks different kinds of questions. Foremost among them is this: Based on what we hear the Spirit of God saying to us through this biblical text, how might we need to reimagine liturgy?

Genesis

Once we received the green light to move forward with this gathering, we had some important decisions to make. The first was the physical location of the worship gathering.

I had learned from many in Buckhead who did not attend church that they were open to spiritual and communal engagement but that the physical presence of churches like ours was intimidating. WRBC's whitewashed façade, waves of crown molding, and glistening steeple were antithetical to how most folks in the neighborhood perceived God. Diana Butler Bass would write a book several years later that would corroborate the theological shift I was sensing in my on-the-ground experience: a shift from a vertical/transcendent to a horizontal/immanent understanding of God.[2]

We settled on the church's fellowship hall for our worship space because it gave us the greatest flexibility for the kind of liturgical environment we were envisioning. While the location was sufficient, the room's decor was totally out of sorts with the ambiance we were seeking to create. The room boasted enormous gold sconces and teal wallpaper reminiscent of one of Louis XIV's palaces. I went all-in to argue for an extreme church makeover, and with the help of my friend Carolyn Meaders, we redecorated the worship space with warm earth tones and contemporary lighting that made the space much more open and inviting for those averse to the accoutrements of institutional religion.

---

2. See Diana Butler Bass, *Grounded: Finding God in the World—A Spiritual Revolution* (New York: HarperOne, 2015).

The last major decision we had to make was when this community would gather for corporate worship. I argued for Sunday evenings, and I did so for five reasons:

1. Brunch is a huge facet of Buckhead culture, and I saw no need to compete with this form of community. In fact, I saw ways that we might work alongside this neighborhood rhythm if we were not already committed to Sunday morning worship.

2. Many Buckhead folks, I learned, are night owls. Given that WRBC's traditional worship service was already situated at that sanctified hour of 11 a.m. on Sundays, I could not imagine wrangling a bleary-eyed community to worship at 9 a.m.

3. Some in leadership positions at WRBC were far too traditional and conservative to abide the levels of liturgical and theological innovation I foresaw emerging from rechurch. I feared that we would get into trouble if we began to reimagine the sights, sounds, smells, rhythms, and practices that constituted "proper Baptist" worship. Considering the church's recent strife, I worried that some might try to squelch the Spirit's movement before we even got this gathering started. I argued that hosting worship in the evening would infringe less upon the status quo.

4. I had learned from leading experiential worship in Little Five Points that time constraints could be the enemy of liturgical expressiveness. If we had to ensure that everything was wrapped up within one hour so that folks could bustle off to Sunday school, we would stifle our capacity for liturgical innovation and, concomitantly, meaningful spiritual encounters. If you create a worship station, for instance, in which you invite a community to open themselves to prayerful, reflective engagement with God, it is bad form to cut them off midway through a body prayer or stifle the work of artistic exegesis. This stuff takes time. And while you can get better at estimating how long this or that worship element will take, you cannot account for the Holy Spirit's uncanniness.

5. By the time we arrived at this stage of the planning process, we had called four new staff members, each of whom brought much-needed energy and insight to our liturgical imaginations. Matt Rich was our new Pastor for Spiritual Formation. (This was another huge shift at WRBC: Spiritual Formation rather than Christian Education.) Shelley Woodruff was hired to revive WRBC's singles and young adult ministry. Andy Smith, a good friend of mine from undergrad, was fast at work in revitalizing WRBC's youth ministry. And Marti Andrews joined the staff to assist in children's ministry. If we were serious about conceiving rechurch as more than a worship service, and given these new members of our pastoral team, I reasoned that a Sunday evening service would afford us opportunities to reimagine church beyond the liturgy. Furthermore, given that we would be operating out of an alternative epistemological and theological paradigm, I argued that the traditional patterns of Sunday school, Baptist potlucks, children's programming, and youth group would not suffice.

Despite these arguments, we opted to host rechurch at 11:30 a.m. This was a risky compromise—so risky, in fact, that when Michael decided that this was what we would do, I was astounded (and impressed) by his temerity. Because he could only be in one place at a time, and because he did not want to split his pastoral presence between overlapping worship gatherings, this displaced the traditional worship service. They got "bumped" to 9 a.m. (I must note that this was far from a unilateral decision. Many of the folks who attended the sanctuary service had already expressed their preference for an earlier worship time.) We would learn later that the symbolic significance of having an empty sanctuary at 11 a.m. on a Sunday was too much for some of our congregants to bear. After months of scheming, planning, and bartering, we hosted our first worship gathering on November 4, 2007.

Process

To broaden both our creativity and (wo)manpower, we decided to form a liturgy planning team. Our liturgy planning team consisted of several standing members, with others invited to help us plan for particular series. The team consisted of nine members: myself; Michael, WRBC's senior pastor; Andy Smith, WRBC's youth pastor; Matt Rich, WRBC's spiritual formation pastor; Shelley Woodruff, WRBC's single and young adult pastor; Marti Andrews, WRBC's associate children's minister; Wes Hunter, the rechurch worship band leader; Ann Canon, the former coordinator for the Corner service; and Belinda McCafferty, a retired executive for the IRS.

The plan for this team was to meet several months out from each worship series to dream and strategize in community. We really did embrace our tagline: "new ideas welcome." The rechurch liturgy planning team remains one of the most meaningful and life-giving aspects of my ministry. Because we were always asking ourselves how we might encounter God afresh, and because we were intentional about inviting new and diverse members of the rechurch community to join our team from series to series, the work was always a joy.

The format for the planning team remained consistent. We often met at Belinda's home on an evening. Belinda has a gift for hospitality, and our most generative conversations took place at her home, which was less than two miles away from WRBC. Let me pause here to note how much space matters—not only worship space, but also the space in which you dream about worship. We tried several liturgy planning meetings in WRBC's Heritage Room, but its aesthetics of posh wallpaper, twelve-inch crown molding, and ornate furniture proved stifling for our creativity. Plus, Belinda always served wine, cheese, and charcuterie.

We would open with prayer, and then Michael would share the scripture texts that would guide us through this series. Michael often followed the Revised Common Lectionary, but he liked to articulate his sermon series thematically. We discovered that this format was conducive to our liturgical endeavors. It is unsustainable and impractical to lead experiential worship gatherings that must be totally reworked from Sunday to Sunday. Planning early and planning for five- to eight-week series gave us the freedom to build a labyrinth, or a giant wailing wall, or tree of life built to scale.

I would moderate the conversation as we devoted the bulk of our time to dreaming, creativity, and play. This is crucial. When you aim to curate liturgical experiences that will lead your congregants or parishioners to experience the gospel more fully, you must foster an atmosphere where no idea is too crazy and nothing is impossible. The challenge is in guiding the conversation forward, lifting new insights, praising creativity, and drawing connections between team members' contributions.

I discovered that the most generative contributions are often not the first idea that is spoken, nor the second, and perhaps not even the third, but that third or fourth thing that would have only been possible on account of the first, second, or third ideas that were rubbish. We learned to trust one another and the process. For instance, we could always count on Andy to push us outside of our liturgical and theological comfort zones. Andy's ideas were crucial to the group process. As WRBC's senior pastor, however, Michael needed to temper the planning team's vision according to the potential fallout with rechurch's detractors; this was not an easy assignment, and Michael balanced these responsibilities well.

Variables

One of the most exciting aspects of our liturgical planning process was in discovering fresh ways to foster engagement with God, with one another, and with the world God loves. We chose not to view the variability of worship possibilities as an obstacle to be overcome but a gift to be embraced. In the words of Keith Pierce, the rechurch band's bassist: "Every Sunday we show up and create a beautiful mess." That says it all.

Even as we embraced a certain chaos in our liturgical planning process, we needed to provide some degree of structure to move us toward execution. As we worked to curate liturgies that would connect with our community, we learned to ask ourselves certain kinds of questions:

- *How might we need to situate ourselves in relation to one another?*
  Should we sit in concentric circles? In the shape of a boat? Facing one another?
  Do we need to be on couches? In chairs? On pillows strewn across the carpet?

- *What kinds of music might allow us to experience this saying and doing of God in this gathering or throughout this series?*
  Do we need a steel drum for this series?
  How about a sitar?
  Will bluegrass or jazz create the sound we need?
  Do we plug in or go acoustic?
  Where should the band position themselves? On stage? In front of the stage?
  In the back of the room?

- *Who should read scripture, and how should he/she/they read it?*
  Should the text be acted out?
  Should more than one person read the text?
  Where should the lector stand in relation to the congregation?
  Should worshipers even see the lector during his/her/their reading?

- *What should the sermon look/sound/feel like this week?*
  Should it take place early in the liturgy and lead us to some experiential action?
  Should it take place all at once or in a series of shorter reflections?
  Who should preach this sermon and why?
  Do we need to identify other voices in the sermon? Whose voices do we need to hear?

- *What aesthetic would best support this gathering? What elements could we add to make this gathering more experiential, contemplative, empowering, etc.?*
  What stations could we create to enhance the look and feel of this gathering?
  Do we want full house lights? Dimmed lights? Candlelight only?
  What art should we create/provide that would foster a deeper connection to the liturgy's focus?

- *How might technology support the work of this liturgy?*
  Do we want PowerPoint slides that will facilitate learning?
  Do we want to have images rolling throughout the gathering?
  Of what?
  Should we share a video clip?

- *What is the function of this liturgy, and what elements do we need to put in place as a response?*
  Should it lead us to the Lord's Table?
  Do we need to provide cards and envelopes so that worship participants may write to their congressional representatives?
  Ought we provide a way for folks to sign up for service opportunities in our community (e.g., Habitat for Humanity, Buckhead Christian Ministry, Atlanta Union Mission)?

- *What should our hospitality time look like this week?*
  Should we employ a traditional greeting and response (e.g., "The peace of Christ be with you" or "He is risen")?
  Might we structure hospitality with a guiding question that sets up for what follows or builds upon an earlier moment in worship?
  How much time should we budget for hospitality and why?
  What concessions can be made to keep the introverts from curling into a fetal position or fleeing the worship space in terror?

These are examples of the kinds of questions we asked ourselves during our liturgy planning sessions. In all honesty, we were better at asking such questions than we were at answering them. Sometimes the logistics impeded our vision. Maybe that person we'd identified to lead us in a part of the liturgy was unavailable on the week we needed her/him/them. Or maybe the fabric we wanted to purchase to black out the windows would put us way over budget. Our inboxes were full of e-mails about what needed to be done and who was responsible for what. Early on, I developed a Detailed Liturgy Template. This allowed us to keep ourselves and others (e.g., greeters, sound techs, etc.) organized and on task.

Results

The results? rechurch *thrived*—and I measure my words here. The community was life-giving to most, if not all, who shared in its "beautiful messiness." Not every worship gathering was a success, at least not by the liturgy planning team's definition of success (we had to use a fire extinguisher more than once). What I loved so much about rechurch was its many and varied serendipities. Worship surprised us. Even when things went "wrong," we marveled at the community's resilience and God's faithfulness to work despite our numerous failings. But rechurch was always more about qualitative than quantitative success. When the gathering officially ended in 2010—on Valentine's Day, no less—it was thriving by all accounts and growing to the point that we were preparing to launch a second rechurch gathering on Sunday evenings.

Such was not to be. The financial market collapse in 2008 had strained the church's finances to the point where we had to reduce the salaries of three staff members. The numerical growth of rechurch was also a major point of contention among WRBC members who attended the traditional service. There was a growing fear that Michael and I were plotting to do away with the traditional service (which was utterly false). Some of our members began to withhold their tithes in protest. Animosity swelled. Eventually, I realized that my presence on the ministerial staff was synonymous with all the discord and anger permeating the church. I resigned in January of 2010. rechurch died a month later.

Within a year, nine of the ten pastoral staff members resigned. Today, WRBC is on life support. Recently they voted to decide whether to sell their property, which is worth tens of millions of dollars. In a move beyond irony, WRBC voted to stay, and they have called a new staff member to help them connect with the very kinds of people whom they feared at rechurch.

Thankfully, many of rechurch's community members have found other meaningful ways to worship God and to serve their communities. Even though it has been more than a decade since rechurch hosted its first worship gathering, I still receive e-mails and Facebook comments about how meaningful rechurch was for those who were a part of it. While this community no longer worships together, we remain invested in one another's lives through social media and occasional gatherings.

I liken rechurch's demise to something I learned at a ranger talk at Yellowstone National Park some years later. The ranger informed us that the only way for the park's coniferous trees to reproduce was through fire. Forest fires, which are incredibly destructive, also foster new life. These fires cause pinecones to explode, spreading new seeds. This is what happened at rechurch: the fires of church conflict spread and spread until our gathering exploded.

But death was not the end. God has used this grand dispersal to plant seeds of innovation in other churches, blessing other communities.

The following experiential gatherings are intended to offer you a glimpse of the curatorial imagination that developed alongside the rechurch community—indeed, the imagination and the community emerged in tandem and sustained each other much as an electric current and a magnetic field work in concert to power an electromagnet. Among the many liturgies I could have chosen, I have selected the four that follow to highlight our liturgical diversity and to illustrate how our worship followed the ebbs and flows of the liturgical calendar.

"Advent People"

This was our first Advent season at rechurch, and we wanted to think creatively about how we might help the community to experience this season anew. Many Baptist churches do little to stress the season of Advent in worship; what I mean is that we tend not to stress the feelings of hope, yearning, and anticipation that other church communities who are higher up the liturgical candle emphasize. Furthermore, much Baptist theology inclines toward the historicity of Jesus's birth, muting the eschatological dimension of Advent. We wanted to curb this trend.

Our curatorial imagination took shape as all such imaginations must: with an eye toward engagement, conservation, and transformation. Our "ah-ha" moment that wove these three elements together was that Advent invites us to become hope, joy, peace, and love for others, to be the light that shines in the darkness in witness to the radical in-breaking of God in Jesus Christ. To borrow Karl Barth's dialectical construction (which he borrowed from the Lutheran German preacher/theologian Christoph Blumhardt), the church is called into the tension between hastening and waiting. In other words, we are compelled to act now for the liberation announced in Jesus's birth. But we cannot inaugurate God's kin(g)dom by ourselves; thus, we are also called to await God's coming fulfillment of God's promises. With our liturgy series "Advent People," we sought to help our worship participants experience this tension.

Liturgical Vision

For the Advent season, we wanted to do something that would draw our congregants more fully into the spirit of Advent. In our initial planning meeting, Michael led us to reflect on a very commonplace aspect of the Advent season, one that we were certain would connect with our community's collective experience: Advent wreathes. Even for those of us who were unfamiliar with the liturgical elements or theological significance of Advent in the life and work of the church, we knew about Advent wreaths. We hang them on our doors and some of us place them on our dining room tables to structure our evening prayers.

Our liturgy planning team also recognized that this was an excellent opportunity to retrieve a beautiful and theologically rich aspect of the church's life that had gone largely ignored by us Baptists. Somewhere amid our conversation, we got the idea to create a *human* Advent wreath. To do this we decided to arrange chairs in concentric circles in the center of our worship space. Though we do not have any seating charts from the earliest church gatherings in Corinth or Philippi or Ephesus, we were confident that these believers did not arrange themselves in linear pews facing an elevated pulpit. These were house churches, and so we imagined men, women, and others gathering together around a table to share meals, struggles, and hopes. The curricular configuration we adopted for this liturgy series was no mere gimmick; we wanted to *embody* an aspect of Christian fellowship that we had lost.

We also had the idea to build four, eight-feet tall Advent candles. Yes, eight-feet tall. We created an experience of putting us into the Advent wreath when we gathered for worship. (I'll say more about this facet of our liturgy in the logistics section below.) Following Marti's creative insight, we used green fabric and lots of greenery to decorate the chairs and sitting space to make it look and feel like an Advent wreath. The smell of fresh-cut pine boughs fostered a multisensory experience that did not go unnoticed by our worshipers.

One of the serendipities of this worship time was the role children played in helping us become God's Christmas message. Our associate children's minister, Marti, worked with the children in advance to decorate the "Advent candles." They covered each of them in the appropriate colored construction paper—purple and pink—and then the children were invited to write messages, draw pictures, and otherwise share their hopes of what we might say to one another and to our world during this Advent season. The first week of Advent focuses on hope. And here we asked folks to reflect on how they might embody hope for a world that so often feels hopeless. By the second week in Advent, where we focused on peace, we had ironed out many of the kinks.

Logistics

There were many moving parts to this liturgy series. First, we had to figure out how to build giant Advent candles. Chuck, one of the members of WRBC, owned a heating and air conditioning company. A few weeks before the series began, I drove out to his workshop and together we constructed the candles. On top of a 4x4 foot platform base we affixed an eight-foot piece of ten-inch cylindrical ducting. At the center of the base we attached a simple light receptacle that we connected to a switch. This allowed us to turn on the "candle" at just the right point in the liturgy. We made four of these, one for each week of Advent.

As mentioned above, we also needed to switch up the room configuration. We moved the chairs to form rows of concentric circles. Not only would this force us to be closer to one another—physically, at least—it also reinforced the vision for this liturgy series: To call us to be Advent people, shining with hope, peace, love, and joy in a world that can often seem so dark.

Liturgy

At Advent, we introduced several rituals and aesthetic elements that connected week-to-week while allowing room for thematic fluctuations. Our community was growing weekly at this point in rechurch's life—both numerically and spiritually. Those who had initially resisted the pragmatic implications of our tagline ("new ideas welcome") had come to appreciate, if not wholly embrace, rechurch's liturgical variety.

I'm including the worship elements for the second week of this Advent series. The liturgy for this worship gathering was as follows:

Pre-worship music

Upbeat opening song

Advent litany

Two songs connecting with the day's theme (in this case, peace)

Praying with eyes wide open

Performance song

Sermon

Experiential time—Hospitality/Passing of the peace

Closing song

Benediction

We experimented with different styles, and we eventually settled on producing pre-worship announcement slides and background music to greet rechurch participants as they trickled into the worship space. Our worship gathering started at 11:30 a.m. Some of our folks elected to attend Sunday school beforehand, and they would enter worship in waves depending on when their classes let out. Others would arrive early to sip coffee and to fellowship with others prior to worship. Setting announcement slides of upcoming events at WRBC added to the ambiance while also getting the word out about the various programs and initiatives going on at the church. Beyond aesthetics, the slides served another purpose. Since we did not produce worship bulletins or orders of worship (we liked to keep everyone guessing what might happen next), we lost that opportunity to let rechurchers know how they could plug in.

Advent Litany for Peace

One of the great blessings of curating worship in a Baptist church is that there are very few liturgical fundamentalists (now, theological fundamentalism is a different matter entirely). We had the freedom to move up and down the proverbial liturgical candle as it facilitated the aesthetic and theological tone we were envisioning from series to series.

For this series, I wrote a litany for each week. Here's the litany for week two of Advent:

LEADER: Last Sunday we lit the first candle in our Advent wreath, the candle of hope. We light it again as we remember that Christ will come again to fulfill all of God's promises to us.

(A person lights the candle of hope.)

PEOPLE: *O Come, O Come Emmanuel. We are your people and our hope remains in you.*

LEADER: As members of Christ's body and harbingers of God's holy kingdom, all of creation looks to us to set the world right. By the way we love one another, our God, and our neighbors, we are a visible sign of God's advent.

PEOPLE: *Come swiftly, Lord Jesus. Come swiftly.*

LEADER: The second candle of Advent is the Candle of Peace. Peace is not merely an absence of strife, but a state of wholeness in which all of creation is set right.

PEOPLE: *To a world in turmoil, we are the Advent wreath. As a community centered on God's peace, we are whole. As a community verdant with missional fruitfulness, we transform division and discord into unity. May peace reign on earth as it does in heaven.*

LEADER: Our hope is in God and in God's son, Jesus Christ. Our peace is found in him. We light this candle today to remind us that Christ brings peace to all who trust in him.

(A person lights the second candle.)

All: *Loving God, thank you for the peace you give us through Jesus. Help us prepare our hearts to receive him. Bless our worship. Guide us in all that we say and do. We ask it in the name of the one born in Bethlehem. Amen.*

Corporate Worship through Song

As I've already noted, the style of music fluctuated from series to series. We sampled every musical style from bluegrass, to jazz, to reggae, to straight acoustic. Wes did a fantastic job helping us find the right sound for each worship experience. This was no easy task when you consider that every musical selection also had to fall within the skills of the volunteer band members and their limited availability for rehearsals.

For this second week in our liturgy series, Wes and the rechurch band led us in a Dave Matthewsy version of "O Come, O Come, Emmanuel" and "Come, Thou Long Expected Jesus." During high liturgical seasons like Advent, we frequently opted to sing songs that were a part of the church's deep reservoir. One of the blessings we received from our talented band members was the gift of hearing these classic hymns and praise songs set to different tunes and performed with a variety of instruments.

Praying with Eyes Wide Open

For this liturgy series, we invited Paul Wallace to join in our liturgy planning team. A former physics professor turned seminary student, Paul energized us all with his creative insights and suggestions. One of his ideas that tied in particularly well with the idea of becoming a living Advent wreath was that of praying with our eyes open.

Paul led us through a prayer while we viewed images on the screens of various forms of discord and strife—from interfamily drama to global warming to conflicts in the Middle East. This form of prayer moved us from thinking of prayer as an internal activity to something that we ought to do with our hearts and minds attuned to the realities of the world around us.

Sermon[1]

The Apostle Paul often offers a greeting in his letters of "grace and peace." This offering integrates the typical Gentile greeting of God's grace

---

1.   This is a condensed version of the sermon Rev. Michael Tutterow preached in the Sanctuary service at Advent, December 13, 2009. Used with permission.

with a typical Jewish greeting of offering peace. Generally, we think of peace as the absence of conflict. But the Bible speaks of peace in terms of the fullness of life. To speak *shalōm/eirēnē* means more than a hope that one's life would be free of trouble. To speak peace to someone was to wish them everything that makes for their highest good: health and security; the basic needs of food and shelter; a life of fairness and justice; a life of love and friendship; and a right relationship with God. Peace, then, doesn't come from the absence of bad things from life, but rather the presence and fullness of good things.

When Paul and Silas were imprisoned and chained, they demonstrated their own peace by singing. After an earthquake broke their bonds and they did not flee, the jailer received their message about Jesus. He and his family became followers. The Bible links our lack of peace to a broken relationship with God. At the heart of this breach in our relationship is what the Bible calls sin. Sin isn't the individual acts we may commit that leave us feeling guilty or ashamed. Those are only symptoms. Sin is our decision to place ourselves at the center of our lives rather than God. Sin is the attempt to live life by our own terms rather than by God's guidance. Reconciliation of people who are at odds with one another requires sacrifice. God provided that sacrifice for us. Have you made peace with God?

Ultimately, peace in all its forms is about the future. Focusing on the future more than the past God extends peace to us through Christ because he is more interested in our future than our past. Remaining tied to our past hurts fills us with regrets or resentments, neither of which give us peace. But Christ's peace, ruling in our hearts, enables us to see others as God sees them. Perhaps that's why Paul began his letter with the two words "grace and peace"—one word each from the Gentile world and the Hebrew world, now joined together because of Jesus. And when anxiety about the future would rob us of peace, Paul urges us to focus on the things that make for peace. Focusing on them, imagining them for ourselves and others, will bring to us God's peace.

Can you imagine what might happen if you and I actually permitted Jesus to be the Prince, the leader, the captain, the commander, the master of peace in our lives?

- When facing hardship, we would sense God's presence and find ourselves calm instead of anxious.

- When facing unfairness, we would respond with kindness instead of retribution.

- When facing uncertainty, we would turn to prayer and God's strength for assurance.

- When circumstances didn't turn out as expected, we would respond with gratitude and thanksgiving—and thereby transform our circumstances.

- When facing conflict, we would "bury the hatchet" and take the initiative to turn retribution into reconciliation.

Living with such peace would indeed be good news of a great joy, and may prove to be the most priceless gift we could receive this Christmas. So, I join Paul in saying, "May God our Father and the Lord Jesus Christ give you grace and peace."

Experiential Time

One of the few consistent elements from week to week was the need for a performance song following our hospitality time. This was necessary to allow a natural transition out of the hospitality time, giving folks a few minutes to wrap up their conversations and find their seats. Because this liturgy focused on the action of passing the peace, the hospitality time merged with the experiential time.

Hospitality was one of our cardinal virtues at rechurch, by the way. Each week we would engage in extended fellowship and welcoming of newcomers. This time in the liturgy often surprised long-time church members. We allotted around five to seven minutes for this element of our liturgy. What we hoped to embody as a practice was that relationships really mattered here. We sought to transcend the perfunctory greeting time we had experienced in other evangelical contexts along with the passing of the peace others had experienced in mainline contexts. We wanted folks to engage in substantive conversation rather than shake a few hands and then quickly return to their seats. I should note that some of our more introverted worship participants struggled during this time in the liturgy and so we would announce that folks could also head back to grab a second cup of coffee, if they preferred.

With this ecclesial emphasis on hospitality in mind, we were able to shake things up a bit during this Advent liturgy by introducing the practice of passing the peace as a mode of hospitality and missional living. To get here, Michael segued from his sermon into the experiential time. He introduced the traditional greeting ("The peace of Christ be with you") and the response ("And also with you") and unpacked the meaning of these words in terms of the missional thrust of our Advent worship: to extend Christ's peace through eye contact, touch, and the sharing of breath situates the church at the epicenter of God's mission of restoration and healing.

When a congregation is used to having an extended period of informal chatting over coffee and tea, and they are led to look one another in the eyes and pass the peace of Christ, the ritual takes on greater significance. This is what we observed during the passing of the peace of Christ during this liturgy. Because it was both old and new, it enabled us to experience on a deeply personal and congregational level that we are called to make Christ's peace manifest in the world.

Reflection

This series was one of our more highly liturgical experiences that we would celebrate in rechurch. There was great excitement and energy around embracing the church's traditions around Advent, especially among those who had formerly been Catholic or Episcopalian. Once everyone came to understand the flow of the liturgy, we were able to settle into it and engage one another in this season of hope, peace, love, and joy.

One of the greatest surprises in the series was the impact of the children's involvement. When we began rechurch, led by Marti and Belinda's compelling arguments, we made the bold decision to let the children remain in worship throughout each gathering. Many parents struggled with the idea of having their children in the same room and yet not sitting together (Marti often created activities for children in the back of the worship space). Because kids are kids, they did contribute to the chaos that seemed to accompany every worship series. However, when given the space and permission to participate in worship, they often surprised us.

During that Advent season, our rechurch kids contributed much beauty and joy to our corporate worship experiences. It took a while for folks to get comfortable with the prominent roles we trusted our children to take up in our worship gatherings, but by this point in rechurch's lifespan everyone had experienced the joys and surprises that accompanied the children's leadership. Through the entire liturgy series, our rechurch kids served as greeters, helped to decorate the worship space, served communion, and remained after the service to help with the lengthy tear-down process.

We did experience some logistical and technical challenges during this worship series. For instance, we learned that the electrical system in our worship space was ill-equipped to handle the Advent candles we created. If we plugged in more than one candle to the same receptacle, the breaker would trip and we would be thrust into total darkness. So, we were forced to purchase incredibly long extension cords and run them into different parts of the church facility. These then became a tripping hazard, so we had to tape them to the carpet before each worship gathering. Despite these logistical complications, the effect outweighed the challenges.

One of my favorite takeaways from this Advent series was the opportunity it afforded us to introduce a piece of the church's tradition that many of our worshipers who came from more evangelical contexts had never experienced before. Here, I witnessed the power of curatorial conservation to create opportunities for spiritual and congregational transformation.

I recall a heated conversation that ensued between a concerned congregant and me after one week in the series. He was angry that I was turning his Baptist church Catholic. While this was by no means one of my more pleasurable moments in ministry, this confrontation taught me a valuable lesson: a positive correlation exists between shocking, and even offensive, liturgies and spiritual insight. By creating space for this man to encounter otherness in a way that was praiseworthy rather than denigrating, he was forced to see what was beautiful and life-giving in another worship tradition. Furthermore, our conversation uncovered the extent to which his self-understanding was built upon the exclusion of others and otherness.

"In Her Shoes: Hagar, the Biblical Hero"

During the summer of 2008, we launched a summer series that ran from June until August. This was by far rechurch's longest series to date. Following all the creative work and logistical challenges of Lent, Easter, and Pentecost, for this post-Pentecost series we decided to focus less on coordinating several distinct series, and instead to focus on consistency of theme and thematic elements through a single, longer series. The summer series was entitled "In Search of Heroes: Biblical Models for Life." The focus of the series was to explore the life, faith, and influence of notable biblical characters as a way to broaden our congregants' biblical literacy and deepen the connections between biblical characters and contemporary persons. We didn't just want to teach these biblical characters; we wanted our folks to engage their stories in meaningful ways.

During this series, we focused on Old Testament/Hebrew Bible characters such as Adam and Eve, Noah, Abraham, Jacob, Joseph, Miriam, Moses, David, and Esther. To provide opportunities for connecting the lives of these characters to the "heroes" in our own community and in our own families, we constructed what we called a "wall of heroes." This ten-foot by twenty-foot wall made of folded construction paper was decorated by the children in the weeks leading up to the launch of this series. We used this wall a bit differently during each week of the series, but in general it became a space where people could post pictures and offer testimonies about how certain people had spoken meaningfully into their lives.

We set up the room in what became our "standard rechurch setup." We employed a fan-shape design that allowed us to be in symmetrical proximity to one another, to experience the facial and bodily expressions of others during the worship time, while also keeping us close to the preacher for the day. This contributed an intimate feel to our fellowship. The rechurch band remained on the main stage, several feet behind the small platform.

During one week in the series, Shelley Woodruff, our associate pastor for singles and young adults guided the planning process, as she was slated to preach while Michael Tutterow, our senior pastor, was out of town. This fell several weeks into the sermon series, and we on the liturgy planning team sensed that people were growing comfortable with the setup and the consistent liturgical movements. So, we decided to shake things up a bit. What emerged was a liturgy we titled "In Her Shoes."

Liturgical Vision

The "hero" upon whom we were to reflect during this liturgy was Hagar. In our planning process, we reflected on the ways that Hagar remains on the margins of biblical consideration for many in our ecclesial context. Some even voiced their surprise that Hagar "made the cut," that she was being included in our "hero" series at all. Shelley explained that within womanist scholarship Hagar is at the center of many conversations.[1]

Our liturgical vision emerged out of the dissonance we perceived between Hagar's marginality in some kinds of faith communities and centrality in others. We wanted to create a worship experience that would allow folks to see the world through Hagar's eyes. Beyond sympathy, we sought to help our community to develop empathy for her: to "walk a mile in her shoes." But how to do this?

One of the insights that Matt had during our planning process was that in the Muslim faith, when people make their annual pilgrimages to Mecca,

---

1. See, for example, Delores S. Williams, *Sisters in the Wilderness: The Challenges of Womanist God-Talk*, anniv. ed. (Maryknoll, NY: Orbis Books, 2013); Renita J. Weems, *Just a Sister Away: A Womanist Vision of Women's Relationships in the* Bible (Philadelphia: Innisfree, 1988), 1–23; and Wilda C. Gafney, *Womanist Midrash: A Reintroduction to the Women of the Torah and the Throne* (Louisville: Westminster John Knox, 2017), 33–44.

there is a practice of walking back and forth three times along a long arc to symbolize the movement of Hagar in the desert as she responds to God's call and promise of provision. Matt led us in exploring the text together by helping us attend to the movement depicted therein. This led us to our central theological insight: Hagar is included in the biblical text because she bears witness to the plight of those marginalized in all communities and to God's sustaining presence and provision thereto.

Logistics

The logistics for this liturgy were rather minimal. We moved the chairs back into a large fan shape configuration to allow a large space to emerge in the room's center. The shape drew everyone's gaze to the center, which is where the preachers took their place among us as the liturgy progressed. Our Hero Wall remained where it had been, at the back of the worship space farthest from the main stage.

During the service, we planned for Shelley to ask the congregation to remove their shoes and place them in large baskets that a few guys would be wielding once worship began. Shelley would later dump the shoes in the center of the room, and we made plans for the rechurch kids to redistribute the shoes at random. People would be invited to retrieve their original shoes during the hospitality time, with the hope that they would strike up conversations with the person who had literally walked in their shoes.

We sensed the tension mounting in the room immediately. We learned that many of our worship participants had feet issues of one kind or another. Some worried about hygiene. Others fretted about having their expensive pumps stretched out. Even though these people had grown to expect—if not always appreciate—that improvisation and adaptation were written into rechurch's DNA, the handling of one another's feet set anxieties to their boiling point.

Another logistic that we needed to carry out was the recruitment of "others" who would participate in the liturgy by performing a vignette. This proved more challenging than we imagined, which I discuss in greater detail below.

For this entire series, we created "Midrash stations," which we adapted every week according to the sermon topic. These were spaces that we set up around the worship space for people to journal or otherwise reflect on what they were experiencing on a personal level. This week we worked off Matt Rich's suggestion that we confront worshipers with the question "Where are you?" With this station, we hoped that the homiletical vignettes would stir our congregants' hearts by encouraging them to reflect on the ways they have been marginalized or oppressed on account of demographic markers and/or the ways the church has been and remains complicit in allowing said marginalization and oppression.

Liturgy

During the worship time, rechurch participants were invited to listen to a series of vignettes about those "others" in our contemporary vicinity who are often relegated to the margins and forced into their own existential and spiritual desert wanderings. rechurch lay leaders took turns reading vignettes written in the second person, addressing congregants as if each were Muslim or homeless or gay or immigrant.

The experiential element of walking in another person's shoes was equal parts joyous and repulsive. During a group processing time that my wife, Abby Myers, led at the end of the gathering, we learned much. For some the experience was too much to bear, and they retrieved their shoes and exited the circle. For those who persevered, much understanding emerged about our differences as a community. Watching tiny women and girls schlep around in men's size 13 loafers, and watching men with NBA-proportioned feet try to cram into size 6 pumps was quite a spectacle to behold. The sermon and vignettes intentionally avoided a "this is the point" moment. When Abby began to ask open-ended questions about what people saw/realized/felt/disagreed with, a meaningful conversation emerged that let the congregation connect their own dots and define their own "this is the point" moment. It also gave people the opportunity to express their feelings in their own words.

The scripts from each of the vignettes are included as follows:

A Gay Clergy Person

You were born the child of a Baptist pastor in North Carolina. When you were twelve years old, you sensed a calling to ministry yourself while serving on your first mission trip with the church youth group. As you grew into your teen years, you wrestled with this call because you could not imagine your so-called "lifestyle" being accepted by those who shared your father's ideology and theology.

In high school, you struggled to fit in. You had lots of friends because you were garrulous and fun-loving, but still you always perceived yourself as an outsider. At seventeen, you sat both of your parents down and shared these identity struggles you had been having with them: about how you sensed God calling you to the pastorate and yet you couldn't imagine a church ever accepting you for who you are. Your mother cried; your father said nothing. Your parents immediately put you into therapy, praying that a professional counselor could help you discern the "right path" to follow.

At eighteen, you enrolled in college and decided to major in English education, but still you felt God's calling upon your life. At twenty-two, you became a high school English teacher and moved into a house with your partner. One part of you felt whole because you were in love, another part of you felt broken and incomplete. At twenty-five, you decided to surrender to God's relentless calling upon your life, and so you entered seminary, trusting God to help you reconcile your calling with who you knew yourself to be.

At twenty-seven, you stood before your ordination council and spoke openly about yourself, your life choices, and your calling. Sadly, the council voted against your ordination to the gospel ministry. All you could muster was one word: "Why?" The question, however, was unrequited, along with your nonverbal pleas for understanding, for tolerance, for sympathy.

At twenty-eight, you graduated from seminary. You spoke to your father about the possibility of working in his church as a non-ordained minister. Your father, fearing the political backlash, refused. At twenty-nine, you again found yourself teaching English to high school students. You are depressed, confused, and angry at God for making you who you are and daring to call you to God's ministry.

What is your name?

A Homeless Person

You rush down the street, braced against the sleet and freezing rain, struggling not to be late for the party. It's Christmas, and you know that three blocks away is a community of friends and laughter—a reality that is warming to the soul on such a cold day. In a few moments, you have arrived, and a group of smiling faces welcomes you into their home and hands you a glass of warm cider. The joy that you feel is indescribable—to be smiled at, to be served, to be welcomed.

Later in the evening, the group begins to sing Christmas hymns. You are asked if you have a favorite one to sing. Your eyes widen and you suggest "Adeste Fidelis," and then proceed to sing three verses with a strong, practiced voice, in Latin.

As the party comes to an end, you reluctantly leave the warmth of the hall and return to the street. You have nowhere in particular to be, so you begin to walk slowly down the sidewalk despite the cold. You relish in the new memory of the warmth of the party . . . it almost felt like family. It has been so long since you have felt any sense of a family—it's been over twenty-five years since your siblings decided that they could no longer deal with you . . . stopped allowing you into their homes . . . stopped returning your calls. You understood. Mental illness is a tough thing to deal with, they said.

Further away from the warm memories, you begin to hustle down the sidewalk. You try not to notice how cold your toes are, or the shivers that rack your body. Your clothes are inadequate, even with the newspapers lining the insides of your shoes and shirt for extra warmth. Your teeth chatter. You briefly stop at a bus stop for a breather. It has been a long walk, and you are exhausted. Only a few moments to catch your breath. You barely notice the lady sitting on the bench, bundled up against the cold, and waiting for the next bus after what has obviously been a long day of Christmas shopping. She gets your attention when she looks over at your unkempt beard and your ratty knit cap, audibly sniffs, and moves farther down the bench. It is difficult to make out her facial expression due to the cataracts that have progressed without care, but you can imagine what that expression shows. One eyebrow and one nostril half raised in a look of disgust, partnered with a subtle flash of fear in the eye. You understand. You would probably react the same way, you tell yourself. And you rise from your seat and continue on . . . to somewhere . . . at least for a few hours.

What is your name?

An Immigrant Person

You are an eighteen-year-old girl with the rest of your life in front of you. Since childhood, you have taken the road less traveled, made the difficult decisions. As a small child, your parents removed you from the corruption and poverty of their homeland in search of a better life in America. After the dangerous and difficult journey to your new home, you enrolled in school there, only to be told by your teacher that the rest of your class was ahead of you and that she could not afford the time to teach you the native language of your new teachers and classmates. So, at nine years old, you made the decision to teach yourself the language.

In school, as the burdens of poverty, strange customs, and a language barrier convinced some of your siblings that the educational system of their new home held no hope for them, you decided that you would have hope, that you would seize it. When many of your friends were resigning to the notion that they could not succeed, you were an honors student, in advanced classes, on the path to a college education. Then, at sixteen, when your dad explained that he needed you to drop out of school to serve as translator for the family's landscaping business, you decided not to let it be the end of your story. So, you went back to high school on your own time and graduated.

All your life, you have made the difficult decision, taken the road less traveled, but now, at eighteen-years-old, that road is closed to you. As your classmates pack for college, discussing their fear and excitement about this new stage in their lives, you can't help but think that your life has reached its final act.

You were not born in what has become your homeland. You didn't choose to live there, but you did choose how you would live there. After all, this new land is a place where anyone who is willing to work hard is supposed to be able to realize their dreams. Right? But, since you weren't born there, all paths to further education and legal, gainful employment are closed to you.

You remark to a friend, "My father moved our family here, so that my brothers and I could have a better life than he had, and I want my children to have a better life than I have. There is no shame in working like my father does, but I want to do something special, to make a difference." You are an eighteen-year-old girl with the rest of your life in front of you, and you feel like your fate is already sealed.

What is your name?

A Muslim Person

You *used* to fit in. Life *was* normal. You would go to school, hang with your friends, help your mother bake sangak, and play games like most other little girls. It was all so normal . . . until one day . . . until *that day*.

You see, your family has been through a lot—they made some big changes to provide you the life you have. Your mom and dad met in a war-torn country (which was his homeland). Hedging her bets, however, your mom convinced your dad to move from his home to her home, the United States, to lead a better life.

Despite all the challenges of adjusting to a new country, things have gone well. Your family has even grown more religious since you moved—there's something about change that drives a person to rely on God. Though your religious customs are somewhat different from many of your classmates, you've enjoyed close friendships—sleepovers, parties, swimming, playing ball.

Then, one day . . . *the* day came. And suddenly your friends, whom you once trusted with your secrets, viewed you with suspicion. In an instant, you were no longer an insider—your name no longer defined you—you became simply "one of them."

Your teacher even began viewing you differently. Your parents tried to stand up for you, but your school did little to prevent the other kids from picking on you. One teacher even told the other students that your religious customs were wrong—and told your friends misleading information about how you thought about others.

Since then, there has been so much strife in your family that your parents have split up. Your dad is moving back "home" where at least he feels like he can be himself. It's really sad . . . because you love your family, and your friends, and your life.

What's your name?

Hagar Sermonette[2]

You are a young woman born far away from democracy and an articulated notion of human rights. You have found yourself in the service of an older family as a slave. It's not a pretty reality, but it is indeed your reality. But the family is a very religious one that you hope will treat you with some respect, despite your role in their household.

You overheard your boss arguing with her husband over their infertility. This topic is always a source of bitter strife between the two—and you grieve for their frustration, confusion, pain, and continual disappointment. After this argument, though, you sense that something is different, a truth that is confirmed when you are summoned to your boss shortly afterward.

She stands in front of you but will not look you in the eye. You barely notice this disregard. It's normal. She explains to her husband that he can have you to solve their infertility problem. You panic—you are slave, not a concubine! But you cannot bear to utter an objection because you know that you have no choice. And any objection would probably go unnoticed anyway. After all, your mistress and her husband stand in front of you, discussing your body and your fate, and never bother to address you directly or even look into your eyes. You hear the stinging words of your mistress calling you over and over again *my slave*—each word like a whiplash to your heart. You relent. Soon, you discover that you are pregnant.

In moments that you dare to slip into your own thoughts, you grieve for the way your life has unfolded. You used to dream, as a child, of finding a man who would love you and respect you. You used to dream of children running around your feet. You used to dream of being a musician in the temple, or perhaps a weaver. But now, dreams are of little importance. You have found a man—an owner whom you belong to. You have the promise of a child—a life in your womb from a forced arrangement. But you will make sweet music for this new child to comfort him . . . and you will clothe him in the most beautiful clothing you can make.

What is your name?

Who are you?

---

2. This sermonette is taken from Rev. Shelley Woodruff's "In Her Shoes" delivered at rechurch on August 17, 2008. Used with permission.

What are you?

Is there a distinction?

This woman is the subject of our text this morning. This is, admittedly, a venture away from the big, bold heroes that we have been studying this summer in this series. The text is found in the sixteenth and twenty-first chapters of the book of Genesis. This is such a rich set of texts that I urge you to read it in entirety on your own.

But we have already heard her story. She is an Egyptian slave-woman, who is given to Abraham by her mistress, Sarah, in order to conceive a child. What our text tells us is intriguing and appalling.

Once Hagar becomes pregnant, she is treated so poorly by Sarah that she flees from the household. Alone, frightened, and certain that death is around the corner, Hagar cries out in the wilderness.

And God calls back to her. "Hagar! Where have you come from and where are you going?"

In this exchange, three things happen: God tells Hagar to return to Sarah; God names the unborn child "Ishmael," which means "God who hears"; and Hagar, in a bold move, names God. She calls God El-Roi, which means "God who sees."

Hagar returns to the home of her mistress and bears a child for Abraham. We think that all is settled . . . until Sarah herself finally gives birth to Isaac—the promised son. It does not take her long to realize that she no longer needs Hagar or Ishmael, and Sarah convinces Abraham to banish the two forever. It's biblical déjà vu. Hagar finds herself back in the wilderness—along with her son, scared to death, and certain that time is running out. And once again, God sees. The Lord is there to whisper her name like a caress and to provide for her.

The story of Hagar should make us uncomfortable. I won't apologize for that. If we call ourselves children of God, then we most naturally identify with Abraham and Sarah—the great patriarch and matriarch of our faith. Heroes, even. If we have grown up in the church, then we have heard sermon after sermon on these two individuals—don't forget, we even heard one on Abraham earlier this very summer as an example of biblical heroism.

But here we see the chosen ones of God treat another human being like property. It's ugly, isn't it? It's embarrassing. It's needless. It is one of those biblical stories that we ignore or sanitize so that we don't really have to deal with the vile reality of the decisions made in it.

Hagar serves as a barometer for our society. She is the prophet who points to our weaknesses and says, "See that? That's not right!" In our text, we know Hagar's name because the author records it, and because God himself speaks it in the wilderness.

But did you notice that Sarah never once calls this woman by name? When she wants something out of her (a child), Sarah calls her "my maid-servant." And when she is threatened by her and angry, Sarah calls her "my slave." This is a story where a human being—with a history, with a family, with emotions, and intellect, and desires, and faith, all of the stuff that goes into being human—is reduced to mere property. This woman is never looked at as something greater than her role—slave. She is given over to Abraham as a means to an end and not elevated from the category of "thing," even by another woman, Sarah.

I hope this text discomforts us all. That's a promising sign that we will not repeat the same mistakes of Abraham and Sarah. This text reminds us that we each receive opportunities all the time to treat others with dignity and the price others have to pay when we fail to do so. The challenge of Abraham and Sarah is that all too often, we as the chosen ones of a loving God, fail to see the humanity residing behind the eyes of another individual because we cannot get past that individual's category, stereotype, or role. I will be the first one to admit my guilt here. I encounter Hagars every single day!

This is really where Abraham and Sarah are at fault. Yes, they physically used her. They treated her as a means to an end. And they banished her to the wilderness. But those shocking actions were a result of the way they saw Hagar—or did not see Hagar, rather. Sarah, especially, fails to see Hagar as a fellow human and only sees her as a servant. A thing. A category. Hagar is wholly "other."

These stories that we have experienced today invite us to share in their narratives. That is why sympathy is not enough for Christ's church. Sympathy sustains distance. We can keep our "others" at arm's length. We can relegate them to a demographic feature. Or a crime. Or a religion we have not taken the time to understand.

I am sure we can all add to this list. The unwed pregnant woman. The prostitute. The refugee. The AIDS patient, and on and on and on. Hagar implores us to ask, "Do they have a name? Who are they? What are they? Is there a distinction?"

Reflection

The political fallout from this service was tremendous. Michael deserves an honorary firefighter's commission for all the fires he had to put out with the existing WRBC members. People were affronted at our temerity. *How dare we walk in another's shoes—literally or metaphorically?*

Some in attendance were brought to tears. The liturgy allowed them to reflect on those nameless "others" whom we ignore on our way into Home Depot and at busy intersections. Several others shared during our reflection time that they could not focus on the vignettes because they were so worried about their shoes. This serendipity forced them to deal with how thoroughly American consumerism was consuming them, forcing them to confront their tendency to construct their sense of self out of the things they buy rather than the people they are called to love.

What I find fascinating is the sustained impact of this liturgy. It's been ten years since this liturgy took place, and whenever I am around former rechurch attendees, this worship experience always seems to come up. Despite the congregational pushback, this liturgy succeeded in helping us to imagine life in another person's shoes. Unfortunately, for some at least, their foot issues made them so uncomfortable that they were not quite able to participate on the spiritual and interpersonal level that genuine empathy demands.

At the same time, this liturgy troubles me. Knowing what I know now about intersectionality and the propensity of Western Christianity to reduce the otherness of the other to an adjective (the poor, the gays, etc.), I cringe at some of the ways we characterized—even caricatured—those whom we deemed "other." I now know that such efforts to draw us toward those whom our encultured context has pushed to the margin can often produce more rather than less alienation. If I were given a do-over for this liturgy, I would have insisted that we create a space for folks in our rechurch community and beyond to offer their own testimonies, in their own words.

"The World Comes to (the Lord's) Supper"

For a new liturgy series centered upon justice, the liturgy planning team decided to shift things up dramatically. And here is a good place to say something about liturgical seasons. The amount of creativity, coordination, and effort to execute these curatorial liturgical visions is only sustainable if you build in time for rest and recovery. We learned to resist the temptation to *out rechurch* rechurch. In other words, if you are always seeking more elaborate and seemingly farfetched worship experiences, both you and those brave enough to serve alongside you will burn out. We elected, for the most part, to follow the rhythms of the liturgical calendar, a novel approach for this Baptist church.

As I noted above, I worked hard to keep the liturgical planning team several months ahead of schedule. This was a challenge: both logistically, in finding a time when so many people could meet, and practically, in sustaining the energy levels of my liturgical planning teammates and myself. Remember, too, that rechurch was only half of my job at WRBC. I also coordinated and recruited folks to participate in local, state, national, and international missional engagement. Sometimes, when I was still jet-lagged from a mission trip to Liberia or Sri Lanka or Morocco or Mexico, the rechurch liturgy planning team refueled me. But this also made it that much more important that I had all the logistics nailed down before I left to lead a mission trip.

Following the liturgical season allowed us to plan accordingly for high, holy seasons with all our creative energies and to embrace "ordinary time" as such. Thus, the liturgical calendar provided an ebb and flow to the elaborateness and time-intensiveness of our liturgies: Advent and Lent were "go big or go home" seasons for us, while the eleventh Sunday after Pentecost took on a much more subdued feel. To be clear, we weren't afraid to innovate during these times; but we did try to build in some periods of rest and recuperation—both for ourselves and our fellow congregants. This was one of those "ordinary" times in the life of rechurch.

Liturgical Vision

With major preparations already underway for both Advent and our one-year rechurch anniversary, we used the month of October to tackle some issues and themes that had yet to make an appearance in rechurch. We hosted a gathering centered on forging deeper relationships by setting up "speed dating" stations for people to try to get to know as much about one another as possible in two-minute intervals. We hosted a roundtable conversation on dealing with difficult people that ended up being far more emotionally and communally significant than we had planned. This led us to our week on justice.

The liturgy I'm now describing happened to fall on World Hunger Sunday. We wanted to take advantage of the rechurch dynamic to help those gathered to experience, albeit partially, the realities of global poverty and food scarcity. One of our planning team members shared a resource written by Aileen Van Beilen, entitled *Hunger Awareness Dinners: A Planning Manual*. The book was published in 1978. (Pay attention to this publication date; it will be important later.)

Logistics

Before the worship gathering, we transformed the worship space into a dining hall. We arranged sixteen large banquet tables in four rows in the center of the worship space. We left a large section empty between the tables and the stage, and at the front of the room, just below the stage, we set up a large rectangle table.

We prepared a slide to go on each of the screens with the following statistics concerning the world's population[1] in 2008:

WORLD Population—2008: 6,705,000,000			
Regional Population (millions)			
AFRICA—967			(14.4%)
	Northern Africa	197	
	Western Africa	291	
	Eastern Africa	301	
	Middle Africa	122	
	Southern Africa	55	
ASIA – 4,052			(60.4%)
	Western Asia	225	
	South Central Asia	1,683	
	Southeast Asia	586	
	East Asia	1,558	
EUROPE – 736			(10.9%)
	Northern Europe	98	
	Western Europe	188	
	Eastern Europe	295	
	Southern Europe	155	
AMERICAS – 915			(13.6%)
	Northern America	338	
	Central America	150	
	Caribbean	150	
	South America	387	
OCEANIA		35	(.05%)

1. World population statistics are from the Population Reference Bureau's "2008 World Population Data Sheet," accessible online at https://www.prb.org/wp-content/uploads/2008/08/08WPDS_Eng.pdf.

We procured groceries, linens, and dining accouterments in preparation for our liturgical meal. We also planned for folks to arrive an hour early to begin the set-up process. Some began cooking. Others cut out strips of paper with numbers on them and created placards for each of the regions of the world.

We also had to do some math based on global dietary statistics.[2] What we wanted to do was to transpose the caloric intake of each global region into the number of people we anticipated for worship. We sought to paint an accurate picture of how much and what kinds of foods one would eat if one happened to live in a particular part of the world. Since we knew that Americans constitute a small percentage of the world's population and at the same time consume far more calories on a daily basis than the rest of the world, we figured that by illustrating this among our worshipers we might foster empathy for those in the world having to make due with far less material resources.

Liturgy

When folks entered the worship space, they were handed a slip of paper with a number written on it and were instructed to find the placard that corresponded to their number. We recruited children to hand out the numbers. What this meant was that families were forced to sit apart from one another, disrupting their normal routine.

A team had already been hard at work in the church kitchen, which was located right next to the room where we hosted rechurch. As the worshipers entered, they were greeted with the smell of baking bread, grilled garlic and onions, and filet mignon.

The numbered placards were scattered all around the room: one each at the round tables, many more strewn across the empty carpet, and at the head table, which had seating room for only six. The head table was covered in a white linen tablecloth. It featured an ornate crystal candelabra, and each of the place settings consisted of china, crystal goblets, and expensive silverware, courtesy of Belinda. The houselights were dimmed.

---

2.   Global dietary statistics are drawn from data collected by the Food and Agriculture Organization of the United Nations. See http://www.fao.org/docrep/018/i3107e/i3107e.PDF, accessed July 12, 2018.

The rechurch band opened with a song, and then our senior pastor Michael Tutterow read the day's scripture passage. He began Part One of his sermon by noting the world population statistics on the screen. As he spoke, three teams entered the worship space. One team carried in a communion table to the front left of the worship space. They slowly worked throughout the service to make elaborate preparations for communion. A second team entered and replaced the numbered placards on each table with the name of a region of the world. The third team entered the worship space dressed as waiters at a formal restaurant, wearing tuxedos and elegant black dresses. This team, too, went about their work of serving each world region their respective lunches as the liturgy progressed.

The head table was served their meal first. Each received a steak, baked potato with all the fixings, grilled mushrooms and onions, and a glass of sparkling grape juice (remember, we were in a Baptist church, so no wine). This was the "North America Table." Next, our waiters served the "Europe" tables. They each received a bowl of vegetable soup, a roast beef sandwich, fresh fruit, and tea. The "Latin America" table was served next. They were served a bowl of beans and rice and a cup of coffee. The "Africa" group were seated on the floor, and they were either given a small bowl of plain mashed potatoes and water, only water, or nothing at all. The final group was also seated on the floor. This was the "Asia" section. They were given a small bowl of rice and a small cup of tea. Many were given nothing to eat.

While these sections were being served, group members were invited to stand and read statistics about the food situation among its inhabitants. All were invited to eat as they were served, and the band played a reflective song while slide images showed people living in each of these regions.

Part Two of the sermon was led by my wife, Dr. Abby Myers, who is a licensed psychologist. She led the community into a group processing time, inviting worship participants to share their reactions and feelings about what we had just experienced. I was astounded to hear how the liturgy had affected our worship participants. Many were in tears. Others promised to alter their lifestyles in light of all they'd learned and experienced.

The liturgy ended with Michael Tutterow inviting us to receive communion, reminding us of the common table we share, and sending us out to support the efforts of Bread for the World, an NGO dedicated to the alleviation of global hunger through advocacy and intervention efforts.

Reflection

We on the liturgy planning team could feel the discomfort in the room throughout this worship gathering. Buckhead, as I have mentioned, is one of the most affluent areas in Metro Atlanta, and few were emotionally prepared for this confrontation with the bitter realities of global inequity.

Several things happened during this gathering that we did not anticipate. One of those lucky few who was seated at the head table, the "North America" table, was a teenage girl. Her aunt, it just so happened, ended up sitting on the floor in the "Asia" region. The aunt was in the third trimester of her pregnancy. During the reflection time, spontaneously, this teenage girl stood up and offered her place at the head table to her aunt as she took her aunt's place on the floor. That's when everything went crazy.

Worship participants began to move around, shifting tables and moving chairs. Chaos ensued as folks tried to squeeze more people around their tables or took their meal to share with one who had nothing. People were crying and hugging and sharing. Rarely have I caught a glimpse of what Dr. King called the "Beloved Community." But here it was, at the corner of Peachtree and Wieuca Roads. In Buckhead, of all places.

During the reflection time, Abby could barely keep up with all who wanted to share. One worship participant used to be a professional body builder. He has maintained his mammoth physique. Through tears he shared that people in his "region" only received five hundred calories a day. He confessed that he eats over five hundred grams of protein a day! Others were action-oriented. They wanted to know how they could do something about the economic disparity they had just witnessed. I'm thankful that we had planned for this, as many of those gathered signed up to support the global efforts of Bread for the World.

"The World Comes to (the Lord's) Supper" liturgy remains, all these years later, one of the most frequently mentioned worship gatherings at rechurch. The liturgy we created allowed our worship participants to experience economic disparity inductively. Had we presented this issue more directly, I fear that many would have retreated to the sanctity of their political party's platform. Furthermore, a direct approach would have allowed many of us to intellectualize global hunger without having to hold these messy truths existentially. I think that this worship experience made such an impact because we did not over-script it. We curated space for engagement with a polarizing issue, and through this space the Spirit moved us to respond.

At the same time, I'm horrified by this liturgy. Years later, in a worship class I taught at Columbia Theological Seminary, one of my students confronted me about the stereotypes this liturgy perpetuated. As a first-generation Korean immigrant, she was offended by how this liturgy perpetuated ethnic stereotypes that neglect the great cultural and economic differences between Asian peoples. My student was absolutely right, and I was mortified that I had never in the intervening years spotted this glaring misrepresentation in "The World Comes to (the Lord's) Supper."

In her illuminating book *The Making of Asian America: A History*, Erika Lee contends that US perceptions of Asian-Americans undulates according to the waxing and waning of the political tide.[3] During different eras, some Asians have been presented to the US cultural imaginary as "good Asians." Others were regarded as "bad Asians." Each of these determinations ebbs and flows in response to the shifting and often contradictory politics behind the immigration and settlement practices thrust upon various Asian communities. In light of Lee's deep historical and cultural research, it is inconceivable to lump all Asians into a single cultural or economic category.

Furthermore, our liturgy neglected to nuance the economic and cultural differences within Asian countries. As with every country, and perhaps most visibly in North America, economic stratification shapes a national landscape. To decide, in abstraction, that all Europeans or Africans or South Americans enjoy a uniform level of economic privilege is just plain wrong. Furthermore,

3. Erika Lee, *The Making of Asian America: A History* (New York: Simon and Schuster, 2016), 7–9. She includes an important reminder, especially for those who minister in the American South: "Race has never been just a matter of black and white in the United States. Asian Americans have been both included and excluded from the country, sometimes simultaneously. In exemplifying this complicated and contingent history of American race relations, Asian Americans remain absolutely central to understanding the ongoing ways in which race works today."

we failed to attend to the ways our liturgy reinforced stereotypes about people from other countries.

Here, more than in any of the liturgies I present in this book, we can see the insidious and noxious effects of white privilege and white supremacy most clearly. Harlon Dalton writes in ways that inform this "failing to see" that I perpetrated and perpetuated in this liturgy. Dalton makes a helpful and important distinction between ethnicity and race:

> Ethnicity is the bearer of culture. It describes that aspect of our heritage that provides us with a mother tongue and that shapes our values, our worldview, our family structure, our rituals, the foods we eat, our mating behavior, our music—in short, much of our daily lives. We embody our ethnicity without regard for the presence or absence of other ethnic groups. Of course, ethnic groups influence one another in myriad ways, and more than occasionally come into conflict. But they do not need each other to exist.
>
> In contrast, races exist only in relation to one another. Whiteness is meaningless in the absence of Blackness; the same holds in reverse. Moreover, race itself would be meaningless if it were not a fault line along which power, prestige, and respect are distributed. . . . While ethnicity determines culture, race determines social position.[4]

In "The World Comes to (the Lord's) Supper," we conflated ethnicity and race, ignoring the ways in which food cultures and economic positioning shape diverse people groups—even within the same country.

This liturgy highlights what author Tim Wise rightly labels the "virtual invisibility of whiteness," which functions for those of us who have "psychological money in the bank, the proceeds of which we cash in every day while others are in a state of perpetual overdraft." Wise continues, writing in ways that ought to both chasten and shape our curatorial imaginations. He avers that it is insufficient just to see these things, or think about them, or come to appreciate what whiteness means. "If we recognize our privileges, yet fail to challenge them, what good is our insight?"[5] These and similar discernments

---

4. Harlon L. Dalton, *Racial Healing: Confronting the Fear Between Blacks and Whites* (New York: Anchor Books, 1996), 107–8.

5. Tim Wise, "Membership Has Its Privileges: Thoughts on Acknowledging and Challenging Whiteness," in *White Privilege: Essential Readings on the Other Side of Racism*, 4th ed., ed. Paula S. Rothenberg (New York: Worth Publishers, 2011), 134.

ought to have guided our liturgical planning. I offer this reflection here to show how easy it is for a well-intentioned group of ministers and church leaders to stir a congregation to action and, at the same time, marginalize others in our midst. This liturgy bears witness to the importance of racial and ethnic diversity at the heart of every liturgy planning team. Without incorporating multiple modes of difference into the DNA of your leadership, your liturgies cannot help but reflect the ideologies and biases of those in power at your church.

"Ancient-Future Wisdom: Life Lessons from the Man in Black"

This would be my last liturgy series with rechurch and my final days on the pastoral staff of Wieuca Road Baptist Church. This saddens me most because with this series we were really hitting our stride. Attendance was higher than ever. More and more folks were volunteering to serve as greeters, liturgists, or members of either our technology or logistics teams. Some longtime church members who attended the traditional service would remain after Sunday school to help with setup and serve in rechurch. For these folks, even though this was not their preferred worship style, they had come to see the impact it was having on others, especially on their children and grandchildren.

Coming out of a powerful Advent series, the liturgy planning team opted to shift things up as we headed into a new year. Many churches, and many contemporary evangelical churches in particular, feature New Year's series that try to capitalize on the whole fresh-start, New Year's resolutions shtick. We decided to play with that. We had no interest in offering "eight tips for a happy marriage" or how to have "your best life now." That's not what rechurch was about.

Instead, we offered a teaching series that participated in a certain deconstruction of New Year's wisdom—not *destructive*, but deconstructive in its attention to questioning those assumptions and ideologies that get in the way of meaningful, authentic existence before God and alongside others. The

47

five-week series was entitled "Life Lessons from the Man in Black." In it we hosted a mashup of two preachers: one ancient, the other far more contemporary. These were Qohelet, the preacher from Ecclesiastes, and Johnny Cash, the Man in Black.

Liturgical Vision

We wanted to provide our worship participants with a form of wisdom that doesn't immediately lend itself to commodification. Having decided to focus on texts from the book of Ecclesiastes this series, we realized that the preacher Qohelet would not be welcome to preach in Joel Osteen's, Andy Stanley's, or Steven Furtick's churches. Wisdom, Qohelet declares, adds vexation and sorrow to its beholder. But how do you share this without causing everyone to want to slit their wrists?

One of our planning team members—probably Wes, whose musical knowledge is borderline encyclopedic—suggested that we play a song or two by Johnny Cash during the series. Many of our rechurch gatherings featured a "secular" song that was performed at the opening of the service. Our liturgies opened with everything from Coldplay's "The Scientist" to Radiohead's "Fake Plastic Trees" to Michael Jackson's "Beat It" (the traditional folks at WRBC just *loved* that last one).

As our conversation and the Holy Spirit would lead us, we realized that Johnny Cash's life and witness provide a sort of contemporary corollary to that of Qohelet. Each "preacher" spoke from practical experience and was only positioned to pass on that wisdom near the end of his life. Furthermore, neither preacher painted a Pollyanna picture of the world, having each endured much hardship and suffered great pain and personal loss.

We paired the following texts from Ecclesiastes with corresponding songs from Johnny.

Week One:	Eccl 1:12-18	"Wanted Man"
Week Two:	Eccl 3:1-8, 11	"Hung My Head"
Week Three:	Eccl 7:1-14	"I Walk the Line"
Week Four:	Eccl 3:12-13; 9	"Hurt" (written by Trent Reznor)
Week Five:	Eccl 6:7-12	"The Beast in Me"

Logistics

From a logistical standpoint, this was one of our lighter series. The first obstacle we faced was in deciding who among us could actually sing like Johnny Cash. All the rechurch band members were in our twenties and thirties, and none of us could sing bass. We ended up inviting my good friend Jim Wallace to play the Man in Black. Jim attended the traditional worship service, but his children and grandchildren were active in every facet of rechurch from planning to performing to preaching. Jim was loved by all, and he was one of a growing cohort of more senior members at WRBC who supported rechurch even though it was not their preferred style of worship.

With our texts and music in place, the liturgy planning team discussed ways that we might help those gathered to experience the wisdom at work within the text in fresh ways. We decided to solicit the skills of some of our more dramatically gifted participants. For each of the weeks of the series, the worship element immediately before the sermon would combine a Johnny Cash song with a monologue writing by a rechurch participant. Below is an example from Week Two. In this instance, we interspersed the song's verses and chorus with the dramatist's monologue, which was performed in the dark with a spotlight on the performer.

....

"Hung My Head" Monologue

Verse one through "I hung my head, I hung my head"

Monologue:
Things just happen. I don't know why I did it. If you want to know . . . that's all I can tell you. Sometimes I just don't think. I figured I'd work at it for a few months, a year max, then . . . (sigh) well, something else would come along. Things just . . . happen. You know how it is. . . . One minute you're in the back of a car, and the next . . . Well, you know how it goes. . . . Things just happen.

Verse two through "I hung my head, I hung my head"

Monologue:

Things just happen. I didn't mean to take it this far. . . . Nobody tells you to think before you act. . . . Well, okay they do, but who really listens to that kind of advice? . . . I took off, had to get away from . . . well, you know. Sometimes things just happen. What can you do about it? People will shake their heads, some will whisper, some will call you a . . . well, you know. Things just happen.

Verse three through the second set of "I hung my head, I hung my head"

Monologue:

Things just happen. One day you die. . . . We all die. No point in second-guessing. What's done is done. Let sleeping dogs lie, I say. When you look back over all the stupid things you've done . . . well, you know. Things just happen. Of course, I would do things differently. Who wouldn't? . . . Advice? You're asking me for advice? Huh. . . . No point in worrying. Of course, if it were me, I would . . . well, you know, sometimes things just happen. Then you die. We all die.

Liturgy

As mentioned in the introduction to this Gallery, we tried to keep things simple leading up to and following the seasons of Advent and Lent. This was for pragmatic as well as liturgical reasons. Accordingly, the "Life Lessons from the Man in Black" liturgy series featured our "standard" room configuration: rows of chairs fanning out in expanding half-circles from the stage, with couches and Ikea recliners interspersed among them.

To open worship, we featured an upbeat song that connected with the day's theme. The songs ranged from "Turn, Turn, Turn" by the Birds (based off of Ecclesiastes) to "Less Like Scars" by Sara Groves. Next, there was a welcome and an invocation followed by corporate singing. Then the day's scripture lesson was read, and hospitality time followed. The band would call us back to our seats with a performance song, or they would tag one of the group songs we sang earlier in the worship gathering. By the end of the song, folks would have returned to their seats (in theory). The house lights were dimmed, and the musical monologue would begin. Next was the sermon, which in this series led to an experiential time intending to help the worship participants engage with the day's theme.

Like the musical monologue, the experiential time shifted each week. The first week Michael invited us to stations, where we were led to write a letter to ourselves in the future, reminding ourselves what was important to us and what we regarded the meaning of life to be. In Week Two, Michael led us in writing our own eulogies, asking us to reflect on what we would want folks to say about us after we die. Marti led the experiential time on Week Three, which played off the "Walk the Line" song to help us consider the relational impact of our choices. On Week Four, Matt helped us to create a pie chart of our time commitments. This led to a brief reflection on wholeness and the degree to which we were pursuing that in our lives. During the final week in the series, Matt invited everyone to participate in one of three worship stations dedicated to body prayer, art, or journaling.

Sermon[1]

Time seems to be in short supply. Even young people speak about how fast the year is flying by. "Can you believe it is mid-January 2010 already?" And the faster time flies, the faster we try to live. Time becomes a precious commodity with little to spare. Or else we turn time into an opponent or an enemy: We "race against time" so we can "beat the clock"; we "seize the day" and "strike while the iron is hot." But still time marches on, marches over us, until it simply passes us by.

In our fear that time will slip by us, we try to manage time, try to organize our lives for more efficiency. We buy calendars, Blackberries, iPhones,

---

1. Rev. Michael Tutterow would often adapt his sermon in the WRBC Sanctuary service at 9 a.m. for his sermon in rechurch. In the later sermon, he would draw from pieces of his manuscript, but much of his preaching was more conversational. This text is an abbreviated version of a sermon he preached on January 17, 2010. Used with permission.

and computer software to help us make the most of time. But though we may find ourselves doing more and more, the feeling of satisfaction seems illusive. Are we spending our time on the things that really matter? Is this really how I wanted to spend my time—spend my life? Qohelet, the speaker in Ecclesiastes, found himself there, too. Time had become a tyrant. He felt the pressure of time slipping away from him. And he realized that in the process of pursuing many good things, he had somehow missed the best things. Time had been the only real currency of his life, and he found himself dangerously close to bankruptcy with nothing to show for all his investments. Qohelet's search for meaning offers some clues for how we avoid the tyranny of time. Making the most of time is more than learning time management, we learn from reading Ecclesiastes.

In chapter three, Qohelet observes that life is in a constant state of change. It is always one time or another. In other words, time never stands still. It is in constant motion. But he reminds us that while time may be in constant motion, that motion is not without meaning. Because God is present in the seasons of our lives, each change in time possesses beauty and purpose. Because Jesus Christ is the Alpha and Omega, the beginning and the end, all time finds its meaning in him. All the seasons of our lives find their hope in him.

It is the movement of time that alerts us to the true value of time. The book of Ecclesiastes reveals that we live our lives between two time zones. One is called *chronos*—as in "chronology"—the clock and calendar time of each day. But there is another time—*kairos*, which means "the opportune time." In his book *My Name Is Asher Lev*, Jewish author Chaim Potok writes of a child's first encounter with death. As a boy and his father return from synagogue one Sabbath, they chanced upon a bird "lying on its side against the curb near their house." And the child asks his father:

> "Is it dead, Papa?" I was six and could not bring myself to look at it.
> "Yes," I heard him say in a sad and distant way.
> "Why did it die?"
> "Everything that lives must die."
> "Everything?"
> "Yes."
> "You, too, Papa? And Mama?"

"Yes."

"And me?"

"Yes," he said. Then he added in Yiddish, "But may it be only after you live a long and good life, my Asher."

I couldn't grasp it. I forced myself to look at the bird. Everything alive would one day be as still as that bird?

"Why?" I asked.

"That's the way the Ribbono Shel Olom made his world, Asher."

"Why?"

"So life would be precious, Asher. Something that is yours forever is never precious."[2]

For Ecclesiastes, the beauty of death is that it creates an urgency for life, a recognition that we savor the moments happening to us with family and friends precisely because they don't last forever. Ecclesiastes spends a lot of time on the subject of death not because he wants to be morbid or negative. It is because death creates a reality that, when faced, changes how we live. That's why he says if we really want to make the most of time, then face death—start living with the end of life in mind. How do you want to finish life? What do you want your life to say in the end? What do you want to be remembered for by others? Determine the finish you would like to have, then start collecting the building materials toward that kind of life.

A second lesson Qohelet teaches us emerges out of the first. Grief and sadness "sharpen understanding" and remind us not only of the things that matter in life, but the true values of life that last: faith, hope, and love, as Paul would later say. That's why Ecclesiastes says we can learn more about living in a house of mourning than a house of laughter. For there, in the end of things, we understand the law of the farm: we reap what we sow.

I find this law of the farm well-illustrated in a quote from Madame Chiang Kai-shek, a Chinese political figure whom many regard as the First Lady of the Republic of China (Taiwan). She writes,

If the past has taught us anything, it is that every cause brings its effect, every action has a consequence. We Chinese have a saying: "If a man plants

---

2. This excerpt is from Chaim Potok, *My Name Is Asher Lev* (New York: Knopf, 1972), 196.

melons, he will reap melons; if he sows beans, he will reap beans." And this is true of everyone's life; good begets good, and evil leads to evil. True enough, the sun shines on the saint and the sinner alike, and too often it seems that the wicked prosper. But we can say with certainty that, with the individual as with the nation, the flourishing of the wicked is an illusion, for, unceasingly, life keeps books on us all. In the end, we are all the sum total of our actions. Character cannot be counterfeited, nor can it be put on and cast off as if it were a garment to meet the whim of the moment. Like the markings on wood which are ingrained in the very heart of the tree, character requires time and nurturing for growth and development. Thus also, day by day, we write our own destiny; for inexorably, we become what we do.[3]

We become what we do. Or, in the words of the law of the farm, "we reap what we sow." What are you sowing with your lifestyle, the habits you practice? There is no waiting until fall to plant if one expects a harvest. This is not something we can "cram" for. Perhaps a good exercise is to write your obituary, to write down not just the accomplishments for which you wish to be remembered, but to ask what others will remember of you—your reputation for fairness and honesty, compassion and justice, friendship and loyalty.

Ironically, Jesus said that those who save their lives, who keep trying to hold all the good of their lives only for themselves, will lose what they seek to keep. But those who lose their lives, those who give their lives up not just for any cause but for his cause, for the sake of God's kingdom, these are the ones who will find their lives. These are the ones who discover the meaning of life, the joy of life. And at the end of their days, they do not feel they have misspent the currency of their lives. The Bible has offered us some knowledge today to make the most of our time. Happy are you who take the time to put that knowledge to use for yourself, and for the sake of others.

Experiential Time

Following the sermon, the band members took up their instruments and began to play softly the melody from "Hung My Head." As the band played,

---

3. Cited by Joi Tania Sigers, "You Are What You Do," *Self Help Daily*, February 18, 2006, http://www.selfhelpdaily.com/you-are-what-you-do/.

we allowed worshipers a few minutes of quiet reflection. Michael then led us into our experiential time. In light of the scripture, sermon, and Johnny Cash monologue, we were directed to write our own eulogies. Given death's inevitability, we invited worshipers to consider what things we hoped others would say about us when our time on earth was at an end. The band continued to play while we wrote. After several minutes, Michael encouraged us to read the eulogies each of us had written once a day as a way to direct our daily activities and decisions in the direction of the person we were striving to be or become. The band then closed out the service with a final corporate song.

Reflection

This liturgy series played off a common practice in many churches. Especially in evangelical settings—oriented as they are to pragmatic, teaching-focused worship gatherings—New Year's series focus on getting one's life in order, considering the past year and looking forward to the future year, and making greater efforts to live one's life in the way of Jesus. Where we diverged was in the use of Ecclesiastes as the scriptural basis for discerning this New Year's wisdom and in allowing the introspective and frequently melancholic songs of Johnny Cash to enhance our corporate worship experience. Each of these were welcomed in rechurch; in fact, I cannot recall any significant criticism about this series at all. Perhaps this had less to do with the ethos this series presented than the presence of Jim Wallace, a pillar of WRBC, at the center of the series.

Jim, our resident Johnny Cash, passed away in 2016. Michael preached his funeral sermon. This was the first time so many former members of WRBC had gathered together in one place after rechurch ceased to be. Both at the viewing and during the funeral, several former rechurch participants mentioned this liturgy series. It stuck me then as it strikes me now how fitting it was that Jim participated in these liturgies. He lived an incredible life. He loved people. He served his church and his community. Rest in peace, Jim!

Tips for Curating Liturgical Possibilities

I make exhibitions as both a seismographer and entertainer,
putting all my energy, knowledge and experience into the process,
working with the artists and the space to create one "work."

—René Block[1]

Drawing together the liturgical takeaways from these four worship experiences and looking toward the curatorial imaginations that we'll explore in Gallery II, we may discern several strategies to help us conceive Christian worship in these polarizing times. The visions we discern from both liturgical and art curators can be distilled into several tips that we may use to guide our liturgical and theological conversations as we seek to become a curating church.

Tip One: Ask Better Questions.

Good questions help us resist the all-too-common impulse to take things for granted. Questions can open us up to forging unexpected connections, particularly at the intersection of worship and culture. Even if the questions seem unanswerable—those are often the best questions, by the way—they set

---

1. René Block, "Art is beautiful . . . but it makes a lot of work: Interview with Lois Schwarz," in *The Readymade Boomerang: Certain Relations in 20th Century Art* (Sydney: Biennale of Sydney, 1990), 10.

us on a path of exploration guided by curiosity and wonder. And in any event, a question is not genuine if you already know the answer. My Columbia Theological Seminary colleague Bill Brown puts this marvelously in his book *Sacred Sense: Discovering the Wonder of God's Word and World.* He encourages us to allow a sense of wonder to situate us before scripture and nature, noting how such will make us more comfortable with ambiguity and difference. Brown adds,

> Reading with wonder shies away from leapfrogging toward a specific resolution or a single answer to a quandary. It is a way of abiding in the text while also bumping around within it, feeling the text's jagged contours, peering into its dark crevices, looking for anomalies and subtleties that raise eyebrows as well as, on occasion, the hair on the back of the neck. In wonder, the text provides space for wondering.[2]

This is what I mean by asking better questions.

Or consider a historical example. In 1928, Lincoln Kirstein and two of his friends founded the Harvard Society for Contemporary Art. This society was, in many respects, a prototype for what Alfred Barr would set out to create years later in the Museum of Modern Art. When Kirstein wrote to announce the founding of his society, he declared that it was dedicated to "art that was decidedly debatable."[3] That's not a bad way for a curating church to think. Think about it. What's the point of gathering together for worship week after week if we already have God all figured out?

We do our churches and the world a disservice when we avoid debate or difference. Curation can help us to interrogate our points of difference and disagreement, helping us foster spaces for discovery and even revelation. When we embrace uncertainty and undecidability in a congregational or parish context, we move away from defending our preexisting beliefs or holding our ideological ground. Hereby, we move toward an ecclesial way of being/becoming that is exciting and transformative.

2. William P. Brown, *Sacred Sense: Discovering the Wonder of God's Word and World* (Grand Rapids, MI: Eerdmans, 2015), 11.

3. Cited in Robert Storr, "How We Do What We Do. And How We Don't," in *Curating Now: Imaginative Practice/Public Responsibility*, ed. Paula Marincola (Philadelphia: Pew Center for Arts and Heritage, 2001), 11.

Another of my friends and Columbia Seminary colleagues, Mindy Mc-Garrah Sharp, offers an ingenious way to help her pastoral theology students interrogate their racist biases through an interrogatory writing prompt. At the beginning of class, she invites students to respond to a series of questions with brief words or phrases (e.g., Who am I? What impact do my attitudes and behaviors regarding racism have on my vocational call? How can I better use my institutional power to enhance the lives of all people?). These questions move her students to reflect on their self-identities, the impact of their racist attitudes and beliefs on their vocation, and how the students' models for pastoral caregiving might perpetuate racist attitudes and institutions. But McGarrah Sharp adds a twist. She asks her students to respond to these questions by writing with their non-dominant hand.

McGarrah Sharp has found this embodied practice to foster greater empathy in her students, opening deeper conversations and readying them to have their dominant/dominating worldviews challenged. In moving her students toward "courageous self-awareness," she models a helpful framework that we might introduce to our curatorial leadership teams. Quoting a colleague, McGarrah Sharp writes, "Before we can scale the walls that divide us, we have to see what bricks we are living behind. . . . Only through honest self-examination can we move to confess where and how we have practiced exclusion in our own lives."[4] This is precisely where better questions lead us.

Tip Two: Aim to Foster Discovery.

Liturgical curation is not about delivering pre-packaged answers to life's questions. Its very purpose is to kindle the interrogatory spirit, creating space for theological exploration and spiritual discovery. One of the major differences between curation and art is the former's focus on exposure: *how* we present a work becomes just as important as the work itself.

Theological educator Kate Siejk contends that when something "other" enters our field of consciousness, we are struck with mental and emotional

---

4. Brita L. Gill-Austern, "Engaging Diversity and Difference: From Practices of Exclusion to Practices of Solidarity," in *Injustice and the Care of Souls*, ed. Sheryl A. Kujawa-Holbrook and Karen B. Montagno (Minneapolis: Fortress, 2009), 37–38, cited in Melinda A. McGarrah Sharp, et al., "Race Matters in the Classroom," *ARTS* 26, no. 2 (2015): 34.

dis-ease. We may respond to this dis-ease in one of two ways. We can attempt to control or dominate what we experience as other, or we can surrender to wonder, which she describes as an intuition that otherness is sacred and revelatory. She writes, "If religious educators value the latter position over the former, then they will create a pedagogy that aims at stimulating wonder and transforming people from controllers into attentive and interested 'inquirers.'"[5] A "liberating pedagogy" emerges when we:

1. Stimulate wonder by posing a variety of questions that move believers to understand, to judge, to evaluate and to make decisions in an intelligent and responsible manner;

2. Encourage believers to articulate their unclear thoughts and to raise their own questions about the meaning and value of their own religious tradition; and

3. Encourage believers to share their own stories of faith and to express their own ideas and counter-ideas so that a variety of models and motives for the decisions and actions that shape our lives are shared.[6]

When we aim to foster discovery rather than provide answers, we enable our worship participants to chart their own courses and to pursue the questions that are most intriguing to them. If your curatorial team represents the diversity of your congregation or parish, then you can be sure that the time you allot for discovery will not be spent in vain.

A great art exhibition begins by seizing my attention. It grabs me by the lapels or pulls the rug out from under my feet. Likewise, curation that embraces the Spirit's instruction that is at once within and beyond both the words of scripture and the world of experience ought to challenge us to imagine both scripture and experience otherwise. The movement, then, is from disorientation to reorientation or from confusion to insight. Worship *must*

---

5. Kate Siejk, "Wonder: The Creative Condition for Interreligious Dialogue," *Religious Education* 90, no. 2 (1995): 234–35.

6. Ibid., 235.

forge a connection, however. No one wants to feel excluded or left out of the picture, as though the feeling of disorientation were a function of one's ignorance.

Virgil Thompson, an avant-garde composer and collaborator with Gertrude Stein, worked by a rule of thumb that is equally important for ministers: *Never overestimate the information your reader has and never underestimate their intelligence.* It has been my experience that congregants will rise to the level of our expectations and would rather be challenged than patronized.

We foster discovery aesthetically, intellectually, and spiritually when we expose our congregants and parishioners to the "fold." This is a term I borrow from contemporary philosophy. The fold expresses an irregularity, a ripple in the epistemological and/or cultural landscape. When we create spaces for people to discover this fold for themselves, we enable them to discern those points of resistance to God's sustaining and creative Spirit. We cannot deliver transformation. That is God's work. We can, however, nurture environments that compel us to pursue God deeper into the biblical text and out into the world.

Tip Three: Go Big or Go Home.

Curation that embraces its charge to both *care* and *cure* pursues the BIG questions. One of the criticisms leveled against curation is that it can narrow the scope of a subject matter. Curating church ought not be *about* a particular subject or issue (nuclear disarmament, human rights, etc.). In such, the subject matter presented is reduced to the level of mere illustrations of some theme. This significantly limits the congregant's or parishioner's imagination and his/her/their possibility for surprise and discovery.

We must resist the temptation to curb the hermeneutical framework for worshipers. Ralph Rugoff, director of the Hayward Gallery in London, writes, "Our encounters with art are never innocent of expectations and presuppositions, or of our knowledge about how different genres of art have been historically categorized or classified."[7] Much to the same point, our theological education sometimes constrains our presentation of liturgical-theological

---

7.   Ibid., 48.

artifacts. While contextual cues can serve to orient folks to a scripture passage, theologian, or hymn, they can also delimit the scope of our liturgical imaginations.

When I suggest that we go big or go home, I mean that we must resist dispensing a version of the gospel that Gardner Taylor once likened to opium, which stimulates even as it gives a false sense of what life is really about.[8] Philosophical theologian Vincent Lloyd has argued recently that ignoring the lived realities of marginalized and oppressed persons misses entirely one of two legitimate sites for genuine theological reflection.[9] Accordingly, when liturgies numb us to the pain that human and non-human subjects encounter on a daily basis, we fail to live up to our calling as church to provide both *care* and *cure*. We can and must do better.

Tip Four: Aim for Re-sponse.

All of these tips—asking better questions, aiming to foster discovery, going big—addresses a certain intentionality behind our curatorial imaginations. The final tip gathers these all together in terms of response.

The word *response* bears significant theological freight. Etymologically, the word arises from the Latin word *respondere* = *re* ("again") + *spondere* ("to pledge"). Thus, it connects with primal theological and ethical themes and commitments, both reminding and deconstructing earlier responses.

Curation participates in the original vocative dimension of church. As those who have been and continue to be *called out, ek-klesia,* the church is nothing less than a community of response. Robert Storr puts it well when he writes that the best exhibitions "have the most friction and show the most sparks."[10] That doesn't mean that folks will always *like* an exhibition or a liturgy. In my experience, some of the most meaningful worship moments appeared amid disquiet—or anger, even.

---

8. "Revered Gardner C. Taylor Extended Interview," Religion and Ethics Newsweekly, August 18, 2006, http://www.pbs.org/wnet/religionandethics/2006/08/18/august-18-2006-reverend-gardner-c-taylor-extended-interview/1881/.

9. Vincent W. Lloyd, *Religion of the Field Negro: On Black Secularism and Black Theology* (New York: Fordham University Press, 2017), 6–7.

10. Storr, "How We Do What We Do," 13.

Embracing Theological Multiplicity

Advancing what they label a "responsible pluralism of interdependence and uncertainty," theologians Catherine Keller and Laurel Schneider urge us to *embrace* the multiple expressions of God's work among us. They write, "What had always seemed a liability for Christian theology—multiplicitous differences contending from within and competing from without—has miraculously turned into theology's friend. Indeed, an emergent commitment to the manifold of creation as it enfolds a multiplicity of wisdoms may be functioning as a baseline requirement for theological soundness."[11] To Keller and Schneider's theological soundness I would add liturgical possibility.

Embracing a "theology without walls," comparative theologian John Thatamanil challenges the notion that an "orthodox" understanding of God ever existed. Rather, he contends, "Virtually all of our religious traditions have been marked by considerable porosity and a long history of mutual contact."[12] He continues, "My sense is that the trinity can indeed be an open site of interreligious dialogue and exchange but not so long as Christians bring to dialogue a finished conception of the trinity that can in no way be enriched by way of dialogue and comparative theology."[13] Though I did not have this vocabulary at my disposal at the time, I can now think of no better way of describing the rechurch ethos than that of embracing theological multiplicity. Depending on your cultural and denominational context, these liturgies may not seem all that radical; but in the context of a wealthy, formerly Southern Baptist church in Atlanta, it sure felt radical to us.

---

11.   Catherine Keller and Laurel C. Schneider, introduction to *Polydoxy: Theology of Multiplicity and Relation*, ed. Catherine Keller and Laurel C. Schneider (London: Routledge, 2011), 1.

12.   John J. Thatamanil, "'True to and True For': The Problem and Promise of Religious Truth for a Theology without Walls," *Journal of Ecumenical Studies* 51, no. 4 (Fall 2016): 462; Idem, "God as Ground, Contingency, and Relation: Trinitarian Polydoxy and Religious Diversity," in *Polydoxy*, 239.

13.   Ibid.

Curating Cultures: Lessons from the World of Art

The process of curating cures the image's powerlessness,
its capacity to present itself. The artwork needs external help;
it needs an exhibition and a curator to become visible.

—*Boris Groys*[1]

Culture and curation relate like precipitation and evaporation. Droplets of culture accumulate like dew on land and cityscapes. The friction of economics, politics, technologies, and socio-ethnic spaces of belonging and exclusion produce the energy necessary to send the otherwise disparate droplets into the atmosphere, where they are in turn accreted and descend in concentrated form. In other words, curation gathers and intensifies manifestations of culture. Curation gives what it receives from culture, and herein lies its power to shape—and even deconstruct—culture. Consider the following examples.

In 1995, Lorna Ferguson and Christopher Till curated the first Johannesburg Biennale. This exhibition took shape following South Africa's first multiracial elections, marking the historic day that Nelson Mandela became the president of South Africa. The exhibition was titled *Africus*, and it aimed

---

1. Boris Groys, "The Curator as Iconoclast," in *Cautionary Tales: Critical Curating*, ed. Steven Rand and Heather Kouris (New York: Apexart, 2007), 49.

to inaugurate the country within the larger global community following the former's deep estrangement with the later through Apartheid.

The Inaugural Gwangju Biennale, also held in 1995, was entitled *Beyond the Borders*. This exhibition attempted to bring forward art from the "Western World" together with that of the "Third World." *Beyond the Borders* conveyed a message of global citizenship that transcends divisions between ideologies, territories, religions, races, cultures, peoples, and the arts. Aesthetically, it manifested art's ability to overcome meaningless pluralism and intended to establish new orders and relationships between the arts and humankind.

In 1996, a team of curators presented an exhibition called *Manifesta*. This was a roving exhibition, which took shape in different sites across Europe. It took the fall of the Berlin Wall as a cue for reconsidering a new Europe in terms of political ideologies, economic structures, and novel communication technologies.

In 2009, twenty years after the fall of the Berlin Wall, a curatorial team worked to host *Integration and Resistance in the Globalization Era* in Cuba. The 10th Havana Biennial Art Exhibition took place from March 27 to April 30, 2009. Experts from the Lam Contemporary Art Center reviewed more than four hundred proposals submitted by artists from forty-four nations. For the first time, the organizers decided to include Western countries. Common topics included the tensions between traditional and contemporary realities, challenges to the historical processes of colonization, the relationships between art and society, individuals and memory, the effects of technological development on human communication, and the dynamics of urban culture.

Despite their temporal and geographical differences, these exhibitions participate in what I am labeling a curatorial imagination. Such an imagination coalesces around the tasks of engagement, conservation, and transformation. Without cultural engagement between artists, cultures, and their potential audiences, nobody shows up. Furthermore, if these curators were not concerned with conserving something quintessential from their respective cultures, there would be nothing to display. Lastly, and this is particularly evident when one reads the work of the curators themselves, success or failure is measured in terms of existential, interpersonal, and political transformation. This last point is key.

Curators are united in their conviction that an exhibition ought not leave audiences unchanged. For instance, in his book *Thinking Contemporary Curating*, Terry Smith explains that the art exhibition "works, above all, to shape its spectator's experience and take its visitor through a journey of understanding that unfolds as a guided yet open-weave pattern of affective insights . . . that accumulates until the viewer has understood the curator's insight and, hopefully, arrived at insights previously unthought by both."[2] Smith's declaration of curatorial intent maps perfectly onto my own hopes and dreams for liturgical curation. Such a "journey of understanding" constitutes a communal world view that in turn shapes a community's experience of and orientation to the gospel.

These three necessary components of artistic curation—engagement, conservation, transformation—develop along the trajectory innate to curation: to care for people, their cultures, and their mutual thriving and to provide cure for people and cultures in some sense. The (post)modern ailments to which curation responds as cure vary from locale to locale. Whether it be xenophobia, racism, heterosexism, environmental apathy, or some combination thereof, curators do what they do because they want to make a positive impact on the way we think, speak, and behave. Herein lie the most salient points of congruence between art curators and pastors: We do what we do because we care and what we offer (in museum galleries or worship spaces) constitutes our best efforts in pointing toward the cures for personal and societal ills.

In the five installations that I sketch below, we will be less concerned with content than process. In other words, I'm not interested in describing every piece of art these curators employed to fashion their aesthetic worlds. More important for curating church is nurturing a curatorial sensibility that these experts have spent years honing. Accordingly, the chapters will move from the curators' vision for their installations to a description of the installations themselves to the critical receptions their exhibitions received. We will end each treatment with liturgical takeaways. My hope is that by leading you into these curators' heads, so to speak, we will begin to grasp that curatorial

---

2. Terry Smith, *Thinking Contemporary Curating* (New York: Independent Curators International, 2012), 35.

intuition that facilitates the tripartite aims of engagement, conservation, and transformation.

Dispelling Myths About Curation

Before we proceed to examine the five art installations I've curated for your reading pleasure, it is important to name and then dispel some common myths about curation.

1. Curators are aesthetic snobs who believe that their opinion trumps all others.

Okay, this myth is kind of true. Art curators are also art critics. Accordingly, they have tended to elevate certain kinds of art above others. Artists and their works go through a process not unlike canonization. Here the curator/ critic's aesthetic judgment is paramount. This Picasso. That Dali. This work of Chopin. That poem of Angelou. We find these so-called "masterpieces" in art, music, and literary anthologies, at national galleries and symphonies.

Even as the work of filtering and privileging is essential to the curator's role, this is not the entire story. Heather Kouris notes, "A good exhibition is not merely a gathering of works of the fifty greatest artists, but should involve some reflection of societal input, and/or a certain recognition of art history, geography, and culture, not to mention sharing some sort of personal perspective." In other words, the myth of the lone curator displaying his favorite works without regard for their public reception does not hold. Curators need to hold in balance their own aesthetic tastes with those of the population at large.

Curators must also be able to articulate the reasons why *this* work is better than *that* work, or why *this* work makes more sense than *that* work given the overarching curatorial imagination in play. Kouris continues, "Those acting in the role of curator should be able to communicate their ideas or intentions easily and openly with the public who sees their exhibition."[3] This is true also for pastors and church leaders conceiving liturgies: We must know why we are doing what we are doing and be able to articulate those reasons in a way that those who have not been privy to our training can understand.

---

3. Heather Kouris, introduction to *Cautionary Tales*, 11–12.

Pastors are not that different from art curators, and let's be honest, we can be just as snobbish. Both pastors and art curators are trained professionals—most with Master's degrees and some with earned doctorates. We, like them, have spent years studying and honing our professional (theological) sensibilities. Who among us has not felt a least a slight twinge of exasperation when a congregant or parishioner has challenged our liturgical judgment? Pastor, I think we should've sung "Just as I Am" after the offertory. You smile and nod in that perfectly pastoral way you've been trained, but inside you are thinking of the theological dissonance such a decision would have created. Not all snobbery is ill-founded, and not all judgment is unassailable.

2. Curators believe that whatever is new is inherently better than that which is old.

There is an avant-garde bias that elevates that which is new and original over that which is perceived to be old and hackneyed. We must never forget that the curator's aesthetic judgment remains a judgment. There is no objective, universal reason why the performance art of Carolee Schneemann or the photographs of Robert Mapplethorpe deserve pride of place above Cézanne or Van Gogh. The avant-garde movement that came into mainstream prominence during the early twentieth century took specific aim against the elitism and bourgeois aesthetic and political sensibilities of so-called "classic" art.

Curator Okwui Enwezor adds further complexity to the myth that whatever is late is necessarily great. He writes, "Today's avant-garde is so thoroughly disciplined and domesticated within the scheme of Empire that a whole different set of regulatory and resistance models has to be found to counterbalance Empire's attempts at totalization."[4] This astute observation focuses our attention on the discursive regimes that govern our ways of theological/liturgical thinking before we even begin to approach our ecclesial calling to care and to cure. We may think that we are pushing the boundaries of liturgical innovation, but this confidence can blind us to who placed the boundaries there in the first place.

---

4. Okwui Enwezor, "Tebbitt's Ghost," in *The Manifesta Decade: Debates on Contemporary Art Exhibitions and Biennials in Post-Wall Europe*, ed. Barbara Vanderlinden and Elena Filipovic (Cambridge, MA: MIT Press, 2005), 176.

In his critical assessment of contemporary curatorial practice, David Balzer argues that contemporary curators must understand the avant-garde aesthetically and commercially, "combining the two to turn something that is new and thus vulnerable into something that is nothing short of invincible. The curator ushers forth the avant-garde, not making, but shaping, it new."[5] It is partly this relentless quest for innovation and novelty that Balzer finds so disturbing about the newfound ubiquity of curation.

While the drive to innovate is certainly a defining aspect of contemporary curation, much more important is the effort to help us experience older works in new ways. As philosopher and art theorist Nicolas Bourriaud points out, there remains an internal tension between art and history. Art makes history even as it refracts the colors and contours of life with a critical light. Commenting on major, epoch-defining works in art history (e.g., Picasso's "Guernica," Malevich's "White on White"), Bourriaud observes that what sets certain works apart from the historical circumstances that informed them is that these were not just works but events that "irreversibly modified" what emerged after them. He writes, "Although they started out as consequences, they became first causes and brought forth manifold effects in other artists and works; in turn, these effects spread and came to be part of the atmosphere of a general sensibility."[6] Thus, even though it might seem that novelty is curation's Great Commandment, curation is better equipped at helping us discern how the ideological and cultural conditions that constitute a societal epoch produce the conditions for certain kinds of art and how such works of art lend fresh ways of thinking and expression to cultures.

3. Art leads; curation follows.

Another myth related to curation concerns sequencing. There is a general assumption that first someone produces a work of art and then someone else comes along to display it. While this is true, it can also lead us to overlook the formative and generative aspects of curation along with the ways that curators solicit works of art as often as they present preexisting works.

---

5. David Balzer, *Curationism: How Curating Took Over the Art World and Everything Else* (Toronto: Coach House Books, 2014), 51.

6. Nicolas Bourriaud, *The Exform*, trans. Erik Butler (London: Verso Books, 2016), 29–30.

Hans Ulrich Obrist contends in his book *Ways of Curating* that curation boils down to this: forging cultural connections. In other words, curation creates opportunities for different elements to touch, thereby leading the observer to dance upon the line between order and disorder—indeed, the order created is disorder. Thus, Obrist argues that curators also create something new. Contemporary curators traffic in what Obrist labels "feedback effects" between local and global cultures, forging spaces to encounter otherness without assimilation.[7] The central tasks of curation are thus cultivating, growing, pruning, and trying to help people and their shared contexts thrive in generative conversation with one another.

Obrist exemplifies the effects of collaboration between curators and artists when they share in one another's creative processes. Out of the influence of the Italian conceptual artist Alighiero Boetti, Obrist begins his work by helping artists imagine those projects that they could not realize under existing conditions. Obrist writes, "I don't believe in the creativity of the curator. I don't think that the exhibition-maker has brilliant ideas around which the works of artists must fit." Rather, the curatorial process always starts for Obrist with a conversation, out of which he discovers his task: to find the means to realize such artistic visions.[8] For example, in 1994 Obrist curated an exhibition entitled *Do It*. The entire exhibition was comprised of do-it-yourself descriptions and procedural instructions. As the exhibition moved from city to city, new DIY pieces were added by artists from each locale. Thus, we find in *Do It* an empirical challenge to the notion of the artist's primacy. Obrist's open, exhibition-in-process model challenges the very possibility of firmly differentiating between artist/curator and between original/copy.

4. Curators operate on the outermost frontier of the artistic universe, challenging institutional mores with utterly original expressions of aesthetic panache.

Curatorial iconoclasm is not as radical as it thinks it is. Many contemporary curators and artists share a common bias—a disdain, really—against traditional museum galleries. Some contemporary art curators denigrate gallery installations as prosaic. There is thus a tendency for curators to seize

7.   Hans Ulrich Obrist with Asad Raza, *Ways of Curating* (New York: Farrar, Straus and Giroux, 2014), 15.

8.   Ibid., 10.

the would-be observer by the ankles and bash his head against the rocks of aesthetic norms. Such curators seek to challenge a dogmatism they perceive in their curatorial forebears.

While seeming to eschew the undeniable reality of capitalism embraced by traditional galleries, some contemporary curators market themselves and their artistic collaborators as above such petty concerns as money, while furtively boosting the market value of their anti-market, non-commodifiable products. It is important that we recognize the internal tensions at work here. I see very much the same thing occurring when some evangelical women hit the speaking circuit with a message about the importance of women to remain at home to care for their children and husbands. The exception undercuts the rule.

Freestyle
The Studio Museum, Harlem

An exhibition is in many ways a series of conversations.
Between the artist and viewer, curator and viewer, and between the works of art
themselves. It clicks when an exhibition feels like it has answered some questions,
and raised even more.

—*Thelma Golden*[1]

Thelma Golden curated an exhibition entitled *Freestyle* in 2001 at the Studio Museum in Harlem. Golden formerly served as an associate curator at the Whitney Museum, where she exhilarated the art world with her provocative 1994 exhibition, *Black Male: Representations of Masculinity in Contemporary Art*. In that exhibition, she worked to subvert stereotypes about black men and black sexuality by placing them in a fresh context.[2] In many ways, Freestyle continues and expands this earlier conversation.

Curatorial Vision

The *Freestyle* exhibition featured twenty-eight, up-and-coming artists, exemplifying a shift that is as much epistemological as aesthetic. The product of

---

1.   Suzanne Rust, "The Art of Being Thelma Golden, Director and Chief Curator of the Studio Museum in Harlem," *The Trio* (May 16, 2013), http://thegrio.com/2013/05/16/the-art-of-being-thelma-golden-director-and-chief-curator-of-the-studio-museum-in-harlem/2/.

2.   See Thelma Golden, *Black Male: Representations of Masculinity in Contemporary American Art* (New York: Whitney Museum of Modern Art, 1994).

Golden's labors, along with the artists whose work she exhibits, ramify according to a new designation: *post-black*. By this neologism, Golden points to artists who resist the reductionistic label of "black artist" even as their work has been steeped in and deeply interested in redefining complex notions of blackness. Golden's exhibition declared boldly that "post-black was the new black."[3] *Freestyle* pushed the art world beyond a cultural essentialism that reduces postmodern art—along with the Black Arts Movement—to a generic multiculturalism.

Lowery Stokes Sims, who was then director of the Studio Museum in Harlem, wrote at the time that *Freestyle* tackles many of the familiar issues of postmodern exhibitions: identity, culture, and aesthetics. Sims notes that what sets *Freestyle* apart from artistic expressions along the "well-trodden paths in the postmodern world," is that:

> These artists are as much rural as urban in their perspectives, "First" World as "Third." Their work is informed as much by western theater as African masquerade, by consumerism as much as metaphysics, by abstraction as much as narrative and storytelling, by fairy tales as much as the reality of social surveillance. Unexpected materials—from digital media to sound, from paint to pomade—enrich our experience of race and gender, as do considerations of sexual orientation, multi-racialism and transnational experience, power and dominance, narcissism and surrogacy.[4]

The works that constitute *Freestyle* displayed a commitment to *intersectionality*, which transcends monolithic designations of the works of African and African American artists beyond the delimiting designation: "Black art." Golden notes the multifarious influences of the artists entrusting their work to her care. She writes, "They are influenced by hip hop, alt rock, new media, suburban angst, urban blight, globalism, and the Internet—the felicitous device of international communication and new optimism in the wake of the initial postmodernist urge to define the avant-garde as dead."[5] *Freestyle* points beyond postmodern aesthetic expression to something else, something that is "both post-Basquiat and post-Biggie."

---

3. Thelma Golden, introduction, *Freestyle* (New York: The Studio Museum in Harlem, 2001), 14.

4. Lowery Stokes Sims, foreword, *Freestyle*, 12.

5. Golden, *Freestyle*, 15.

Description

Examples from this exhibition reveal the aesthetic breadth and diversity of Golden's artists. For example, Golden selected several works by Laylah Ali from the latter's "Greenheads" series. These are a series of drawings that depict the ambivalence of brown-skinned bodies in American society. Critic Olukemi Ilesanmi aptly characterizes Ali's drawings as "iron fists briefly disguised as a velvet glove," as "allegories of power," and as "parables of race as experienced in America." Indeed, Ali's works have a way of sneaking up on the viewer; they draw us in, and once they have our full attention, they reveal something shocking and terrible about the realities of African-American experiences. Her paintings highlight the objectification, surveillance, and betrayal of black bodies.[6]

In one of Ali's drawings, for instance, we encounter an androgynous figure running. The figure wears a light blue button-up shirt and dark blue pants, which fall undecidable between work clothes and prison uniforms. The figure's expression is one of fear, and it is unclear whether the figure is running away or toward something. Another of Ali's drawings in this series features three lynching victims. A fourth figure, whose forearms and one leg are missing and which are held by each of the three lynching victims, is forced to behold this gruesome spectacle by a fifth figure who stands sentry. All, save the dismembered figure, wear masks. Ali's drawing haunts the viewer even as it solicits an interpretation.

Another example in Golden's exhibition is a photograph by Rashid Johnson entitled "Jonathan's Eyes." In it an African-American man glares into the camera in a way that seems simultaneously to demand that the viewer see him as a man (not a homeless man) and to solicit the viewers' concern—care, even. Critic Sylvia Chivaratanond comments, "Jonathan, the sitter, not only emphatically returns the viewers' gaze but he exposes different sides of his personality . . . enabling Jonathan to take possession of his own image."[7] The photograph disturbs the objectifying gaze of the viewer, reclaiming Jonathan's subjecthood.

---

6. Olukemi Ilesanmi, "Laylah Ali" in *Freestyle*, 20.
7. Sylvia Chivaratanond, "Rashid Johnson" in *Freestyle*, 49.

Playing through an overhead speaker in another part of the exhibition hall, the participant hears an audio exhibition created by Nadine Robinson that mixes political speeches by George W. Bush and the Rev. Martin Luther King Jr. against laugh tracks. Along this line is a video created by Susan Smith-Pinelo. The video is entitled "Sometimes," and it features a video loop tightly framed on the artist's own breasts, which jiggle and bounce beneath a white V-neck T-shirt to the rhythm of Michael Jackson's *Working Day and Night*. The video says much. It addresses the objectification of Black women in hip-hop videos and at the same time embodies a certain embrace of Black women's sexuality. As critic Claire Gilman comments, "Perhaps what is most unsettling is the way in which, refusing to adopt the didactic approach that has traditionally been expected of minority artists, Smith-Pinelo shifts the focus from dogmatic societal attitudes to our personal and ultimately more nuanced responses to the world."[8] Whatever the viewer's reaction to this piece, *some* reaction is called for.

Even as the art displayed during the *Freestyle* exhibition reflects a turn in contemporary art, it is also avowedly guided by Golden's dissatisfaction with the whole enterprise. In particular, Golden pushes against the dogmatic insistence for multiculturalism, which seemingly embraces cultural diversity while simultaneously protecting the political and economic "core" of the dominant culture.[9]

Golden is not alone in her distaste of multiculturalism. In his introductory essay "Renigged" in the exhibition book *Freestyle*, Chicago-based curator and critic Hamza Walker writes, "I arrived at the doorstep of diversity very angry. I experienced multiculturalism as the sound of a door closing rather than opening." Following a default on promises made during the Civil Rights Movement and a burgeoning post-racial impetus overtaking popular and political discourse, Golden sought to articulate something more. Walker comments,

> Just as representations of blackness mediate black-white relations they also mediated black-black relations and ultimately the relationship I had to myself. Each and every image of someone black was speaking to me, at me and

---

8. Claire Gilman, "Susan Smith-Pinelo" in *Freestyle*, 73. See http://www.dailymotion.com/video/x2o3r5z.

9. See Walter D. Mignolo, *The Darker Side of Western Modernity: Global Futures, Decolonial Options* (Durham, NC: Duke University Press, 2011), 35.

for me. A "we" was assumed, imposing itself of whatever meager sense of self I could muster. "I" could start the morning as Michael Jordan or Michael Jackson (or Michael Jordan Jesse Jackson) and end the day a crime statistic.[10]

This quotation highlights an essential feature of *Freestyle*. Walker names a space of continuity of the central affirmation of the Black Arts Movement concerning the innate value and beauty of Black cultures and Black bodies. At the same time, *Freestyle* carries this conversation forward by examining the intersectional dynamics at play.

Critical Reception

New York Times critic Holland Cotter describes *Freestyle* as being "ahead of the curve." He praises Golden, both for her curatorial insight and for her vision for emerging trends and techniques looming on the artistic horizon. While acknowledging the physical constraints with which Golden had to work (the Studio Museum was undergoing expansion in 2001, forcing her to cram twenty-eight artists' works into a very small space), Cotter lauds Golden for the depth and breadth of her selections. Noting the many styles and mediums, Cotter writes, "It's best to take *Freestyle* as a loose assemblage, an anthology of individual styles and sensibilities, some more interesting and assertive than others, going in different directions." This, he recognizes, fulfills Golden's curatorial intention: to trouble facile notions of "black art" by highlighting the complexities, tensions, and diversity celebrated among African-American artists. Cotter concludes:

> This is important stuff. Maybe that's why there's a sense that the best artists in the show—along with the young curators, scholars and critics who contribute to its slender but spicy catalog—are operating beyond the level of conceptual noodling that seems to be endemic at present. They're actually talking about something— life—and we're sure to be hearing from many of them again soon.[11]

---

10. Hamza Walker, "Renigged" in *Freestyle*, 17.

11. Holland Cotter, "Art Review: A Full Studio Museum Show Starts with 28 Young Artists and a Shoehorn," *The New York Times*, May 11, 2001, http://www.nytimes.com/2001/05/11/arts/art-review-a-full-studio-museum-show-starts-with-28-young-artists-and-a-shoehorn.html.

In his review for *The Village Voice,* Jerry Saltz offers tentative praise, writing, "There is enough dynamic and promising art on hand to say it's a good show, and enough not-so-good work to say it could have been better."[12] His major critique comes at the end of his review. Saltz writes, "In spite of Golden's claim that *Freestyle* is *post-conceptual,* much of the work in it is nothing but hackneyed conceptualism." This critique notwithstanding, Saltz's review is positive. He praises Golden and her team for curating an exhibition that "stands on its own." He continues, "Like a lightbulb, it needs no explanation: The minute you see it, you know why you needed to see it." He singles out Laylah Ali's work in particular, labeling them "meticulously rendered nodules of narrative ambiguity."

These are merely a sampling of critics' responses to the exhibit and its catalog. What I wish to underscore is that even as it receives widespread approbation, critics still find faults and room for improvement. On the one hand, this is germane to the critic's vocation: critics critique. On the other hand, and given the pressure of art critics to find fault, the overall positive nature of these reviews suggests that Golden succeeded in her work of engagement, conservation, and transformation.

Liturgical Takeaways

A defining feature of Golden's curatorial prowess transcends her eye for great art and her capacity to structure points of engagement between such art and her audience. Her work pushes the very definition of *art* and the conceptual parameters that constrain certain art and artists to certain categories. In so doing, Golden allows the artists' visions to transform the viewers' assumptions. This, I believe, is a model for liturgical curation: not resting with variations but in questioning the nature, function, and reception of Christian worship itself.

Golden exhibits a deep historical consciousness that explores how Black artists participate in contemporary notions of blackness arising out of the Civil Rights Movement of the '50s and '60s, the essentialism of the Black Arts Movement of the '70s, and the vagaries of postmodern multiculturalism

---

12. Jerry Salz, "Post-Black," *Village Voice* (May 15, 2001), http://www.villagevoice.com/news/post-black-6415619.

and globalization of the '80s and '90s. And at the same time, she shows the ways in which her artists challenge these movements in the worlds of art and culture.

I find a parallel between Golden's work here in *Freestyle* and the work of Andrea C. White, associate professor of theology and culture at Union Theological Seminary in New York City. In her forthcoming monograph *The Scandal of Flesh: Black Women's Bodies and God Politics*, White both draws upon and challenges the theological anthropologies of Karl Barth and James H. Cone from a womanist theological frame. In so doing, White names what is good and life-giving in each of these theologian's work, while also highlighting the points of dissonance such thinking structures for African-American women.

What can Golden's curatorial approach teach ministers about curating church? There are (at least) three takeaways we ought to consider.

1. Curating church ought to take a point of view without constraining that of its participants.

Golden makes no attempts to hide her curatorial labors; rather, she names her ideological commitments in her introduction to the exhibition catalogue. The curatorial biases of *Freestyle* manifest according to Golden's concept of *post-black art*. Remember that this show took place a full eight years before pundits would employ the term *post-black* to signal a *post-racial* America under President Obama.

My central takeaway from this exhibition centers around vision casting. Golden is not afraid to name what she sees in the worlds of culture and art. She names "post-blackness," and she offers an overarching vision that is assertive without being totalizing. Naming the exhibition *Freestyle*, for instance, (a word used in hip-hop cultures to describe a way with music and dancing that frees the emcee or dancer to improvise within certain acoustical boundaries), casts a vision for artists both to work within and also to subvert preconceived artistic paradigms. For pastors and church leaders seeking to curate worship experiences, Golden embodies a form of leadership that evokes innovation and gives space for improvisation.

What might it look like for a liturgical curator to name and create space for a post-Baptist, post-Catholic, post-Episcopalian worship experience?

How might this free worship leaders and worship participants to see their denominational blind spots, to imagine new ways of being within their respective theological tribes? Or, imagine worship that might unfold beneath the banner "Re[form]ations"? What would this title evoke? Where might the creative folks in your church take this? How might such a title enable a liturgical vision that sees the sixteenth and twenty-first century in one glance?

2. Curating church ought to blur the lines between conservation and transformation.

Golden wished to express the nuanced ways that contemporary notions of blackness manifest in the works of her artists. Her exhibition embraces a diachronic dimension of so-called "black art," acknowledging how historical developments structured the possibility of such art. At the same time, Golden's exhibition transforms the viewers' notions of blackness by highlighting artists who transcend a facile racial reductionism. This undecidability forces the viewer to think, to examine their epistemological, cultural, and aesthetic assumptions.

This helps me imagine several exhilarating worship possibilities. Dream with me a worship space that featured several large images and blown-up quotes by a seminal figure in your tradition. Maybe that would be John Wesley or Jonathan Edwards or Dorothy Day. Now consider the potential impact of filling all of the remaining wall space with less prominent but equally poignant leaders and thinkers before, during, and after the time of these great church fathers and mothers. Would not something like this lend color and contrast to overly simplified notions of Methodism, the Great Awakening, or Catholic Social Teaching?

Or, imagine with me the potential impact of drawing Augustine, or Anselm, or Teresa of Avila into a dialogue with a contemporary theologian like Mayra Rivera or Brian Bantum. What if in your homily or sermon you hosted an exegetical roundtable about the Apostle Paul's ethnic identity in Acts between John Chrysostom, James D. G. Dunn, and Eric Barreto? Golden's curatorial imagination opens up that of liturgists and worship curators by drawing elements of our past into dialogue with our present and future. The possibilities are limitless.

3. Curating church ought to resist the modern liturgical and homiletical propensity to articulate a singular point.

One critic of the show described Golden's exhibition as a "loose assemblage, an anthology of individual styles and sensibilities, some more interesting and assertive than others, going in different directions."[13] The works of the *Freestyle* exhibition press against homogeneity and integration—and this is by design. They express humor, rage, desire, and hope; they feature class, sexual, racial, ethnic, and aesthetic difference. We who would curate worship and spiritual formation opportunities would do well to trust our participants to forge connections with our liturgical or homiletical selections and to receive the space to draw their own conclusions.

Ambiguity and uncertainty can lead a worshipping community into exciting, sometimes scary, places. Our theological training—in fact, Western education in general—militates against equivocation and undecidability. This binds liturgical leaders and participants alike with epistemological and theological fetters, and that is why manumission has been a driving impetus behind my first two books.[14]

We should not avoid but expect criticism from worship participants when we allow works, ideas, and hymns to remain in tension with other liturgical elements. Such tension is more than obfuscation. Liturgical and theological tension are generative. They give rise to new thoughts and new ways of being.

As a concrete example, imagine a liturgy that led worshipers into the thorny thicket of marriage equality. Such an experience would encourage reflection on sex/sexual embodiment, narrative identity and selfhood, covenantal fidelity, rites of passage, identity politics, and a politics of radical difference.[15]

---

13. Cotter, "Art Review."

14. See Jacob D. Myers, *Making Love with Scripture: Why the Bible Doesn't Mean How You Think It Means* (Minneapolis: Fortress, 2015) and idem, *Preaching Must Die! Troubling Homiletical Theology* (Minneapolis: Fortress, 2017).

15. Consider, for example, the following conversation partners: Robyn Henderson-Espinoza, "Difference, Becoming, and Interrelatedness: A Material Resistance Becoming," *Cross Currents* 66, no. 2 (June 2016): 281–89; Thelathia Nikki Young, *Black Queer Ethics, Family, and Philosophical Imagination* (New York: Palgrave Macmillan, 2016); and Melissa Browning, *Risky Marriage: HIV and Intimate Relationships in Tanzania* (Lanham, MD: Lexington Books, 2013).

By no means would you want to—nor could you—resolve these important issues. And it is here, at this point of dissemination that blurs any and every point, that something transformative might emerge. There are no guarantees, of course; but that is true even with the most focused and singular sermon or liturgy.

EXHIBITION 2

Unmapping the Earth
2nd Gwangju Biennale,
South Korea

*Curators should not only concentrate on the culture of our times and radius,
i.e., western culture, but also on the culture of non-western societies.
I see an essential duty of curatorial work in discovering the diversity of aesthetic
expressions of, in our eyes, exotic cultures.*

—*Jean-Hubert Martin*[1]

Unmapping the Earth upended traditional paradigms for artistic curation.[2] Rather than flowing from the vision of a single curator, this exhibition took shape according to a polyphony of curatorial imaginations. The exhibition, hosted in Gwangju, South Korea in 1995, followed a trajectory set by the Biennale's artistic director, Youngchul Lee. Rather than curating the entire exhibition himself, Lee invited five other curators to develop their own unique exhibitions within the larger exhibition. These were organized around five sub-themes: speed/water, space/fire, hybrid/wood, power/metal, and becoming/earth. Over 108 artists and eleven art groups would contribute.

---

1. Jean-Hubert Martin, "Independent Curatorship," in *Cautionary Tales: Critical Curating*, ed. Steven Rand and Heather Kouris (New York: Apexart, 2007), 44

2. The Gwangju Biennale Foundation funds the Gwangju Biennale in South Korea, Asia's oldest biennial of contemporary art.

83

What is unique—and fascinating—about this exhibition was its freeform, "chaosmic" character (to borrow James Joyce's neologism[3]). The installations emerged as a multiplicity added to multiplicity in that each curator curated a space for curation by other curators. Lee, as harbinger and visionary of this Biennale, "mapped" his exhibition with the intention of having it "unmapped" by his curatorial collaborators who worked under their own autonomy. At the same time, Lee's original vision could not be completely "unmapped." His cartographic influence was evident throughout the installations, and the visions of his curator-collaborators served to enhance his creative insights. Accordingly, *Unmapping the Earth* has much to teach liturgical curators about process and collaboration, about how to engage otherness while affirming a unifying vision.

Curatorial Vision

Lee's curatorial vision combines Eastern and Western artistic paradigms and people to create an exhibition that troubles overly simplistic aesthetic cartographies. He explains that the sub-themes he chose for the exhibition connect with the five elements of Eastern cosmology: water, fire, wood, metal, and earth. He chose these themes to interrogate fractal and crossing forces, to touch upon all of a person's senses, and to create a space where meaning could erupt in many and varied ways. He writes, "Within rapidly changing global circumstances, my intention was to put 'I' and 'non—I' together—contact zones where distinction between inside and outside have no sense—with 'singular' speeds, spaces, hybrids, powers and becoming into a 'contact zone' where art is the core side of subjectivity."[4] Lee embodies here something that is central to the curatorial imagination: forging engagement. By "allowing different elements to touch" along the "twin poles of order and disorder," Lee allows that which is old to become something new.[5]

---

3. James Joyce coined this term in his 1939 novel *Finnegans Wake*.

4. Youngchul Lee, "Unmapping the Earth," in *97 Kwangju Biennale: Unmapping the Earth*, trans. Lee Young Jun (Kwangju, South Korea: Kwangju Biennale Press, 1997), 33. Note: In some of Lee's interviews and essays, he (or the publisher) follows the Asian convention of placing his last name first and his first name last (i.e., Lee Youngchul). For the sake of consistency and his more recent practice of following Western conventions when authoring essays and books, I designate the works bearing his name as Youngchul Lee.

5. Hans Ulrich Obrist with Asad Raza, *Ways of Curating* (New York: Farrar, Straus and Giroux, 2014), 11. Here Obrist is drawing on the curatorial vision of Alighiero Boetti.

By juxtaposing contemporary issues with traditional Eastern ideas, Lee was not intending "to romanticize nature while rejecting the ills of modern civilization, but rather to investigate the mechanisms of various powers generated and emitted in the present age."[6] Lee was able to see, moreover, how certain ways of thinking and being are mapped too easily and too often onto "eastern" or "western" longitudes. Part of contemporary life that he hoped to transform—or at least to trouble—was this problematic bifurcation that divides peoples, religions, and ways of knowing from their perceived "others."

Lee recognized that the objectifying and "essentializing" logic of postmodernism was not much better for the non-Western "other" than modernism. So, part of his curatorial vision was to perform a kind of deconstruction on the governing logics of the art world itself, to "unmap" the map.[7] One way to disturb this logic is to create spaces for artists and other curators to exercise their own aesthetic imaginations. This is precisely what Lee did.

In his introduction to *Unmapping the Earth*, Lee writes, "To some degree, this Biennale distances itself from the interest in the 'Other' which is emphasized in multiculturalism, and its diverse strategies of cultural politics."[8] He goes on to explain that art that merely considers the other and otherness cannot endow a subject with identity. All that an art curator can do is to host events wherein individual identity may reveal itself. Such was a central aim of Lee's exhibition.

In service of Lee's curatorial vision, the exhibition was realized without any intentional moves toward consensus, whereby the participants would consciously engage the work of one another. At the same time, they made no attempt to construct a boundary between the five exhibitions. Again, Lee writes that his wish was to curate a "relationship solely among the parts," a "network among relationships," an "open system." Lee sought "to make a transversal diagram rather than a totalization or integration, to plunge into an 'adventurous

---

6.   Lee, *Unmapping the Earth*, 30.

7.   In his own words, "before the logic of multiculturalism which hypocritically claims an equal distribution of rights (in which the center conceals the dichotomy of center and periphery, while the periphery makes use of that logic in the context of cultural politics), can be a new humanist technique of domination used to assimilate the periphery into a logic of value established by the center." Lee, *Unmapping the Earth*, 30–31.

8.   Ibid., 31.

game' for which no one can predict the result, and to have everyone participate in a creative 'play' of pure difference, so that the exhibition itself spontaneously proceeds to a mysterious state."[9] Lee sought to create a method without setting up a model. Ultimately, the aim of this biennial was to produce unexpected mergers and exchanges, which could constitute rather than minimize ambiguity.

Description

Unmapping the Earth was not only thematic but structural as well. Es-chewing the traditional national pavilions and competitive judging typical of other biennales, Lee subcontracted the curatorial tasks to figures from Asia, Europe, and America. He thereby challenged the whole concept of a bien-nale itself—*unmapping* the central feature of a biennale: its location. The exhibition took shape following an initial meeting with the five curators, wherein they discussed the basic concepts and themes of the exhibition. Sev-eral months later they met again, and the five curators presented their own concepts for the exhibition. This meeting lasted fifteen hours. Out of this, a skeletal structure emerged, and the curators were given free-reign to add flesh, blood, and organs to these bones.

What was common to the five sections of the exhibition was their fluid-ity, contingency, and non-fixity. They hereby contributed to the Biennale's overall complexity of social, cultural, positional, and sexual boundaries and scales, which contemporary societies are constantly policing and disciplining. Generously housed in a series of massive sheds in a large park at the center of Gwangju, the exhibition provided ample space for the complex installations, multimedia presentations, and conceptual provocations that constituted art at end of the twentieth century. Such international stars as Cindy Sherman, Chris Marker, Yves Klein, Joseph Beuys, Bill Viola, John Cage, Louise Bour-geois, and Bruce Naumann were shown alongside lesser-known artists. By drawing these different artists into one exhibition, Lee and his curatorial agents were able to exploit the tensions between progressive theories of the so-called "first world" and the cultural politics of the so-called "third world."[10]

---

9.   Ibid.

10.   In his essay, "Curating in a Global Age," Youngchul Lee writes, "Despite the fact that these progressive theories have legitimacy in anti-modernism movements, it was not clear

86

Lee's Biennale also attempted to link several topics in cultural studies and contemporary art by exploring ways to deconstruct a hierarchical dualism that strengthened the regime of modernization. As a result, exhibits emerged that challenged and subverted modern categories by embracing indeterminacy and hybridity.

The Speed/Water "contact zone" was curated by Harald Szeemann, who is arguably the most famous curator in history. In his introduction to his section of the Biennale, he explains that he chose works that "transpose the click of instantaneous exposure out of the material world and into the spiritual."[11] This union—reinforced symbolically by the *I Ching*, which connects speed with water—led him to select works in a number of mediums that bear witness to the mellifluousness of life. In, for instance, Pipilotti Rist's video stills *Sip My Ocean*, Szeemann was drawn to sensual and flowing lines that seduce the viewer to enter the water with the artist. In stark contrast, an installation created by Serge Spitzer (*Reality Models*) features a room wherein ten tennis training machines are hidden behind walls. Balls fire toward spectators with various arcs and trajectories. This installation forces the spectator to become an active participant in the work, moving, dodging, and ducking the volley of fuzzy yellow balls.

Curated by Kyong Park, the Space/Fire exhibit attends to urban life in light of global migration, technological change, and economic shifts. Park explains that he did not invite artists into his exhibit, per se; he invited cities. Thus, his section of the Biennale features a wide range of photos: buildings in ruins in Sarajevo, Beirut, and Rome are positioned alongside urban planning maps for Macau and thriving urban landscapes in Beijing. Park aimed to highlight the complexities of postmodern space and the metaphorical alluring and repelling force of fire vis-à-vis urban existence.

The Hybrid/Wood exhibit focused on the ecological overtones conceptualized by various forms of hybrid art, which combine distinct artistic mediums (e.g., painting, performance, video) into one work. Much as agricultural hybrids exhibit humanity's efforts to control nature, hybrid art presents

---

whether so-called post-modern theories would be capable of contributing political resistance against eurocentrism or if they were just another reflection of hegemony of the west." Young-chul Lee, "Curating in a Global Age," in *Cautionary Tales*, 109.

11.   Harald Szeemann, "Speed & Water: A Saga," trans. David Britt, in *Unmapping the Earth*, 60.

the illusion of mastery. This exhibit's curators, Richard Kolashek and Erica Clark, explain that the relatively recent phenomenon of hybrid art relies on the artist to innovate with mediums, styles, and forms to force the spectator's participation. Accordingly, the works they assembled break in certain ways from old patterns while also expanding the boundaries of artistic disciplines. Employing the works of artists like John Cage and Rosângela Rennó, the curating duo address the audience member's unfolding subjectivity. Kolashek and Clark explain,

> The viewer's questions are not just part of the engagement with the work; they are the transformative act that fulfills the work's intentions, the fusion of artist and viewer in yet another hybrid process. Questions engender other questions, and these produce new possibilities for action. But who is the viewer? There is, of course, no single answer—precisely the point of hybrid art as well. Hybrid art points to each of our infinite differences, creatures of our past, and of the fleeting moment at hand.[12]

Central to this exhibit is the question of identity, which, like wood, can be at once hard and brittle yet porous and malleable.

The Power/Metal section of the exhibition helps the viewer to reflect on themes of survival and violence amid flux. Curated by Sung Wan Kyung, this zone relates artists to moments and movements of political turmoil from across the world. He features, for instance the Argentine comic strip artist Alberto Breccia alongside the Russian painter Erik Boulatov, resisting military despotism and Soviet totalitarianism, respectively. Kyung also couples works by the French filmmaker Chris Marker with the paintings of Manuel Ocampo, whose murals gesture to the quest for survival amid colonial violence in the Philippines.

Lastly, the Becoming/Earth exhibit followed the curatorial vision of Bernard Marcadé. Emerging out of a series of hypotheses that tether becoming to a certain femininity and femininity to the earth, Marcadé features works by an array of artists who reflect on migration, proliferation, abjection, and contamination. Despite the negative feelings these words connote, his selections evoke a sense of hope and even joy amid the global changes afoot. He includes pieces by artists like Annette Messager, Cindy Sherman, and Paul

---

12. Richard Koshalek and Erica Clark, "Meditations on Hybrid Art," in *Unmapping the Earth*, 230.

McCarthy with subjects as wide-ranging as stuffed animals and computer-generated cyborgs. Marcadé writes, "In this way, we might then get beyond the oppositions between the mechanical and the organic, the atomistic and the holistic, the natural and the artificial, in which the idea of the Earth has so often been enclosed."[13] In many ways, Marcadé's curatorial imagination works to transpose the artist's vision onto the viewer, leaving him/her/them transformed to consider the world otherwise.

Critical Reception

Unmapping the Earth received a mixed reception from the art community. Even as many marveled at the scope and ambitions of the Biennale, the breadth of the exhibitions kept some viewers scratching their heads. Here's what one critic observed:

> Judging by the exuberance of the crowds, which appeared to manifest the same mixture of fascination and bewilderment that Western audiences display in front of today's cutting-edge art, I would hazard a guess that the de-provincializing intentions of the organizers were bearing some fruit. For at least a few months, in the once remote city of Kwangju in Cholla Province, South Korea, the global cultural world, or at least that associated with the artistic avant-garde, was "unmapped" enough so that center and margins were no longer as rigidly demarcated as before and the métropole and its provinces lost their absolute distinction.[14]

In his review of the Biennale, critic Thomas Wulffen addressed the challenges inherent to conceiving a program that adopts and yet challenges the artistic and curatorial hegemony of Euro-America. He notes that any attempt to mount an "autonomous art project outside the Euro-American art system faces a paradox, one which prevails for every comparable undertaking. On the one hand it has to work with the standards, procedures and regulations of this system, on the other it has to establish a kind of autonomous status."[15]

---

13.   Bernard Marcadé, "Remarks on the Becomings (Woman-Child-Animal-Object) of Art," in *Unmapping the Earth*, trans. Lara Ferb, 437.

14.   Martin Jay, "Kwangju: From Massacre to Biennale," *Salmagundi* 120 (Fall 1998), 19.

15.   ThomasWulffen, "Kwangju," *Art Monthly* 212 (December 1997–January 1998), 20.

While appreciating the curatorial vision underlying the Biennale, Wulffen was also critical. In reflecting upon the "Power/Metal" exhibit, he observes, "The different works did not fit together and apart from those by some of the big names, like Nauman or Bulator, most were indifferent in quality. Even those works by the big names were not really surprising, at least to a European eye."[16] In spite of this and other specific critiques, Wulffen's review was positive. He most appreciated that one could connect specific works on one floor with another exhibition on another floor. In this way, the visitor was able to take in the whole Biennale and was given the opportunity to make comparisons between different concepts of what is significant in contemporary art.

At the press conference following the Biennale, an Indian artist complained about the neglect in this Biennale of "third world" art. Lee's response to this complaint was that so-called "third world" art did not *count* as art. This response reveals a tension that persists across most biennales—and the art world in general—that fails to account for class and educational difference even while valorizing racial, sexual, and ethnic otherness. Arrogant answers like that do not help to "unmap" the earth.

Liturgical Takeaways

We can learn much from Lee's artistic imagination and the impact his curatorial vision has had upon the art world. What is most evident and most promising for our liturgical imaginations is how his exhibition can help us *unmap* the church. Lest we forget, much of our global cartographies result from the work of ecclesial cartographers. Willie James Jennings has made this case most cogently in *The Christian Imagination*.[17]

In this must-read book, Jennings shows how the church is culpable for much of the racial and ethnic injustices perpetuated through history to the present. It is not the case, Jennings argues, that first we have a concept of race and then we begin to think theologically about it; rather, the origins of race and racism emerge out of a "diseased" theological imagination. What I find

---

16.   Ibid., 21.

17.   Willie James Jennings, *The Christian Imagination: Theology and the Origins of Race* (New Haven, CT and London: Yale University Press, 2010).

so promising in Lee's exhibition are the prospects it offers for transforming our theological and cultural imaginations in and through Christian worship. There are (at least) three maxims we may infer from the *Unmapping the Earth* exhibit and approach.

1. Curating church ought to destabilize hegemonic, colonial/imperial ideologies by creating space for marginalized voices to articulate themselves.

To fully appreciate the impact of Lee's curatorial imagination, we must have a bit of background in art history. Leading up to the 2nd Gwangju Biennale, multiculturalism was all the rage in the art world. Desiring to be inclusive and to promote global understanding, many Western art exhibitions would include installations and works by non-Western artists. This is one of the defining features of so-called "postmodern" art.

In the art world, postmodernism both follows after and subverts modern art. At first glance, it may seem that this evolution was a good thing. And it is—to an extent. Only the most insular and xenophobic among us would continue to tout exclusion and segregation. But this is not the entire story. Philosopher Nicolas Bourriaud contends, and rightly so, that in postmodernism, "the other" was valorized on account of his/her/their otherness; but this otherness only exists in relation to the dominant majority, who are able to mark their imagined sameness by segregating and excluding the other in the first place. In postmodernism, and concomitantly with globalization, this process is not overcome.

Othering is intensified with the advent of postmodernism—only now it is perceived as a mode of embrace. Bourriaud writes,

> Lacking a common cultural space since the collapse of modernist universalism, Western individuals have felt obliged to regard the other as a representative of the true, and to do so from a locus of enunciation by which a narrow barrier separates them from the other. . . . Thus, we find ourselves confronting an aporia: although we know the universal master narrative of modernism is obsolete, the idea of judging each work according to the codes of its author's local culture implies the existence of viewers who have mastered each culture's referential field, which seems difficult to say the least.[18]

---

18. Nicolas Bourriaud, *The Radicant* (New York: Lukas & Sternberg, 2009), 28–29.

In sum, the act of judging remains inequitable. Those on the "inside" still wield tremendous power over those relegated to the "outside." To say this differently, the aesthetic monoculturalism of modernism was replaced by an aesthetic multiculturalism in postmodernism, both of which name and marginalize the other as such. The former "Orientalized" the other (to borrow Edward Said's famous term); the latter seemed to embrace the other, but only on the terms of the dominant culture and not for the other's particular contribution.

Moving the theoretical impetus for this exhibition closer to our theological/liturgical concerns, we may find a corollary in the work of my friend Gerald Liu. Liu's monograph *Music and the Generosity of God* challenges the work of such seminal figures as Jeremy Begbie and Nicholas Wolterstorff for privileging certain kinds of music to substantiate their theological claims. If Bach or Mozart produce scores that are to be deemed revelatory, then, Liu contends, we are missing what other modes of musicality may reveal about God. Drawing upon John Cage's landmark work *4'33"*—where the three moves of his composition force audiences to attend to the ambient noise of their environment—Liu troubles both musical and theological exclusionism.[19]

2. Curating church necessitates a critical understanding of historical and global forces.

As Lee puts it in his curator's introduction, his curatorial vision pursued "art as a construct of chaos. An art that critically reflects the present 'disorder of things'—or a new global (b)order."[20] In other words, art presents us with a picture of the world that we all intuit but cannot clearly see because we are so completely immersed in it. A central feature of our global order is precisely the dissolution of borders thanks to transnational corporations, ever-accelerating communications and travel technologies, and consumption practices.[21] Lee helps us see and question our b/orders by casting fresh light upon them.

To fully appreciate the impact of Lee's curatorial imagination at this juncture, we must understand a bit of Korean history. Gwangju (formerly spelled

---

19. See Gerald C. Liu, *Music and the Generosity of God* (New York: Palgrave Macmillan, 2017).

20. Lee, *Unmapping the Earth*, 31.

21. See Zygmunt Bauman, *Globalization: The Human Consequence* (New York: Columbia University Press, 1998).

Kwangju) is a city in the agricultural region of Jeolla Province, located in southwestern Korea. The city came to international attention when, on May 18, 1980, a demonstration against the military regime then in power was cruelly suppressed. Official statistics reported that two hundred people were killed, but in reality the number was closer to two thousand.

Gwangju was selected to host South Korea's—in fact, East Asia's—first Biennale as a way to honor the victims of the city and their role in the democracy movement. The history of the city plays a crucial role in the identity of the Biennale and is sometimes directly paid tribute to in the program (i.e., in special exhibitions). As stated on the Gwangju Biennale Foundation's website, the Biennale aims to contribute to "blurring distinctions between center and margin" as well as to a "break from the past of discrimination and exclusivity."[22] Accordingly, *Unmapping the Earth* challenged the geopolitical and geocultural power dynamics that had relegated South Korea, and a fortiori the capital city of isolated Jeolla Province, to the margins. The center that determined those marginalized by political and economic structures as "other" was imploding.

3. Curating church can do more to subvert binary ways of thinking by forging new connections between non-binary concepts.

As curator, Lee teaches us how creating a "strategic and non-stratified environment" can highlight the deconstruction always already at work within binary logics. Binaries structure much thinking in Western cultures. Black/White. Gay/Straight. Republican/Democrat. Our epistemological foundations are fabricated from somewhat arbitrary divisions and subsequent hierarchies that privilege one of the binary's terms over the other.

This is no different in the church. Orthodox/Heretic. Saint/Sinner. Baptist/Catholic. Sprinkling/Immersion. So much energy is spent in church sessions, general conferences, and (inter)national gatherings to ward off perceived contaminations of an imagined purity. *Unmapping the Earth* reveals another way. Each of Lee's pairs contains a symbiotic relationship in which the elements are very fluid, and at the same time, irreducible to each other. For instance, speed and water exist in close proximity to one another and they

---

22.　See http://www.biennialfoundation.org/biennials/gwangju-biennale/.

are remote at the same time. That is why this relationship appears as a non-relationship. Between speed/water multitudinous interfering, harmonizing, and conflicting forces intermingle. Hereby, numerous new meanings emerge according to the arrangement and alignment of these forces.

This work of forging new connections en route to subversion is crucial for curating church. One of the reasons church leaders and theologians have responded to deconstruction with so much fear and vitriol is because of the void that it opens in the heart of belief and praxis.[23] Such a fear of nihilism may be mitigated, if not avoided, through creative and constructive interactions. For instance, in response to the silo mentality that marks the present—especially online—two colleagues and I are collaborating on a book project that celebrates our points of dissonance and convergence. I identify as a white, mostly straight, currently able-bodied, cisgender man, who works at the intersection of homiletics and poststructural philosophy. My friend Eric Barreto identifies as a mostly straight, cisgender Puerto Rican man, who situates his work at the nexus of New Testament studies and postcolonialism. My friend Nikki Young identifies herself as a queer, African-American ethicist. Together we are reading texts in Acts and 1 Corinthians that refer to speaking in tongues. Central to our project is a critical and generative conversation that includes the biblical text alongside one another's culturally situated interpretations. The results are proving both fascinating and life-giving.

---

23. "This is the greatest gift of deconstruction: to question the authority of the investigating subject without paralyzing him, persistently transforming conditions of impossibility into possibility." Gayatri Chakravorty Spivak, "Subaltern Studies: Deconstructing Historiography," in *In Other Worlds: Essays in Cultural Politics* (London and New York: Routledge, 1998), 276.

The Readymade Boomerang

8th Sydney Biennial, Australia

A great group exhibition . . . asks its audience to make connections.
Like an orgy, it brings things together in stimulating and unpredictable combinations.
It immerses us in an experience of shifting yet interlinked viewpoints, and multiple
climaxes. It juxtaposes works whose overlapping concerns resonate in ways that transform
our experience of them. And it invites us to explore a seemingly newly discovered territory
of art that contains within it more than we can hold in our heads at any one moment.

—*Ralph Rugoff*[1]

You've been there. You turn a corner in a museum or warehouse exhibition space and there it is: some everyday object hanging on a wall. It's titled and framed like the other paintings and sculptures, set apart, drawing your gaze. An ironing board from the 1950s; a warped bicycle wheel, its tire riddled with dry rot; a water-stained edition of *Reader's Digest*. What you are beholding is known to folks in the art world as a *readymade*.

More than a century ago Marcel Duchamp unveiled his (in)famous "Fountain," a "readymade" porcelain urinal. Can you imagine the shock on the spectators' faces at the 1917 exhibition in New York: *This is a gallery not a restroom*, they quip. That, my friend, was precisely Duchamp's point, the raison

---

1. Ralph Rugoff, "You Talking to Me? On Curating Group Shows that Give You a Chance to Join the Group," in *What Makes a Great Exhibition?* ed. Paula Marincola (Philadelphia: Philadelphia Exhibitions Initiative, 2006), 44.

d'être of the *readymade*: to draw our attention to the everyday, commonplace objects of our lives so that we may behold beauty in the "art" that is all around us. Moreover, the readymade situates itself as a challenge to the possibility of defining and delimiting "art" as such.

Who has the authority to delineate art from non-art? Who gets to draw the line dividing the aesthetically mundane from the sacrosanct? Duchamp himself confessed in an interview, "An oeuvre by itself doesn't exist, it's an optical illusion. It's only made to be seen by the people who look at it."[2] Put differently, the force that is necessary to determine that such-and-such is a *work of art* is merely a cultural fabrication. There is no innate and necessary power that constitutes art as such.

In his 1990 exhibition *The Readymade Boomerang*, German curator René Block highlighted the significance of the readymade on art history and art theory throughout the twentieth century using the boomerang as metaphor. It was at once an homage to Duchamp's epoch-shifting genius and a critical investigation of his influence. This exhibition promises to expand our liturgical imaginations by modeling a diachronic intentionality seldom manifested in Christian worship spaces.

Curatorial Vision

Block describes the theme of *The Readymade Boomerang* as one of elliptical movement. The trajectory of a boomerang aligns with that of the readymade, wherein artistic innovation conjoins with an impulse to return always to its source. He describes the impetus for his curatorial vision accordingly:

> The development of western art has often been regarded as a linear process. In my opinion, it takes place in cycles, in rings. When you take a look at the art of the last century, this becomes very clear. The developments are like the annual rings on a tree trunk which differ according to colour. The colours reflect different styles in art. And just as the colours repeat themselves after a few years, so artists constantly return to earlier developments.[3]

---

2. Dore Ashton, "An Interview with Marcel Duchamp," in *Out of the Whirlwind: Three Decades of Art Commentary* (Ann Arbor, MI: UMI Research Press, 1987), 71.

3. René Block, "Artistic Director Forward," *8th Biennale of Sydney*, https://www.biennale ofsydney.com.au/about-us/history/1990-2/.

The works of Marcel Duchamp, Joseph Beuys, Piero Manzoni, and Arthur Köpcke—the evangelists of the readymade, so to speak—challenge us to attend to life as to art: with imagination and irony. They teach us to see the world differently, to engage the stuff of our everyday experience with fascination. They also press us to engage the world of mass production and consumerization that marks our post-industrial age.

Block wanted his audience to ponder several questions. How can you parse the difference between a consumable and an object worthy of preservation? What are the defining limits for a work of art? Who gets to decide what counts as art? These questions invite us behind the wizard's curtain, so to speak, to cast a critical gaze upon those who are pressing the buttons and turning the wheels that surround art with an aura of mystery.

In the 1960s and 1970s, Block was greatly influenced by and contributed to the Fluxus movement in Europe. Fluxus defined itself as an avant-garde art movement by pushing the boundaries of what counted as art (much as Duchamp did in the 1920s). Particularly notable was the group's use of *intermedia*, which combines disparate artistic mediums (e.g., drawing, poetry, theater) to create works that were utterly novel when they first appeared (e.g., visual poetry, performance art). Especially defining for the Fluxus movement was the notion that artwork ought to proceed without a conception of its end, and an understanding of the work as a site of engagement between an artist and his/her/their audience. The Fluxus artists privileged the process of creating over the finished product. The group's contributors also challenged the capitalistic intention emerging in the art world, particularly the production of artwork in unlimited editions at very low prices. Both Fluxus and the creation of multiples have in common the intention of denying a work of art's status as a unique and precious item.

For much of his career, Block's focus has been on taking up the discussion on the status of the object of art as kindled by Marcel Duchamp, a debate continued and expanded on in postwar times by neo avant-garde artists and after them by Piero Manzoni, pop artists, and the Fluxus movement. With *The Readymade Boomerang* exhibit, Block traced the history of the *readymades* and the development of the *found object* as art movement since Marcel Duchamp, Man Ray, and Francis Picabia, displaying and juxtaposing these "original works" with the works of contemporary artists. The portfolio catalogue contained twenty-two sheets that reflected the theme of the exhibition. The results are correspondingly diverse, and the experimentation with various printing techniques gave rise to a set of prints that reflect an entire epoch of developments in printmaking.

Description

The Readymade Boomerang presented works that have critically engaged with Duchamp's readymade. The exhibition unfolded as a series of arch and circles. On the outermost ring were the works of artists such as Koons, Miyajima, and Trockel. On the second most peripheral ring, Block displayed the work of McPherson and Kabakov, among others. The third ring presented the work of artists like John Cage, Andy Warhol, Sigmar Polke, and Bruce Nauman. The innermost circle, the exhibition's holy of holies, featured the work of three artists: Man Ray, Picabia, and, of course, Duchamp.

At the center of the exhibition space, Block displayed Duchamp's famous *Roue de Bicyclette* (1913), which consists of a bicycle wheel affixed by its fork to the top of a wooden stool. Many art historians consider this to be the very first readymade, though Duchamp himself did not immediately recognize it as such until several years later. The entire exhibition spiraled out from here, moving parabolically outward in both space and time.

An exhibition by Richard Hamilton, entitled *Computer DS 101*, not only selected a readymade object (a Swedish-designed computer), he also produced an industrial object as a readymade. In so doing, Hamilton directed the viewer to reflect on the aesthetic and cognitive capacities of this increasingly ubiquitous object (in 1990). Hamilton programmed the computer to carry out the following operations for his exhibition participants: 1) Discuss the artist's concept with the computer; 2) Use the computer as a catalogue of the artist's work and ask for all information; and 3) Look at the artist in a series of specially designed self-portraits based on Polaroids and painted with an electronic paint box.

Hamilton, reflecting on the influence of Duchamp and the latter's readymades on the trajectory of art history, writes, "The studied neutrality of his [Duchamp's] solutions in this area could not be repeated, but the instrument of irony he used so effectively in other works could be adopted with advantage." Hamilton continues, "The phrase from his toes to the Large Glass, 'an irony of affirmation,' was a guiding principle in my considerations."[4]

In another area of the exhibition space, Dale Frank explored the idea of the painting as a readymade, which he related to the notion of painting having its own independent life-world. Here he exhibited paintings leaning against the wall and against each other, arranged like industrial workers on a smoke break. He also made paintings from ready-made carpets and still others from sticky-backed contact paper on canvas. In a later interview, Frank explains that he selected and worked with these pieces that he discovered in a catalogue for Spanish and Italian printed blankets. Each blanket in the catalogue was already illustrated and displayed in heavy gold frames—like paintings in a gallery. He explains, "One could argue that, although individually each painting consisted of some ready-made approach to material and existence, together they became an entity that was not ready-made, but which fulfilled and justified all the traditional qualities of painting. Seen together, they were a new way of painting."[5] In Frank's work and in his own words, we catch a glimpse of this parabolic, boomerang trajectory of the readymade operating not just historically but within works themselves.

Critical Reception

Critics offered mixed reviews of Block's exhibition. This was, in part, due to the subject matter of the 1990 Sydney Biennale. Art scholar and curator Lynne Cooke writes that,

> . . . in the last decade scholars, critics and theoreticians have returned to Duchamp and his work with renewed passion, arguably making of him the central figure in twentieth century art history. Artists too have regained their fascination with that elusive and yet immensely fecund body of work—a fascination not always devoid, however, of exasperation at the way he seems

---

4.   Richard Hamilton, "Concept/Technology > artwork," in *The Readymade Boomerang: Certain Relations in 20th Century Art, 11 April-3 June 1990, The Eighth Biennale of Sydney* (Sydney: Art Gallery of New South Wales, 1990), 32.

5.   Sue Cramer, "Interview with Dale Frank," in *Volume One: MCA Collection*, ed. Ewan McDonald (Sydney: Museum of Contemporary Art, 2012), 266.

to have pre-empted many of art's most crucial concerns and issues with an understandable economic reticence, leaving to the later-comer little more than the possibility of permutation, explication and elaboration.[6]

Thus, much like a treatment of any figure of historical significance whose reception has been ambivalent (e.g., Tertullian vis-à-vis sexism; Thomas Jefferson vis-à-vis slavery; Heidegger vis-à-vis anti-Semitism), focusing on Duchamp was bound to garner a mixed reception.

Eleanor Heartney praises one aspect of Block's exhibition: its aptness for Australian art. She contends that Australian culture bears much in common with Duchamp's readymade. There is a "borrowed, ready-made quality" to Australian culture that "extends to the contemporary art of Australia as well." Heartney continues, however to denigrate Block's work as that which "simply reiterated the rather disturbing art-world tendency, accelerated since the early '80s, to collapse the politically radical into the merely marketable."[7]

In her review, Bernice Murphy observes the workshop feel to the 8th Sydney Biennale, noting an "expansive and historically ventilated" engagement with traditions and themes that have ebbed and flowed through the decades of the twentieth century. She is quick to add, however, that the situation of this exhibition in Australia was "awkward."[8] Noting the particular and complex ethnic, linguistic, and political structures of Australia and New Zealand, Murphy contends that the arrival of the readymade is but another imposition of culture upon the Province. It is hoisted upon an already confused and complicated context.

Murphy observes that objects as quotidian as a bottle rack or urinal in European-American contexts were anything but for residents of the Antipodes. She writes that "one country's banal receptacle may be to the denizen of another a bizarre and mystifying ceramic. . . . It needs to be stressed that the Readymade could only ever claim its radically 'ordinary' status through a

6. Lynne Cooke, "Reviewing Francis Picabia, Man Ray, Marcel Duchamp, Rose Sélavy, Marchand Du Sel...," in *The Readymade Boomerang*, 98.

7. Eleanor Heartney, "The Expanded Readymade: Report from Sydney," *Art in America* 78, no. 9 (Sep 1990): 89.

8. Bernice Murphy, "Marcel Who? (The Readymade in the Context of the Province)," in *The Readymade Boomerang*, 108.

highly privileged discourse."[9] The site of Block's exhibition was in no way like the white cube gallery space, which provides the curator a virginal site for exhibition. Australia and New Zealand are colonial and colonizing spaces: from the British, on the one hand, and against the indigenous aboriginal peoples, on the other. There is no *readymade* in such a context.

Victoria Lynn's review is critical on a more fundamental level. She writes that the historical links between Duchamp's originary vision and its manifestations in later art movements are vague and that the show "tends to overload Duchamp (and to a lesser degree Man Ray and Picabia) with responsibility for almost all the significant art of the '80s, so the historical point of his achievement becomes lost in generalities."[10] Lynn, a native Australian, continues to note that the radically of Duchamp's act of naming quotidian objects as art loses its radicality when every little thing can be set in an exhibition hall and labeled "art." She concludes that the Sydney Biennale "has much exciting, challenging, and unusual work," though she faults Block for the show's conceptual dubiousness.

From these and similar critiques, church curators can learn much about the dangers of filtering histories and theories through a single mind. One of the risks inherent to curation is that the works must stand on their own. Much like the dangers of sending a love letter to one's beloved, the author loses control over the message's reception and interpretation.

Liturgical Takeaways

Block's curatorial vision offers church leaders a way of engaging tradition beyond mere recitation. And let's face it: we know how to do the latter. We all know how to drop in a Wesley, Calvin, or Luther quote to shore up a theological argument. We invoke these authoritative voices much as we cite biblical texts to legitimize our claims. We may be less proficient in articulating how these theological giants on whose shoulders we stand have shaped eras and movements within church history.

9.　Ibid., 112.

10.　Victoria Lynn, "The Readymade Boomerang: Certain Relations in 20th Century Art," *Arts Magazine* 65 (Oct. 1990): 124.

Duchamp famously declared, "Everything in life is art. If I call it art, it's art, or if I hang it in a museum, it's art." What a claim! This declaration—while revolutionary within art history—is far from unassailable. And here's where Block comes in. He assembles a coterie of artists whose work both accedes to Duchamp's dictum and redefines its significance for different times and contexts. By investigating the resurgence and innovation upon the readymade in nouveau realism, pop art in the '50s, the Fluxus movement of the '60s, and by contemporary artists, Block sets a context for examining Duchamp's legacy and aberrations. This opens up several liturgical takeaways for we who would curate church in our respective ecclesial contexts.

1. Curating church ought to enable worshipers to understand the ideological frameworks that undergird contemporary theologies.

My friend and colleague Brennan Breed is a leading voice within a realm of biblical studies called *reception history*. Rather than focusing on what a text meant in its original context, biblical reception historians investigate the multiple ways that texts *have meant* and *continue to mean* in diverse cultural contexts. Reception historians recognize that biblical texts are always being reworked for new contexts and purposes. Texts traverse semantic boundaries and contextual borders. Anchoring texts through appeals to the original text and the original meaning produces "specters" that thereafter "haunt" scholarship, leading to a lack of methodological precision. Breed writes, "The skill of escaping contexts is not an anomaly or problem but in fact a central feature of texts." In fact, "all texts continue to find new contexts regardless of writerly, readerly, and scholarly attempts to pin them down. This is how texts function."[11]

Breed concludes by reshaping the governing metaphor for biblical studies. Texts are neither *exiles* yearning to return home, nor are they migrants who decide to leave their homeland for pragmatic reasons. No. Texts are *nomads*. They have no home because they are never sedentary, nor were they. Inasmuch as homiletics and liturgics are dependent upon the work of biblical scholars, we ought to take Breed's theory seriously. Imagine the homiletical potential of looking to a text's myriad ways of meaning in various times and

---

11.   Brennan W. Breed, *Nomadic Text: A Theory of Biblical Reception History* (Bloomington: Indiana University Press, 2014), 93, 104.

cultures. Breed opens a path beyond theological essentialism by helping us to see texts as *events* rather than *objects*.

Breed would likely concur that biblical texts, like readymades, follow a parabolic, boomerang trajectory. In fact, I can imagine a liturgical series that draws upon Breed's and Block's work. Consider the impact of tracing a single text of scripture through history. How might we teach our congregants to imagine the biblical witness differently if we highlighted a text's use in the writings of Chrysostom, Augustine, Bullinger, Weil, and Schüssler Fiorenza? What could that teach us about the Spirit's sustaining presence throughout history? What might we learn about the role of contextual/historical circumstances in how we interpret scripture?

Or consider another example. In 1896, Charles Sheldon wrote a religious fiction novel entitled *In His Steps: What Would Jesus Do?* The book has sold more than thirty million copies! The story begins at a point of crisis for Rev. Henry Maxwell, a pastor deeply moved by his dismissal of an impoverished stranger. Maxwell thus presents a challenge to his congregation that they do nothing without first asking, "What would Jesus do?" This challenge is the theme of the novel and is the driving force of the plot. From this point on, the rest of the novel consists of episodes that focus on individual characters as their lives are transformed by the challenge.

Now consider the WWJD phenomenon that swept the church in the 1990s. This grassroots movement originated with a youth pastor named Janie Tinklenberg as a way to sharpen her youth's spiritual discernment. How might a critical investigation of the neoliberal ideologies that undergird the WWJD movement challenge it at its core? How has the commercialization of Christianity shaped spiritual practices and congregational commitments? Would Jesus have worn a WWJD bracelet?

Lastly, you might lead your fellow worshipers to attend to philosopher John Caputo's 2007 book *What Would Jesus Deconstruct?* In critical conversation with both Sheldon's book and the WWJD phenomenon, Caputo presents a "hermeneutics of the kingdom of God" that he situates within Jesus's work and witness. Caputo explains,

> The deconstruction of Christianity is not an attack on the church but a critique of the idols to which it is vulnerable—the literalism and authoritarianism, the sexism and racism, the militarism and imperialism, and the

love of unrestrained capitalism with which the church in its various forms has today and for too long been entangled, any one of which is toxic to the kingdom of God.[12]

Such liturgical imagining could link the curative tasks of engagement, conservation, and transformation within the context of Christian worship gatherings.

2. Curating church should adopt a genealogical approach to worship, that is, an approach that helps worshipers attend to the historical ruptures and effects of power that have shaped our understanding of God and the world.

We all tend to speak about doctrines and concepts as if they have always been the way they now are. One of the great contributions that Block's work makes to liturgical theology is the attention it draws to a time when people did not think about art in the critical way that we now do. Before Duchamp, a urinal was just a urinal.

Rather than accepting theologies and "truths" as we currently understand them, a genealogical approach to liturgical design could expose congregants to moments when such concepts were not regarded as truths. The notion of biblical inerrancy did not exist prior to the emergence of the "Princeton Theology" of Charles Hodge and B. B. Warfield.[13] When the Apostle Paul references "sexual immorality" (*porneia*) in 1 Corinthians 6:9, he could not have had in mind committed, covenantal same-sex partnerships that many enjoy today.[14] Attending to the forces of power at work within and behind history, we are able to catch a glimpse of the epistemological and social conditions that made it possible for such-and-such concept to become the "truth" that many in our time now take for granted.[15]

---

12.   John D. Caputo, *What Would Jesus Deconstruct? The Good News of Postmodernism for the Church* (Grand Rapids, MI: Baker Academic, 2007), 137.

13.   See Mark A. Noll, *The Princeton Theology 1812–1921* (Grand Rapids, MI: Baker Academic, 2001).

14.   See Stephen D. Moore, "Que(e)rying Paul: Preliminary Questions," in *Auguries: The Jubilee Volume of the Sheffield Department of Biblical Studies,* ed. David J.A. Clines and Stephen D. Moore (Sheffield, UK: Sheffield Academic Press, 1998), 250–74.

15.   This is known in philosophy as an *épistème*. In his preface to *The Order of Things*, Michel Foucault characterizes *épistème* thusly: "The fundamental codes of a culture—those governing its language, its schemas of perception, its exchanges, its techniques, its values, the hierarchy of its practices—establish for every man [*sic*], from the first, the empirical orders

Consider this: we speak so casually in our churches today about preaching as the "Word of God." The semantic equivalence between preaching and Word has not always existed, however. Historically, Christian thinkers reserved the moniker "Word of God" exclusively for Jesus. See, for instance, St. Irenaeus, *On the Apostolic Preaching*: "For those who bear the Spirit of God are led to the Word, that is to the Son, while the Son presents [them] to the Father, and the Father furnishes incorruptibility."[16] Augustine, too, differentiates between the capital *W Word* and all human words, writing,

> . . . the Father did not beget His one and only Word in the same way He made all things through the Word. For God begot God, but the Begetter and the Begotten are together one God. God certainly made the world; the world, however, passes away while God endures. And so, these things that were made did not make themselves, but by no one was God made, the One by whom all things were made. It is no wonder, then, that a human being [like me], a creature in the midst of it all, cannot explain the Word through Whom all things were made.[17]

It was not until the Second Helvetic Confession (1562 CE) that preaching received a status upgrade. Having asserted that the Bible is the Word of God, Heinrich Bullinger (the confession's principal author) turns to preaching. "The Preaching of the Word of God Is the Word of God," he declares.[18]

---

with which he will be dealing and within which he will be at home. . . . I am not concerned, therefore, to describe the progress of knowledge towards an objectivity in which today's science can finally be recognized; what I am attempting to bring to light is the epistemological field, the episteme in which knowledge, envisaged apart from all criteria having reference to its rational value or to its objective forms, ground its positivity and thereby manifests a history which is not that of its growing perfection, but rather of its conditions of possibility . . ." Michel Foucault, *The Order of Things: An Archeology of the Human Sciences* (New York: Vintage Books, 1994), xx–xxii.

16. St. Irenaeus, *On the Apostolic Preaching*, trans. John Behr (Crestwood, NY: St. Vladimir's Seminary Press, 1997), 44. See also St. Augustine, *On the Holy Trinity*, in *Nicene and Post-Nicene Fathers*, Philip Schaff, ed.; Stephen McKenna, ed.; vol. 3 (New York: Cosimo, 2007), "For it is plain that we are to take the Word of God to be the only Son of God . . . ." 21.

17. St. Augustine, "Sermon 188," in *Augustine in His Own Words*, ed. William Harmless (Washington, DC: Catholic University of America Press, 2010), 128.

18. "The Second Helvetic Confession," in *The Book of Confessions* (Louisville: Office of the General Assembly Presbyterian Church USA, 1999), 53–54.

After Bullinger, Christian theologians rarely questioned the correspondence between preaching and the Word.

These examples lead me to several questions. What is at stake in the contemporary insistence that preaching "is" the Word of God? How has this semantic and theological linkage shaped the role of preaching in your denominational tradition? Following Block's lead would allow worship communities to reconsider why we believe what we believe in light of church history. This is one modality of the curator's efforts at conservation.

3. A curating church should offer its worshipers a frame for interrogating the concept of theology as such.

Block's curatorial imagination offers a final lesson for we who are called to craft liturgical spaces for engagement, conservation, and transformation. Much as he follows Duchamp in forcing his audience to interrogate the concept of art, liturgical curators may curate spaces to interrogate what counts as *theology*.

Our "words about God" are many and varied. How do we adjudicate the truthfulness of such words when they are invoked by Donald Trump? Or Westboro Baptist Church members? Ought these words hold the same theological weight as those espoused by Desmond Tutu or Pope Francis? How do we delineate the theological from the mundane? Who gets to cordon off these areas? What is at stake socially, ecclesiologically, and politically when *this* counts as theology but *that* does not?

I offer two examples. My friend and colleague Tim Hartman wrote an article recently that does much the same work as Block's exhibition.[19] Focusing on the concept of syncretism, Hartman challenges the notion of a "pure Christianity" removed from cultural conditioning. Hartman contends that the process of translation modifies what it means to be "Christian" from culture to culture and that as individuals work to understand and articulate their own Christian identity, these identities are always in flux. In other words, as their culture changes and their understanding of the Christian faith changes, so too does their notion of God: theology. Thus, instead of speaking about a monolithic Christian theology, the various hybrid Christian identities around

19. Tim Hartman, "Synkretismen nah und fern: Betrauchtungen zur christlichen Identität inmitten von Pluralismus," *Salzburger Theologische Zeitschrift* 19, no. 1 (2015): 24–38.

the world point toward multiple modes of theological expression, or "Christianities." Hartman makes his case by engaging the thought of two diverse theologians: Kwame Bediako of Ghana and Karl Barth of Switzerland. He shows how both theologians were equally shaped by their cultures. Hartman offers ways of rethinking Christian identity in our religiously pluralistic, globalized world of the twenty-first century, ways that offer much for liturgical curation.

In a similar vein, Block's *The Readymade Boomerang* helps us reimagine whose work counts as "theology." When I was in seminary, my theology classes included readings from thinkers like Augustine, Luther, Wesley, Moltmann, and Barth—with maybe a little Cone or Isasi-Diaz added at the end. These "theologians" are authorized to speak of God by virtue of their training, their academic positions, and their influence on the guild. Why do *these* voices receive time at the curricular microphone? Who gets to decide that their work counts as theology?

I'm excited about a new initiative to garner theology from those who do not possess fancy titles or endowed chairs. Published by Fortress Press, the First Person Faith series challenges the practice whereby only select people are allowed to offer "words of God." My friend and fellow church member Nikki Roberts is contributing to this series. As a formerly incarcerated person, she has a firsthand perspective on God that challenges abstract philosophical reflections on God. Her working title is *Freed From Within*, and it tethers her experiences in prison with her understanding of God. I can't wait to read the final product!

Inverted Utopias: Avant-Garde Art in Latin America
The Museum of Fine Arts, Houston

> *How does the curator work both within canonical thinking and against the grain of that thinking in order to take cognizance of artistic thought that slowly makes itself felt, first in the field of culture, before it appears to be sanctioned by critics and institutions?*
>
> —*Okwui Enwezor*[1]

Most major art exhibitions are either historic or geographic. That is, they take as their theme some artist or artistic movement (e.g., cubism, surrealism), or they focus on artists from certain regions. More recently, and in the wake of artistic postmodernism, the geographic metric has focused on difference and inclusion. *Inverted Utopias*, an exhibition curated by Mari Carmen Ramírez and Héctor Olea in 2004, was different.

Ramírez and Olea organized the exhibition around six *constellations*, each intending to highlight some ideological, formal, or thematic feature of avant-garde artistic production in the Americas. Each constellation presented an open, flexible, and porous category seeking to hold together a wide range of

---

1. Okwui Enwezor, "The Postcolonial Constellation: Contemporary Art in a State of Permanent Transition," *Research in African Literatures* 34, no. 4 (Winter 2003): 74.

artistic expression *and* specific works belonging to different time periods or geographic locales. These *constellations* included: 1) Universal and Vernacular; 2) Vibrational and Stationary; 3) Geometry and Concrete; 4) Play and Grief; 5) Touch and Gaze; and 6) Cryptic and Committed.

Curatorial Vision

The twentieth century avant-garde movement established itself by pushing against the aesthetic, cultural, and political boundaries constituting the bourgeoisie status quo. Artistic innovation became a mode of sociopolitical critique. Avant-gardism made its mark in overtly challenging mainstream European culture: its essence is its subversiveness. This background information is necessary to appreciate what Ramírez and Olea were envisioning with *Inverted Utopias*.

European avant-gardism was obsessed with the future, and especially a utopian future in which the deleterious effects of modernism might be overcome. The aim was to imagine a future beyond the economic alienation of industrial factory workers and the noxious effects of capitalism. Utopia, for the European avant-garde, was a perfected reality, a place (*topos*) that was other (*u-*) than the horrific realities of World War I.

This utopian vision inverted itself under the brushes, pens, and chisels of Latin American artists of this era. They dis-placed this u-topic gaze in two ways: They shifted the viewer's gaze from the future to the past, and they restored the viewer's consciousness from no place (*u-topos*) to the historically contested firmament known collectively as Latin America—and of course this naming of their place was impressed upon indigenous people much as aesthetic judgments were. This was no mere nostalgia. They sought to return to ancient cultures in service of a vitalized, and distinctively Latin American, modernity. In other words, rather than looking to the future to make sense of the present, the Latin American avant-garde looked to the past to make sense of a (possible) future. The "inversion" captured in Ramírez and Olea's exhibition presented a direct challenge to the European canons, including the ideas of Dadaist "non-participation" and the Futurist "anti-tradition" that drove the original movements' theories during World War I.

At the same time, Ramírez and Olea sought to invert another utopia of sorts. Their exhibition aimed to deconstruct the very notion of "Modern Art" and "The (capital-*T*) Avant-Garde" in art history and contemporary museology. Latin American art in the United States and abroad proliferates in museums according to a "methodological caricature," they argue. Such presentation both *flattens* the heterogeneity of art from South America, Central America, and the Caribbean and *excludes* it from exhibitions focusing on Modernism and/or avant-gardism.[2] In a sense, Latin American art and artists are given *no-place* (*u-topos*). In *giving place* to Latin American avant-garde art, Ramírez and Olea inverted its assignation to *no place*, hence *Inverting Utopias*.

The six "constellations" that constitute this exhibition receive their name from their function. Drawing upon the aesthetic theory of Theodor Adorno, Ramírez and Olea wished to showcase the extremes of Latin American avant-gardism from the 1920s and the 1960s. They label these groupings *constellations* because, by analogy to astronomy, constellations are at once arbitrary configurations of stars and geographic orientations for the wayfarer. This allowed Ramírez and Olea to group the work of artists from different countries and time periods who nevertheless achieve a measure of ideological, aesthetic, or thematic unity.

Olea wastes no time in declaring, "The official history of Latin American art has been not only a lie, but an unfair, regrettable, and reductive lie."[3] The impetus driving *Inverted Utopias*, accordingly, was to expose this lie by revealing the arti(facts) that disprove it. Ramírez writes that *Inverted Utopias* sought to "expand the parameters for understanding our astonishing and matter-of-fact *displaced utopias* of Modernism" and to "displace the conventional syntax of art-historical narratives."[4]

Description

Inverted Utopias set itself apart from other major exhibitions by beaming a spotlight on lesser-known artists of the South American avant-garde.

---

2. Mari Carmen Ramírez, "The Displacement of Utopias," in *Versions and Inversions: Perspectives on Avant-Garde Art in Latin America*, ed. Héctor Olea and Mari Carmen Ramírez (New Haven, CT: Yale University Press, 2006), 123.

3. Héctor Olea, "The Rights of Inversion," in *Versions and Inversions*, 15.

4. Ramírez, "The Displacement of Utopias," 127.

In particular, Ramírez and Olea highlighted the work of artists working in Brazil, Argentina, and Venezuela during the quarter-centuries on either side of the end of the Second World War. Conspicuously absent from their exhibition were the works of artists like Frida Kahlo, Diego Rivera, and Wifredo Lam—staples of most Latin American art shows.

The exhibition drew together over 250 works, books, documents and films by sixty-nine artists from Latin American countries including Argentina, Brazil, Columbia, Cuba, Chile, Mexico, Puerto Rico, Uruguay, and Venezuela. Ramírez explains that despite their chronological and spatial differences, her artists share an ideological critique of European avant-garde movements, overturning the very possibility of a "utopia." This thematic hallmark of avant-gardism underwent a "radical transformation" amid the pre- and postwar Latin American realities. She continues, "Our artists were advocating not an ideal impracticability, but for getting real with regard to a practical approach to society through art and its political schemes."[5]

Some highlights of the exhibition were works of the Otra Figuración group, led by the Argentinian painter and theoretician Luis Filipe Noé. The work of this group of artists from the 1960s ramifies out of a sense of alienation born of the contradictions inherent in Latin American colonial identity. Noé, in particular, forwarded an "anti-aesthetic," which celebrated the openness of chaos to destabilize both the privileged institution of art and the discursive power regimes from which art receives its authority. As a result of this theoretical orientation, Noé's art employed flat and concave mirrors to invert and distort images.

Also, prominently featured were several works by Puerto Rican painter and engraver Carlos Raquel Rivera. A member of the CAP (Puerto Rican Art Center), a seminal group of artists whose works from the 1950s exhibited a radical anti-imperialism—both aesthetically and politically—as well as promoting an overtly nationalistic art. Rivera influenced the development of a Puerto Rican avant-garde consciousness. His featured paintings from the 1960s, including *Paroxismo* (1963), *La enchapada* (1960–62), and *Mala entrañita* (1961–62), depict what Ramírez labels "the monstrous, asphyxiating, political nightmares" of Puerto Rico's colonial condition.[6]

---

5. Ibid., 123.

6. Mari Carmen Ramírez, "A Highly Topical Utopia: Outstanding Features of the Avant-

The exhibition included the subversive political paintings of Chilean artist José Balmes. Art critic and independent curator Justo Pastor Mellado explains that Chilean art had always capitulated to nationalist regimes—the "ventriloquist's dummy to political and literary areas since the time of their formation as state fictions."[7] Balmes changed that narrative. Drawing from modernism, Balmes was able to render a critique of Chilean nationalist historicism through the turbulent years of the 1960s. His paintings feature pages of text that have been painted over, depicting the socio-symbolic collapse of his society.

In sum, the exhibition upended viewer expectations about the representative works and artists constituting Latin American art. Moreover, rather than sustaining the narrative that the avant-garde in South and Central America merely continued the trajectory set by its European forebears, *Inverted Utopias* showed how avant-gardism had been employed to many and varied ends by Latin American artists throughout the twentieth century.

Critical Reception

Inverted Utopias was a critical and commercial success. The AICA (International Association of Art Critics—USA) described it as "the best thematic museum show nationally," and *The New York Times* commended it to their readership, declaring that if they "could travel to just one American museum show this summer, this would be it."[8]

Olga Viso, former director of the Walker Art Center in Minneapolis and an American of Cuban descent, highlights the subversive elements of *Inverted Utopias* in particular. She observes that the exhibition ". . . aggressively attacked many stereotypes of Latin American art. It was eye-opening for those who don't know and affirming for those of us who always believed these artists should get a voice."[9] Allow me to underscore this point: Not everyone

---

Garde in Latin America," in *Inverted Utopias: Avant-Garde Art in Latin America*, ed. Mari Carmen Ramírez and Héctor Olea (New Haven, CT: Yale University Press, 2004), 8.

7.   Justo Pastor Mellado, "The Critical Painting of José Balmes," in *Inverted Utopias*, 403.

8.   Peter C. Marzio, preface to *Versions and Inversions*, 11.

9.   Arthur Lubow, "After Frida," *The New York Times Magazine*, March 23, 2008, http://www.nytimes.com/2008/03/23/magazine/23ramirez-t.html.

arrives at any curated event with the same level of experience and expertise; the challenge, then, is to *engage* this diversity with an eye toward transformation—of the system, if not also the individual.

One of the world's leading exponents of curatorial theory, Robert Storr, describes *Inverted Utopias* as a "landmark exhibition," and that it was "the kind of exhibition that we have been waiting for a long time and of which there needs to be more."[10] Similarly, renowned critic and art historian Terry Smith calls the exhibition "a brave and bold enterprise, grounded in expertise and executed with an entirely appropriate passion."[11] Both their curatorial imagination and the works they selected contributed a fresh perspective to the art world in the summer of 2004. Accordingly, Ramírez and Olea can help pastors and church leaders to think about curating church from new and varied angles.

Liturgical Takeaways

Ramírez argues that the role and responsibilities of curators has shifted, transforming the curator of contemporary art from "behind-the-scenes aesthetic arbiter to central player in the broader stage of global cultural politics." She continues, writing that "more than art critics or gallery dealers, [curators] establish the meaning and status of contemporary art through its acquisition, exhibition, and interpretation."[12] This is a crucial point by which to structure our liturgical gleanings from this exhibition. Curators *make meaning* precisely in their work of aesthetic or liturgical arbitration. By extension, if pastors and church leaders only extol the writings of Tim Keller or the sermons of Adam Hamilton, we are reinforcing hierarchies that may silence alternative perspectives that can also enrich a community's existence. Keeping this in mind . . .

---

10. Robert Storr, "Perspective of Exhibition Craft," in *Versions and Inversions*, 209.

11. Terry Smith, "Better Ideas and Impossible Objects: A Commentary," in *Versions and Inversions*, 245.

12. Mari Carmen Ramírez, "Brokering Identities: Art Curators and the Politics of Cultural Representation," in *Thinking About Exhibitions*, ed. Reesa Greenberg, Bruce W. Ferguson, and Sandy Nairne (London: Routledge, 1996), 15.

1. Curating church ought to learn from other artistic, theological, and liturgical movements and recontextualize them in light of local realities.

Here the possibilities are endless. Consider the historical and theological significance of the Confessing Church movement in the 1930s. Through their famous Barmen Declaration, certain theologians and church leaders refused to capitulate to the *Deutsche Christen* movement, arguing that the German Christians had corrupted church government by making it subservient to the state and had introduced Nazi ideology into the German Protestant churches that contradicted the Christian gospel. This is all well known.

Consider a worship gathering, or worship series, that recast Barmen in Greenville or Tuscaloosa or Raleigh. What might a coterie of concerned theologians and church leaders declare about the gospel in light of the rise of Trumpism? How might our state and national legislatures receive such "primary theology"? How would American cities need to add to Barmen concerns for race, class, gender, ability, and sexual orientation? What institutions could such a worshipping community call out for their unjust practices (for-profit prisons, stop-and-frisk laws, and laws regulating women's bodies come to mind).

Or consider this. Pastors and church leaders are well acquainted with the precipitating events and proceedings of the Third Ecumenical Council held in Ephesus in 431. Herein, the assembled bishops rejected Nestorianism as an adequate understanding of Jesus Christ's divinity and humanity. By way of a refresher, Nestorianism is a form of *dyophysitism*, which holds that Christ had two loosely united natures, divine and human. Nesotorius and his followers maintained that Jesus Christ was not *identical* with the Son but personally *united* with the Son, who lives in him. Recall that this view emerged out of an effort to make sense of the hypostatic union, whereby that which is eternal (Jesus's divinity) and that which is not (Jesus's flesh), came together. This view was again condemned by the Council of Chalcedon in 451.

Contemporary theologians and church leaders are still inquiring into Jesus's hypostasis. Much as the councils of the early church emerged out of critical conversation with philosophical conundrums—especially those of neoplatonism—our contemporary understandings of Jesus grate against the important work by critical race theorists, stand-point epistemologists, and queer theorists. What is at stake *theologically* for a church to proclaim Jesus's blackness, queerness, or colonial identity?[13] How might worship gatherings create space for *engaging* with these pertinent questions, *conserving* the church's robust theological history, but also *transforming* congregational consciousness? These are the central tasks of curating church.

2. Curating church ought not neglect lesser-known voices.

In a *New York Times* article on Ramírez and her influence upon contemporary art curation, she is reported as saying, "My objection to Frida Kahlo is the phenomenon of Frida Kahlo and the way it obscures Latin American art. She was a woman with an exceptional capacity to present her own suffering through an amazing and rather unique style. But she didn't have many followers. You can't use her as an emblem for an entire continent. It's absurd."[14] Her and Olea's exhibition, therefore, omitted Kahlo, creating space for other Latin American artists to shine.

What is more, *Inverted Utopias* troubled a reductionistic and stereotypical assumption about art history itself. The twentieth-century aesthetic and ideological phenomenon captured by the designation "modernism" exists by excluding that which subverts its aesthetic imperialism. As a decidedly European movement, the "historical avant-garde" gathers together such disparate artistic movements as cubism, futurism, Dadaism, constructivism, and surrealism. In order to establish its own independent existence, this movement has coalesced around the exclusion of Latin American art and artists—many of whom studied in Europe with the so-called "masters" of the avant-garde. Nevertheless, art history has marginalized these artists. Ramírez and Olea write that "until such empowerment [of Latin American art] operates in force, and stale remarks—such as 'peripheral,' 'derivative,' 'epigynous,' 'exotic,' and 'outsider'—are forgotten, our task is nothing less than the comprehensive challenge to Latin American art's no-place in history."[15] Hence, the

---

13. See Miguel A. De La Torre, *The Politics of Jesús: A Hispanic Political Theology* (Lanham, MD: Rowman and Littlefield, 2015); and Kathleen T. Talvacchia, Mark Larrimore, and Michael F. Pettinger, eds., *Queer Christianities: Lived Religion in Transgressive Forms* (New York: NYU Press, 2014), as recent examples.

14. Lubow, "After Frida."

15. Mari Carmen Ramírez and Héctor Olea, prologue to *Inverted Utopias*, xv.

exhibition's title, *Inverted Utopias*, plays against avant-gardism in a playfully deconstructive fashion (as highlighted above).

Moving from here to a liturgical curatorial imagination, we have opportunities to expose our congregants and parishioners to those on the margins of church life. Church historians help us immensely here. My Columbia Seminary colleague Haruko Nawata Ward has dedicated her career to bringing the work and witness of sixteenth-century Japanese women religious leaders to light.[16] Consider also the writings of homiletician Frank Thomas. In his latest book, Thomas declares that he is dedicating the rest of his scholarly career to preserving and presenting the best specimens of African-American preaching to the church and the Academy.[17] Rather than setting Rev. Dr. Martin Luther King's sermons on repeat—wonderful as they are!—we also have a responsibility to preserve by presenting the works of amazing preachers and leaders like Adam Clayton Powell Jr., Ida B. Wells, Alexander Crummell, and Ella Pearson Mitchell.

3. Curating church ought to engage traditions (theologies, histories, cultural ideologies, etc.) with an eye to forging new connections.

In her scholarly reflections on *Inverted Utopias*, Ramírez writes that the idea of the show itself "provides an ideal site, an alternative one, if you will, for apprehending previously undetected, dormant, or under-recognized relationships between artists and their production."[18] Such a re-presentation can be productive for new understandings, which may, in turn, generate new possibilities for moving forward as a community.

The possibilities for curating church are limited only by our liturgical imaginations. How might the Social Gospel Movement of the 1920s speak meaningfully to the numerous Occupy movements of late? Could Walter Rauschenbusch share a pulpit with Joerg Rieger? How about Dorothy Day

---

16. Haruko Nawata Ward, *Women Religious Leaders in Japan's Christian Century, 1549–1650* (Surrey, England: Ashgate, 2009).

17. Frank A. Thomas, *Introduction to the Practice of African American Preaching* (Nashville: Abingdon, 2016), 5–6. See also Martha Simmons and Frank A. Thomas, *Preaching with Sacred Fire: An Anthology of African American Sermons, 1750 to the Present* (New York: Norton, 2010).

18. Ramírez, "The Displacement of Utopias," 123.

and Kwok Pui-lan? Or consider how the Ghanaian theology of Kwame Bediako might harmonize with Diana Butler Bass's "grounded" theology.[19]

The point here is not to see how many disparate voices you can invite to the same microphone. Rather, following Ramírez's curatorial insight, forging these connections can offer nuanced appreciations for past struggles and triumphs and theoretically-practical approaches to addressing the same or similar situations in the present. There is something immensely disarming when one comes to understand that this or that contemporary polarizing issue has already been addressed, mutatis mutandis, by church leaders in an earlier era.

4. Curating church may only emerge when indigenous perspectives are included.

It is not by chance that the Mexican Olea and the Puerto Rican Ramírez came to curate *Inverted Utopias*. Their particular ethnic perspectives allowed them to conceive such an exhibition. As Olea contends, ". . . Latin America was able to interpret history not by virtue of its barely perceptible peripheral position, but by the all-encompassing perspective granted by its liminal status. And this sensory threshold to the 360 degrees of art's experimental possibilities is one of the key issues at the core of *Inverted Utopias*."[20] What this means for we who would curate church is that we must nurture relationships with people in our communities who possess different angles of vision on the world. Attending to the particularities of race, ethnicity, gender, sexual orientation, ability, and class will open up liturgical possibilities. When church leaders and pastors confess that we don't even know what we don't know, we foster a space of hospitality that is essential to forging connections and possible transformations.

---

19. See Kwame Bediako, *Theology and Identity: The Impact of Culture upon Christian Thought in the Second Century and in Modern Africa* (Eugene, OR: Wipf and Stock, 1999), and Diana Butler Bass, *Grounded: Finding God in the World—A Spiritual Revolution* (New York: HarperOne, 2015).

20. Olea, "The Rights of Inversion," 17.

In/sight: African Photographers, 1940 to the Present

Guggenheim Museum, New York

Frankly speaking, there is no such thing as a single curator. Even when one person is working, "a multiplicity of anonymous people" are constantly working together in him or her. Collaborators, interferers, opposers, memories, accidental happenings . . . infinitely numerous elements incessantly affect the work. Who can claim a single I in this circumstance?

—*Youngchul Lee*[1]

In/sight: African Photographers, 1940 to the Present is an exhibition curated by an exceptionally acclaimed and diverse team. Together, Clare Bell, Okwui Enwezor, Danielle Tilkin, and Octavio Zaya offered an alternative world—better worlds—of visuality and experience. Central to their curatorial labors was a riposte to (mis)representations of Africa, especially from the period in which African nations had ostensibly freed themselves from colonial rule by Western powers.

---

1. Cited in Christian Haye, "Spin City Survey: The Istanbul, Johannesburg, and Kwangju Biennales," *Trade Routes Revisited, 1997-2012: A Project Marking the 15th Anniversary of the Second Johannesburg Biennale,* ed. Joost Bosland (Cape Town and Johannesburg: Stevenson, 2012), 67.

Hosted at the Guggenheim Museum in 1996, *In/sight* presented the work of thirty ethnically and racially diverse African photographers active on the continent and abroad who employ, critique, and exploit notions of photographic truth concerning African representation. The artists displayed came from many disciplines (including photojournalism, portraiture, documentary photography, and art of the Western gallery variety). The exhibition challenged the dueling narratives presented by *National Geographic* of Africa as a humble utopia and by cable news networks as a dystopia ravaged by war and famine. *In/sight* is significant for many reasons, but foremost among these is that it was the first museum exhibit in the United States to look critically at the work of African-born photographers.

Curatorial Vision

Enwezor, Zaya, Bell, and Tilkin set out to curate a space where Africans could share their own visualization of Africa beyond Western perceptions. To this end, they drew together works of thirty African photographers (including several Afrikaners and other Caucasians) representing multiple layers of diversity: nationality, language, religion, and sexuality, in particular. As the subtitle of the exhibition indicates, the curatorial team selected images dating from the various independence struggles to the present post/de-colonial period.

Photography in Africa has been dominated by anthropologists or Western commercial photographers. While true, Enwezor and Zaya argue, these dominant outlets present a flattened and colorless picture of African life. With *In/Sight* they sought to recast the relationship between the production of knowledge in the West and images of Africa, to give Africans (and the rest of us) a chance to see how Africans have represented themselves through the medium of photography.

In/sight is first and foremost an art exhibition, but it is also an exhibition of an alternative mode of ethnography. Even in the purportedly "scientific" imagery that Westerners discover in our school textbooks, we receive the bodies of Africans as consumables—what Enwezor and Zaya label "the decapitation or cannibalization of the subject." What these anthropologies achieve is a gross misrepresentation of African bodies and communities. Such images stoke the fires of a false imagination, working in consort with the notion of "scientific inquiry."[2]

Photographs are inherently ambiguous: they both represent and misrepresent reality. Such images are tape measures for assessing the cultural landscape of a people and for constraining ideological boundaries. Photographs foster homogeneity; however, curated exhibitions of photographs infuse a degree of movement to such stills, fostering multiplicity and broadening horizons.

Western representations of Africa and Africans constitute a case in point. Such photographs have produced an inherently distorted view and ongoing misconception about Africans. Clare Bell, director of exhibition management at the Solomon R. Guggenheim Museum, notes that, "Geographical considerations and their relationship to identity and culture have also been subsumed into an insulated dynamic that privileges one point of view over another." This is a function of still photography itself; but is also creates an ethical situation for the photographer as to just which slice of life she chooses to capture. She must ask herself what story she is telling frame-by-frame.

Bell continues, "Self-reflexive rather than revealing, the recognition of place in these terms functions as a way to affirm our resolutions about ourselves rather than to tell us about others."[3] Said differently, every photograph is a kind of confession; the click of the shutter reveals those conscious and unconscious ways of thinking and modes of perceiving others that can be as revealing to the photographer as any other who views her work.

In their introduction to the exhibition entitled "Colonial Imaginary, Tropes of Disruption: History, Culture, and Representation in the Works of African Photographers," Enwezor and Zaya write, "Ultimately, what the European powers that conquered, colonized, and exploited Africa produced is a rendering of the continent as an amoral, primitive, and marginal site of dark, brooding forces, misery, and pestilence, a place that both cripples and

---

2. Okwui Enwezor and Octavio Zaya, "Colonial Imaginary, Tropes of Disruption: History, Culture, and Representation in the Works of African Photographers," in *In/sight: African Photographers, 1940 to the Present* (New York: Solomon R. Guggenheim Foundation, 1996), 24.

3. Clare Bell, introduction to *In/sight*, 9.

fervidly arouses the imagination of the traveler, explorer, missionary, bounty hunter, and colonist."[4]

We have all witnessed the spectacle that Enwezor and Zaya describe: images of black children with swollen stomachs on late-night infomercials; bare-chested women in Congolese rainforests; loincloth-wearing warriors with distended earlobes. Enwezor and Zaya advance their own in/sight into the lives of Africans, one that is purportedly less stereotypical because such was captured by Africans themselves. Later in their introductory essay we read,

> In one way or another, Africa as seen through this exhibition is not a mono-lithic supposition, nor is it merely an idea that can be bent to our wishes and desires. Consequently, all the participating photographers touch on the nodes of these demands. They speak from positions that allow us to explore their various cultural and artistic imperatives, while opening up avenues to examine the dynamic relationship between past and present, history and memory, time and space, origin and authenticity, desire and ambivalence, and ethnic and sexual desire.[5]

In concluding their essay, Enwezor and Zaya note, "In examining issues of modern and contemporary African representation and identity, and the interpretation and dissemination of history, [*In/sight*] calls attention to a continent whose long historical traditions have crossed, touched, and influenced all the consequential byways of human history."[6] *In/sight* offers an example of curation that transforms simplistic assumptions about the *other*. Henceforward, the participant must work to integrate this counter-narrative with those images and stories that will continue to shape an understanding of Africa and Africans.

Description

The photographs selected for this exhibition frame a certain ambivalence, deconstructing Western notions of Africans as the quintessential other. Some of the artists perform such a deconstruction explicitly. For example, Nigerian

---

4. Enwezor and Zaya, "Colonial Imaginary," 18.

5. Ibid., 21.

6. Ibid., 29.

artist Iké Udé's installations juxtapose photographs of caricatured images of Africa culled from popular culture with collages of family portraits and snapshots that might appear in any North American or European photo album. When we compare Udé's images with those that have come to represent Africa and Africans, we're reminded that our knowledge of Africa has come to us through gross misrepresentations. Udé challenges the false grounding for Western fantasies and fears by offering his viewers alternative pictures of actual African lives, lives that do not appear all that different from those of Westerners.

A second fascinating example in this exhibition is that of another Nigerian artist, Rotimi Fani-Kayode, whose works focus on the intersectionality of his own sense of otherness (cultural, racial, sexual). In his essay "Traces of Ecstasy," Fani-Kayode writes that "an awareness of history has been of fundamental importance in the development of my creativity. The history of Africa and of the Black race has been constantly distorted."[7] Fani-Kayode experienced this distortion from Westerners, to be sure; but he also felt this within his Yoruba culture, which spurned his sexual orientation. Thus, in photographs like "Tulip Boy," "Abybiyi," and "Every Moment Counts," Fani-Kayode presents images of beautiful Black men alongside imagery that solicits a sense of dissonance for Western and African viewers alike.

Togolese photographer Cornélius Yao Augustt Azaglo offers yet another perspective. His selections include close-up portraits of rural Senufo people in which his subjects peer back at the camera with an appraising eye. The gaze of these men and women haunts the viewer, as if challenging even the possibility of objectification. What is interesting about Azaglo's photographs is that they were taken in the 1960s as ID pictures (for voting purposes). His photographs capture a people en route to the formation of a new country, Côte d'Ivoire. The dignified, almost regal posture of these people belies false conceptions of West Africans as either submissive or savage beings, as well as contemporary standards of DMV photos in America.

Central to the exhibit were a large group of photos taken from *Drum* magazine, dating mostly from the 1950s. Originally published in South Africa, *Drum* later appeared in regional African editions and in the West Indies.

---

7. Rotimi Fani-Kayode, "Traces of Ecstasy," *Ten-8*, no. 28 (1988): 36.

It was a major source for both the production and consumption of new identities in Africa during the early years of national independence. The curatorial team recontextualized *Drum's* imagery to spotlight its distinct aesthetic sensibility.

One feature of the exhibit was an issue of the South Africa Edition of *Drum* dated August, 1958. To put the significance of this magazine in perspective, as one commentator has, *Drum* operated for Africans in the '50s and '60s like *Ebony* does for African Americans today. The magazine's writers refused to shy away from tough issues by putting the most positive face forward in the public image. "It depicted a time when particularly those in South Africa lived in a more hopeful and vibrant period, and a small window for creative and intellectual multicultural freedom existed, before being bricked in by apartheid."[8]

In one example, the curators juxtaposed an advertisement for laundry soap with the caption, "Whites and coloureds come out of those rich suds sparkling clean" with an article appearing on the adjacent page entitled, "Some of Nigeria's Most Successful Women." This juxtaposition is striking when we consider that in South Africa during this era many *Drum* readers would have actually been employed to wash the clothes of white people. Such economic and social conditions beg the question of how these South Africans could have even imagined becoming one of the "Most Successful Women." Through it, the editors of *Drum* bore witness to an alternative reality beyond the status quo, thereby shaping what their viewers regarded as possible.

Critical Reception

Critics offered little but praise for *In/sight*. One such commentator summarizes the scholarly consensus thusly: "The images dispel the myth of the 'dark continent' by revealing its faces and forms with both clarity and resonance."[9] The gift that *In/sight's* curatorial team offer their audience is nothing less than subjecthood. They return the native African to a subject-position, releasing him/her/them from Western objectification. Along the

---

8. John Peffer-Engels, "Recent Exhibitions," *African Arts* 30, no. 1 (Winter 1997): 73.

9. Carol Strickland, "African Photographers Dispel Myth of the 'Dark Continent,'" *Christian Science Monitor* 88, no. 144 (June 20, 1996): 10.

way, they establish the conditions of possibility for a counter-historization of Africa as perceived by its inhabitants rather than by the Western explorers who returned to Europe with tales of the "dark continent."

One critic observes that *In/sight* "provided a quick and efficient antidote to just this sort of watering down of the intellectual and aesthetic achievements of Africans for the American public." He continues,

> To what extent are African artists expected to speak of themselves explicitly for the Western-oriented marketplace of the gallery system, and to what degree is speaking of the self a strategy used by these artists to subvert the expectations and projections of the Western gaze? Though internationalism usually means orientation toward the desires of a Western-oriented middle class, many artists working for the galleries are aware that their practice is ultimately framed by Western aesthetics and standards of quality and content. It is the ways in which academically trained transnational Africans continually challenge this commodifying and disempowering regime of the visual that makes their work important.[10]

Such a postcolonial approach to African photography was most evident throughout the exhibition.

While critics praised *In/sight* for its revelatory effects, they also celebrated the lingering questions the exhibition opened. Writing for *The New York Times*, Holland Cotter lauds *In/sight's* "venture into the terrain." And at the same time, "by sifting themes and raising ideas and remaining determinedly incomplete, it suggests an immense and exciting body of work waiting to be discovered."[11]

Liturgical Takeaways

One of the obvious takeaways from the *In/sight* exhibition for curating church is the importance of curators to collaborate as broadly as possible. We must constantly ask ourselves, "Who is absent from this conversation?" and "How might we present the other (whether ethnic, racial, sexual, or biblical)

---

10. Peffer-Engels, "Recent Exhibitions," 76.

11. Holland Cotter, "Mostly African Scenes, All by Africans," *The New York Times*, July 5, 1996, http://www.nytimes.com/1996/07/05/arts/photography-review-mostly-african-scenes-all-by-africans.html.

in ways that resists his/her/their totalization?" in our liturgies and our sermons. *In/sight's* curatorial foursome offer pastors and church leaders four ways to pursue such a course.

1. A curating church embraces particularity, and particularity begins 'originarily' or it never begins.

The word *originarily* at once signifies and challenges modern Western notions of beginning; indeed, it names the non-simplicity of every beginning. The origin of any concept, act, or way of being can never be simple because there is always something else that precedes it and which structures and troubles that something's beginning. Where we find this in *In/sight* is in the synergy emanating from the ethnic and racial differences between the curators themselves.

Bell is American. Enwezor is Nigerian. Zaya is Spanish. Tilkin shares her time between New York and Madrid. At the time of the exhibit they all lived in New York City. While such diversity alone can in no way guarantee diversity, a breadth of lived experiences from distinct geopolitical purviews can at least increase the likelihood that particularity will be sought in a team's subject matter. Especially for those who must live and work beyond the dominant frame, the desire to hear the other speak in his/her/their own voice is paramount. To underscore this point, consider the following question posed by Enwezor and Zaya: "So how do we address questions of representation, self-imaging, and artistic freedom when those initiatives are counteracted by stronger economic imperativeness, and when the contingencies of social and epistemological control are made to bend to the influence of power and access?"[12] Such questioning drives us to reflect upon material and intersubjective realities of persons.

When we think about beginning to curate worship experiences for and alongside our congregants and parishioners, we ought to consider our team. Who selects the "artists"? How are they chosen? How do they offer ways of seeing the world that help the community to see otherwise? Who makes the final decision about what gets included or excluded? By incorporating differ-

---

12. Salah Hassan, "Vers un renaissance," Ja Taa, Prendre L'image, *Illes Rencontres Africaines de la Photographie* (Bamako, 1998), 8.

ence at the beginning, church curators produce built-in mechanisms to resist the hegemony of the solitary visionary, who creates all by himself.

2. Curating church facilitates thinking along multiple axes of difference.

Bell, Enwezor, Tilkin, and Zaya do not think along only one axis of difference. The participating photographers address us from unique epistemological positions that allow us to explore their various cultural and artistic imperatives. At the same time, their work opens avenues to examine the dynamic relationships between past and present, history and memory, time and space, origin and authenticity, desire and ambivalence, and ethnic and sexual identity. In other words, it is not just ethnic difference, but gender, sexual, and temporal difference that matters. Some of the artists with whom the curators collaborated have remained in their home countries. Others are living in the diaspora. These experiences that their artists bring to the exhibition is not peripheral to the kind of work they produce. Intersectionality is key.

Church curators who seek to expand the interpretive, epistemological, relational, and spiritual horizons of their congregants and neighbors in and through Christian worship would do well to interrogate the way that the makeup of the curatorial team expresses or forecloses upon difference. If our congregation is homogenous, we cannot imagine that it will ever diversify if the leadership reflects the sameness of the congregation. And this is not merely about cosmetic diversity; we have to engage with others who are not afraid to bring that otherness to bear in conceptual and tangible ways. My pastor and colleague Brandon Maxwell labels this the formation of "brave space," which encourages truth-telling and transformative dialogue.

3. Curating church enables worshipers to see the world in different ways, leading to transformed ways of being in the world.

Presenting issues as wide-ranging and complex as apartheid, Yoruba spiritualities, the exploitative mythologizing of black virility, and the vulgar objectification of Africa, the curators offer us a model for imagining worship beyond conventional praxis. *In/sight* did not shy away from a challenge that is just as pertinent today as it was in 1996: How do we fully address "the other" amid structures that have staked claims, appropriated, restricted, and controlled the access, diffusion, circulation and representation of the other?

127

Here we may be so bold as to substitute photography of Africa and Africans for other media and the ways it renders an attenuated identity of other people groups: sitcoms' portrayals of gay masculinity; Fox News's depiction of Muslims; the Gospel's rarified presentation of Judaisms and "the Jews."

American photographer and art critic Max Kozloff praises the work of *In/sight's* curatorial team for having rendered an exhibition that was at once familiar and eye-opening. He writes that here he "was greeted by a spectrum of familiar genres with unexpected points of view. Instead of having to look from the 'outside' at African subjects, a viewer was given perspectives from within their diverse cultures . . ." Kozloff goes on to observe and applaud the ways in which *In/sight* granted the viewer access to "interior horizons" theretofore inaccessible to a Western public.[13] This observation bears greatly upon a liturgical imagination informed by curation.

It is not enough that we simply show images of the "other" and expect our congregants and parishioners to encounter this "other" authentically. If the other is not permitted to show him/her/themselves by and from his/her/their own subject position, what is shown is merely a shade, a projection of the sameness secured by the other's perceived difference. Nurturing a curatorial imagination calls pastors and church leaders to create spaces for others to show themselves as they see themselves—beyond objectification or appropriation.

4. Even as curating church opens itself to new encounters with otherness, such work calls for continued engagement; that is, in its constructs it structures the need for deconstruction.

In a retrospective essay written ten years after *In/sight* first made its presence felt on the art world, curator Vanessa Rocco names several ways that this exhibition has shaped contemporary African photography. She traces the genealogical effects of *In/sight* to major art exhibitions in Paris, Munich, London, Düsseldorf, South Africa, and Mali. She first names a crucial contribution of *In/sight* as that of having "established a lineage of images and influences before moving on to how the contemporary artists of the 1980s and '90s had absorbed those influences in their quest to confront their cur-

---

13.   Max Kozloff, "In/sight: African Photographers, 1940 to the Present," *Artforum International* 35, no. 2 (October 1996), 114.

rent struggles and issues."[14] At the same time, however, Rocco notes how the works and artists that *In/sight* foregrounded in 1998 have become a sort of canon unto themselves. Artists like Keïta, Fosso, Sidibé, Goldblat, and other African modernists have become stable figures of African art exhibitions. The danger of this is that the breadth and vibrancy of other African artists fail to receive their due attention, ostensibly arresting the vitality of African self-representation.

The lure to situate our understandings of peoples and places is enticing, but we must not allow such understandings to ossify. Liturgical curation offers congregants and parishioners opportunities to embrace nuance, to wrestle with ambiguities, and to continually question our understandings. Remembering that we see through a glass darkly (1 Cor 13:12), we must fight against the hubris that convinces us that we have this or that issue settled.

---

14.   Vanessa Rocco, "After *In/sight*: Ten Years of Exhibiting Contemporary African Photography," in *Snap Judgments: New Positions in Contemporary African Photography* (New York: International Center of Photography, 2006), 350.

Embracing a Curatorial Imagination

As curators, our task is to make those tensions [of contemporary reality] clearer, more articulate, and more acute, and to do it on behalf of the art and on behalf of the public, since there is absolutely no purpose in inviting people to come and see something that was intended to stir them up and have them soothed or lulled by it instead.

—Robert Storr[1]

The work of the contemporary curator remains close to the sense in *curare* of *care*—cultivating, growing, pruning, and trying to help people and their shared contexts to thrive. In parallel, the professional curator's role began to coalesce around two functions. The first of these was conservation. Art had come to be understood as a crucial part of a nation's heritage, a set of artifacts that collectively told the story of a country. Thus, safeguarding that heritage became a primary responsibility of the curator. The second task was the selection of new work. As time passes, museum collections must necessarily be added to, and the caretaker of the museum thus becomes the caretaker of the national legacy which the museum represents.

At the same time, curation calls for a second task: that of *cure*. In artistic curation, another word to signal this impetus is *transformation*. The church has need of curators, ministers charged with the holy and difficult

---

1. Robert Storr, "How We Do What We Do. And How We Don't," in *Curating Now: Imaginative Practice/Public Responsibility*, ed. Paula Marincola (Philadelphia: Pew Center for Arts and Heritage, 2001), 10.

task of conserving what is best in our tradition and making that tradition available for our ecclesial and societal constituencies. We are also charged with understanding our contemporary contexts well enough to assess what is ailing society, and increasingly, church. The substance of ministry ought to be that which leads to transformation—note that transformation is not the task of the curator much as physicians do not, or rarely, cure a patient. Doctors and ministers are administrators of cures; we are not ourselves the cure.

This raises an obvious question: How best are we to facilitate the important work of engagement, conservation, and transformation?

Curating "Now"

In a week-long symposium hosted in October 2000 by the Philadelphia Exhibitions Initiative, curators and critics gathered to assess the current state of curatorial practice. The event was named "Curating Now: Imaginative Practice/Public Responsibility." The opening lecture was delivered by Robert Storr, who serves as the senior curator in the department of painting and sculpture at the Museum of Modern Art in New York. Storr's lecture offers many points for us to consider, but I will restrict my observations to two: the generational gap manifesting between both curators and clergy; and the hermeneutical tension inherent in artistic and ecclesial curation.

Generation Gap

Storr began his career as an art critic, where he vociferously challenged the parochialism and conservatism he detected in large institutional museums. His career has led him from that of outsider/iconoclast to insider/iconophile. He recognizes that his earlier critiques facilitated his entry into the very institutions he was critiquing. He is now part of the establishment.

Storr encourages his colleagues in the contemporary art world to listen and learn from the critiques of younger generations of curators. He says,

> All of us work directly with younger colleagues coming up through the ranks as interns and assistants, younger colleagues facing great uncertainties

about the profession and their place in it, and not a few wonder whether there is a tolerable future in museums at all. Some want to know, better than we can probably tell them, what the trade-offs are going to be, and they want to know, having made those trade-offs, if, at the end, there really will be an opportunity to work in a museum context on terms that allow them to do what they do in a manner consonant with their convictions. Having learned what I have learned on the job, I take their doubts and discomforts very, very seriously.[2]

The history of the world takes shape according to generational dissent, appeasement, and transformation. Much as geological strata are formed by the heating and cooling of magma, epochal transitions emerge out of the passionate intensity of younger generations challenging the patterns and practices of older generations. Ironically, as their furor cools and the younger generation ages, they become part of the establishment and find themselves on the receiving end of the emerging generation's vitriol.

This dynamic interplay between the old and the new structures our perception of the present. Take me for an example. At the time of this writing, I am thirty-eight years old. Just ten years ago, I was a rogue church planter working in Little Five Points, the most countercultural enclave of Atlanta. I lectured all over the country about the need for the church to change in light of postmodernity, and I served on the national leadership of the Emerging Church Conversation, co-founding first the Princeton Emergent Cohort with Tony Jones and then the Atlanta Emergent Cohort with Troy Bronsink.

My pushing against certain ecclesial theologies and practices led me into Wieuca Road Baptist Church, one of the most prominent churches in my denomination. I joined this staff as a pastor focused on missional community and alternative worship. There I challenged the institutional church from within the institution, curating a worship space called re-church.

A decade later, I have a PhD and am teaching the next generation of ministers to challenge the very institutions I once challenged. I, like Robert Storr and his symposia participants, am part of the establishment.

---

2. Ibid., 5.

Moreover, I'm on the tenure track, which means I am pursuing a vocational trajectory that will ensure my institutional backing in perpetuity—*Deo volente!*

I share this with you both to underscore a bit about my own ministerial journey that I shared in Gallery II, but also as an offering that might lead you to reflect on the generational gap manifesting in your particular context.

- Where do you find yourself along the generational spectrum, and how does this sync up with your degree of institutionalization?

- What responsibilities does this place on you as you work with younger generations who are challenging what they perceive as outmoded beliefs and practices?

- How do you provide care and counsel to young pastors and seminary interns who are worried about the fate and future of the church as a viable vocation?

Hermeneutical Tension

I find another point of comparison between Storr's observations in the art world with that of church regarding interpretation. Neither art curators nor Christian ministers create *ex nihilo*. We present artifacts to our respective constituencies in the hope that these artifacts will engage our audiences and prompt a transformation in them that may in turn foster community and even transformation.

Storr discusses the hermeneutical tension arising out of his work as an art curator:

I have abiding doubts about many aspects of the relation of modern and contemporary art to the museums and other venues devoted to them. Those doubts become specific when I consider the ways in which what I, in all good will, do as a curator may qualify or denature what the artist has tried to do. This is not a simple problem, and walking away from it won't help matters. All things considered, I would rather be in a position where I can test certain options, in the service of what I believe in and what I think the artist believes in, and use my intuition and expertise to try to minimize the mistakes that can be made in presenting their work than to stand back and let someone else run those risks and indulge myself in the luxury of being right about how they were wrong. The fact is, I have been responsible for having 'framed' or contextualized art in ways that subtly, albeit unintentionally, altered its meaning or diminished its impact. As a practicing curator, one has to be straightforward not only about the potential for but the likelihood of doing this in a given circumstance.[3]

One of the great gifts of curation, one that leans into this hermeneutical tension instead of running away from or ignoring it, is the possibility of collaboration.

Storr argues that the "great institutions"—and, by this, he does not mean just the big ones—are those that "foster internal differences, those that do not operate according to a uniform aesthetic ideology, and do not, in the current fashionable way, think of themselves as a 'brand' with a consistent product, although they may have an overall 'style' or a primary focus on certain kinds of material." Instead, they are ones that encourage a multiplicity of ways of framing and interpreting the material with which they are concerned.[4] This should be a guiding principle for our liturgical curations during the polarizing times in which we live and serve.

Cultivating Aesthetic Judgment

But how, exactly, are we who have been called to serve God's church in and through culture to facilitate the tripartite tasks of cultural curation? How are we to decide where and how to engage? What in our history is worthy of conservation? What calls for transformation?

Theologian David Kelsey offers a theological term that maps onto the element of aesthetic judgment in the art world. He speaks of a *discrimen*, a Latin term that signifies judgment and demarcation. For Kelsey, a *discrimen* marks the criteria by which theological judgments are made. In his book *The Uses of Scripture in Recent Theology*, Kelsey observes that the manner in which we bring scripture to bear on theological argument is inextricable to

---

3. Ibid.

4. Ibid., 9.

our understanding of God's abiding presence. He writes that "the criterion by which the church's current forms of speech and action and reforms proposed in 'doing theology' is a *discrimen* in which the church's use of scripture in her common life is conjoined with God's presence among the faithful."[5] If we are going to think about church as cultural curation—the church as both a cultural quantity and a cultural product—we must interrogate our metrics for aesthetic, theological, liturgical, and homiletical judgment. In short, we must articulate our *discrimen*.

It is only polite that I articulate my own ecclesiological *discrimen*. My approach to curating church is guided by what I would identify as an incarnational-deconstructive *discrimen*. This framework guides my ecclesiological judgments. It shapes my approach to liturgical leadership and preaching. It bolsters my understanding of spiritual formation. In short, my *discrimen* presupposes that God is present among us in our respective particularities/peculiarities as one who is radically other.

What results from this implicit understanding of God in relation to the created order is attention to the word-world of God as an interrogation of articulations of identity and righteousness. Many theoretical resources are ready-to-hand. My *discrimen* is guided by a queer epistemology, which aims beyond identity politics and cultural monism by recognizing identity as a discursive negotiation of particularities. Intersectionality guides me here. I view the work of church in and through culture as deconstructive: theologically constructive in its philosophical deconstruction. In other words, it is not that the church is sometimes constructive and at other times deconstructive; rather, I see the church as we who are called out to participate in God's construction that takes shape through deconstruction.[6]

---

5. David H. Kelsey, *Proving Doctrine: The Uses of Scripture in Modern Theology* (Harrisburg, PA: Trinity Press International, 1999), 167.

6. For a more explicit articulation of this de-constructive orientation, see Jacob D. Myers, *Preaching Must Die! Troubling Homiletical Theology* (Minneapolis: Fortress, 2017); and my forthcoming book co-authored by Eric D. Barreto and Thelathia Nikki Young, *In Tongues of Mortals and Angels: A De-Constructive Theology of God-Talk in Acts and 1 Corinthians* (Minneapolis: Fortress, 2018).

Curating Possibilities for Liturgical Transformation

Throughout this book, I've worked to advance a relatively straightforward thesis: Our polarizing cultural and ecclesial contexts call for an alternative liturgical imagination that is oriented toward both *care* and *cure*—the quintessence of curation. Following from my own experiences of curating church (Gallery I), and building upon the liturgical insights we've gleaned from curated art exhibitions across the globe (Gallery II), it is now time that I pass the proverbial baton to you.

Here in Gallery III, I seek to do two things. First, I want to model a way of engaging matters of contemporary cultural and theological significance oriented toward care and cure. Operating within this intention is an assumption. Since you have stuck with me thus far, I believe you desire to lead your fellow worshipers to engage matters of "ultimate concern," to borrow Paul Tillich's well-known phrase. Unfortunately, such matters are rarely clear-cut. Liturgical curation is especially well-suited for helping pastors and church leaders broach polarizing issues, for which holding care and cure in balance are paramount concerns. Accordingly, it is imperative that we engage such issues with an eye toward *engagement, conservation*, and *transformation*.

As you will have undoubtedly discerned from our discussion thus far, curation demands more of us than merely presenting our congregants/parishioners with a range of theological responses to polarizing issues. Insofar as we don the curator's mantle, we bear responsibility not only for *what* we choose to present but *how* we present it.

Second, in this Gallery I aim to lay the groundwork for you to engage polarizing topics in your ministry context. What I hope you will do is gather a diverse group of people from within and from beyond your community and consider these flashpoints of polarization together. I have discovered that the key to talking about hot-button topics in churches is to begin by peeling away the layers that complicate these topics. This is precisely what I aim to model in this Gallery.

I hope that you will consider these matters culturally, politically, and theologically, with an eye to connecting with your congregants/parishioners. I hope that you will think together about how to resource your fellow worshippers from the annals of church history and theology in response to these issues. And I hope that you will carry out these tasks of engagement and conservation with an eye toward transformation. As my mentor in liturgical theology, Don Saliers, teaches us, "authentic" Christian worship confronts us simultaneously as *threat* and *hope*. He writes, "Christian liturgy transforms and empowers when the vulnerability of human pathos is met by the ethos of God's vulnerability in word and sacrament."[1] Curating possibilities for liturgical transformation calls us to awareness of the lived realities of human suffering and injustice *and* awareness of God's self-giving of God's grace and glory—care *and* cure.

Once you have a group assembled to consider these curating possibilities with you, you'll want to approach these matters with an eye to what care and cure might look like within your ecclesial/liturgical context. More specifically, you'll want to ask each other some version of the following questions:

1) How might we connect best with our congregants/parishioners at this point of complexity and polarization?

2) What resources abound that might best allow us to care for our fellow worshipers while leading them toward a cure for the modern maladies we are facing?

---

1. Don E. Saliers, *Worship as Theology: Foretaste of Glory Divine* (Nashville: Abingdon, 1994), 22.

3) What would genuine transformation look like in our congregational/parish context, and how do we nurture spaces where such transformation might take shape?

Lastly, remember that the following curating possibilities are merely examples to illustrate how I would broach these topics in my liturgical context. As cultures shift and the church responds (or fails to respond), perhaps these matters will cease to be as polarizing as they are in my context in 2018. To God be the glory if isolationism, racism, and alienation give way to hope, hospitality, and embrace. Sadly, I imagine these issues will remain with us into the foreseeable future.

Worshipping God in a World of Uncertainty, Fear, and Isolationism

Thrown into a vast open sea with no navigation charts and all the marker buoys sunk and barely visible, we have only two choices left: we may rejoice in the breath-taking vistas of new discoveries—or we may tremble out of fear of drowning.

—Zygmunt Bauman[1]

People are worried. One of the marks of the past few years is a heightened sense of anxiety and uncertainty about what the future may hold. With the rise of carbon emissions—and the current US administration's withdrawal from the Paris Climate Accord and refusal even to acknowledge the realities of global warming—will the world survive? When our current president openly refutes facts and decries the work of serious journalists as "fake news," who can be certain of the truth? Will the political vitriol between Republicans and Democrats ever diminish? These are difficult days for people of faith, and we as pastors and church leaders bear a responsibility to curate worship experiences able to lead people through this fog of uncertainty.

In his book *Liquid Times: Living in an Age of Uncertainty*, the Polish sociologist Zygmunt Bauman marks the present as a time of insecurity, anxiety, and faltering identity. By this last point, he signifies the erosion of our

---

1. Zygmunt Bauman, *Globalization: The Human Consequence* (New York: Columbia University Press, 1998), 85.

confidence in our own selfhood in the midst of global chaos. While global-ization creates instabilities that create surplus people and stark inequalities, Bauman also argues that globalization erodes the ability of the state and local communities to provide genuine stability and security for individuals. Social institutions such as the family, education, and work dissipate faster than the span of one's life, and it becomes difficult for individuals to construct a coher-ent life-project.

This situation results in what Bauman calls "existential tremors," where individuals do not have a stable sense of who they are, or what they belong to, resulting in increased feelings of anxiety, fear, and uncertainty.[2] As evidence of this, Bauman points out that most of us do not generally perceive the future as a bright place of hope and of better things to come; instead, we see the future as a series of challenges to be endured, of risks to be managed, and of threats to our security. In short, the future is a bleak, dark, and uncertain place.

In the absence of collective security, individuals and families are left to de-velop strategies to find their own sense of security and stability, and thus our focus shifts toward risk management, and our horizons constrict to the ever-narrowing sphere over which we still have some measure of control. Thus, we invest in pensions, become very protective of our children, and grow increas-ingly xenophobic. We're obliged to spend our time doing things to minimize the perceived threats to our safety—to "Make America Safe Again": checking for cancers, investing in home security, and monitoring our children. Our life-project becomes not one of self-development, not one of striving for a deeper understanding of what it means to be human, but, instead, our life goals become limited to avoiding bad things that might befall us.

In his book *After God*, philosopher Mark C. Taylor looks at our grow-ing sense of uncertainty and fear from a slightly different angle, one that is more philosophical than Bauman's sociological analyses. Taylor details an "oppositional logic of self-identity," which is the process of identity formation whereby each side in a conflict attempts to secure itself by negating the other. What neither side understands, Taylor notes, is that such struggles are always

---

2. Zygmunt Bauman, *Liquid Times: Living in an Age of Uncertainty* (Cambridge: Polity, 2007), 14.

self-defeating—"to negate the other without whom one cannot be what one is, is to negate the self."[3] Emerging out of this other-denying movement requires us to ascribe to the dualistic logic of absolutism, marked by a stark either/or. Ironically, this schema forces everyone to stand alone. Autonomy, which seems so central to selfhood, turns out to be a "freedom *from* relationship rather than a freedom *in* relationship." Taylor concludes,

> When this schema is appropriated and adapted to today's world, the proliferation of choices comes to be regarded as an unquestioned good—the more choices, the better. As choice becomes an end in itself, however, it tends to be trivialized. No longer existentially fraught, subjectivity is reduced to style, and choice degenerates into a consumerism that defines individuals by what they own.[4]

To illustrate this point, consider the ways that we have shifted from buying a Mac or PC to becoming a Mac or Microsoft *person*. The things we buy end up defining who we are.

In this chapter, we'll be attending to the ways that curation offers theoretical, practical, and even theological support to the audacious task of worshipping God in a world of existential, political, and economic uncertainty.

Theory Matters

Let us begin by considering some liturgical possibilities that might respond to the sense of uncertainty pervading the minds of our congregants and parishioners. Here, I wish to provide theoretical support for curated liturgical experiences that can lead participants from their cultural and epistemological particularities to encounter God and thereby face the possibility of transformation.

The famed social scientist Clifford Geertz once argued that a symbol system such as we encounter in Christian worship does two things. First, it offers an *embracing worldview*, that is, a coherent framework of general ideas about how the world functions (or ought to function). Second, symbol systems

---

3. Mark C. Taylor, *After God* (Chicago and London: The University of Chicago Press, 2007), 349.

4. Ibid., 350.

induce an *ethos*, a set of moods and motivations. It is in ritual, Geertz suggests, that images and attitudes about the nature of existence are fused with one's actual experiences of the realities of existence. He explains that "in a ritual, the world as lived and the world as imagined, fused under the agency of a single set of symbolic forms, turn out to be the same world."[5]

Alienation from oneself and one's homeland is the definition of exile, which is a prevalent metaphor for our current cultural milieu. We have nothing to ground our identity. Perhaps that is why we carry phones in our pockets and purses, why we are compelled to constantly check them: We need to remind ourselves through Facebook, Twitter, and the like who we are in the new world economy of "likes," "pins," "shares," and "retweets." Worship situates us in relation to God, self, and others in a non-totalizing way. It offers us a crucial modification to René Descartes's (in)famous dictum: We worship, therefore we are.

Worship Is Already Uncertain

Worshipping God in a world of uncertainty is a bold move. Some would call it foolish; but the Apostle Paul has taught us to embrace such foolishness, not as ancillary but as essential to our love of God in the way of Jesus Christ. Curating worship, like artistic curation, is already attuned to a world of uncertainty because uncertainty is at the very heart of both worship and aesthetic encounter.

As minister-curators, we need to lean into this uncertainty, for, paradoxically, embracing uncertainty actually works to counter the epistemological uncertainty marking the present. Curator extraordinaire Hans Ulrich Obrist argues that "Combining uncertainty and the unpredictable with the organization seems an important issue. Instead of certitude, the exhibition expresses *connective possibilities*."[6] So too liturgy.

The performative nature of worship, as Shannon Craigo-Snell reminds us, constitutes its own ambiguity. This element is captured with the term

---

5. Clifford Geertz, *The Interpretation of Cultures* (New York: Basic Books, 1973), 112.

6. Hans-Ulrich Obrist, "Panel Statements and Discussion," in *Curating Now: Imaginative Practice/Public Responsibility*, Paula Marincola, ed. (Philadelphia: Philadelphia Exhibitions Initiative, 2001), 27.

doubleness, which signifies an uncertainty or tension hardwired into worship itself. Performatively, the worshiper at worship is at once performing an act of worship that has been decided in advance (a liturgical prayer, hymn, creed, etc.) *and* achieving something completely novel in his/her/their performance. In other words, we must differentiate between the performer and the role or action being performed.

This is the tension inherent to repetition. Every liturgical behavior is a "twice-behaved behavior," writes Craigo-Snell. In other words, "A performance is an event happening in the present that is also a reenactment of past events."[7] Furthermore, no repetition is ever *merely* repetition. Circumstances change, shaping performance.

Further uncertainty also emerges out of intention and actualization. When we pray, sing, or move in acts of worship we aim toward some ideal performance that is never at ease with the performance itself, that was *never* at ease with itself. The performative nature of worship is eschatological in that such acts orient us toward a future identity that is already present in liturgical events and also not yet.

I like the way that philosopher Paul Ricoeur describes this in his theory of narrative. He explains that all of us are two kinds of self: *ipse* and *idem*. These Latin terms get at a tension at work in the heart of selfhood. In his book *Oneself as Another*, Ricoeur distinguishes between two fundamental aspects of the self, or of identity (i.e., our "I"). Ricoeur explains that *ipse* is identity understood as selfhood, close to our sense of individuality, that kind of inner core that marks us out as what we really are. *Idem*, on the other hand, is identity understood as sameness, as a more external possibility of identifying the self as self despite loss or mutability of the attributions of that self in time. *Ipse* identifies "who" the self is, *idem* "what" the self consists of.

The very uncertainty of liturgical ritual and the undecidability of liturgical symbols facilitates spiritual formation by grounding our *ipse* identities (our who-ness) as those loved by and called of God to participate in God's restoration of all creation. At the same time, worship calls into question a

7. Shannon Craigo-Snell, *The Empty Church: Theater, Theology, and Bodily Hope* (Oxford: Oxford University Press, 2014), 14–15. See also Richard Schechner, *Performance Studies: An Introduction* (New York: Routledge, 2002), 22, from whom Craigo-Snell gets the phrase "twice-behaved behavior."

notion of selfhood preoccupied with sameness (*idem*). Worship challenges our what-ness. It embraces an existential stance of uncertainty because such is the faithfulness of God: to not leave us as we are, but to lead us in our becoming.

Liturgical Possibilities

1. Curating possibilities for worship in an age of uncertainty ought to attend to worshipers' fraught sense of selfhood and identity in our contemporary cultural contexts.

Uncertainty pervades the contemporary person's sense of self and identity. As Facebook and Instagram teach us, and as Judith Butler avers, "there is no self-identical subject."[8] What this means is that our meaning of ourselves is in a constant state of flux, whereby the "I" that I "am" never quite meshes with the material realities that inform my existence. The body's intelligibility is not a given; it is produced. Subjectivity is performed.

I want to suggest that worship provides we who live in liquid, uncertain times with a generative space wherein we perform our identities beyond the Cartesian, modern self that is self-secure in its own thinking—"I think, therefore I am"—and also beyond the postmodern self that unravels the very possibility of selfhood. Worship, and particularly its ritual elements, provide worshipers with a medium for the expression of cultural ideals and models that, in turn, serves to orient, though not prescribe, our way of being in the world.

2. Curating possibilities for worship in an age of uncertainty ought to embrace the (trans)formative capacity of liturgical rituals.

In her important ethnographic treatment of liturgical theology, my Columbia Seminary colleague Martha Moore-Keish makes a seductively simple statement: "Rituals are about *doing*."[9] Building on the work of Eduard Muir (*Ritual in Early Modern Europe*), Moore-Keish writes,

---

8. Judith Butler, *Bodies That Matter* (London: Routledge, 1993), 230.

9. Martha Moore-Keish, *Do This in Remembrance of Me: A Ritual Approach to Reformed Eucharistic Theology* (Grand Rapids, MI: Eerdmans, 2008), 89.

. . . in the sixteenth century, there was a major shift in understanding of rituals. According to the earlier view of the medieval Catholic Church, rituals
made something present; they did something. According to the newer view
of the reformers, rituals communicated meaning; they meant something. As
a result, rituals were no longer conceived as presenting reality. They *repre-*
sented a reality that existed elsewhere.[10]

The last line of Moore-Keish's quote is worth re-iterating: "They [rituals] represented a reality that existed elsewhere." Worship re-presents us to ourselves,
challenging our state of uncertainty by reminding us who we are and who we
are becoming as a church, as a collective of men, women, and others called
out to participate in God's liberation.

Conclusion: Erotic Worship

In conclusion, and in response to our liquid times, I wish to offer a new
epistemological orientation to worship, one that deconstructs many of the
modern church's presuppositions about the self in worship. It participates in
the emerging cultural ethos and draws upon all that we've been discussing thus
far about the self in relation to the God we encounter in Christian worship.

I call this *erotic worship*, which leans into a certain liturgical theology
that takes love (*eros*) as its guiding epistemological orientation.[11] Such a way
of knowing receives theoretical support from the concept of curation, which
is marked, as we've noted, by the twin preoccupations of *care* and *cure*. Getting as far from theory toward practice as I am able, I want to lay this out in
three steps.

Step One: Curate a Stance.
Step Two: Curate an Approach.
Step Three: Curate a Mode of Reception.

Because modernity has drawn the self into the center, we must begin by
placing the self under erasure. We need to curate the stance of selves in relation

---

10. Ibid. Italics in original.

11. See Jacob D. Myers, "Toward an Erotic Liturgical Theology: Schmemann in Conversation with Contemporary Philosophy," *Worship* 87, no. 5 (Sept. 2013): 387–413.

to liturgical phenomena. How we approach other people shapes what we might receive from them. Westerners, following Descartes, have been taught to regard ourselves as subjects and all else that we encounter in the world of our experience as objects. Intersubjectively, modernity keeps us locked in a state of perpetual egocentrism. However, every person we will ever encounter, and of course God, is also a subject and thus radically beyond being objectified by me.[12]

The reason I call this stance "erotic" is because it subverts the will to knowledge characteristic of our post-Enlightenment condition. Said differently, an erotic approach flips the script on how we understand knowledge. We've been trained to believe that so-called *genuine* knowledge must purge all emotion. This might be true when seeking to understand an inert object; but when we aim to know an *other* who must retain his/her/their personhood throughout the process of my striving to know him/her/them, love fosters a different, truer reception that mere logic.

We need to curate spaces that allow us to think the concept of love prior to any a priori bifurcation. Logic and love—*Logos kai Eros*—are often viewed as antonyms. They are folded into a binary logic that divides logic, rationality, sameness, presence, Being, and so on from its imagined opposite: affect, madness, alterity, absence, and nothingness. It is Jean-Luc Marion who mentions repeatedly, "the only measure of love is love without measure."[13]

If you want to know God, you must first love God. If you want to know someone as neighbor, you must first find a way to love her. And, of course, love of God and neighbor are not mutually exclusive. The only way that you can love anyone (or anything) is by first deciding to situate yourself in such a way that the one whom you choose to love is free to exist in and for himself. At the same time, you can only love if you are a subject, an agent capable of acting on the world. This is not easy or simple. Loving is both radically passive and radically active.

---

12.   See Karl Barth, *The Göttingen Dogmatics: Instruction in the Christian Religion*, vol. 1, ed. Hannelotte Reiffen, ed.; Geoffrey W. Bromiley, trans. (Grand Rapids, MI: Eerdmans, 1991), 327: "God's deity or person is never a mere object, never merely His being an It or a He but rather His being an I. In His revelation, precisely in His revelation, God is an irremovable subject that can never be confused with an object."

13.   Jean-Luc Marion, *The Erotic Phenomenon*, trans. Stephen E. Lewis (Chicago: University of Chicago Press, 2007), 10, 46, 92.

Especially in our Western contexts, marked as they are by the will-to-power and control of people, bracketing yourself will require tremendous effort. It's a bit like the act of "apparating" in the Harry Potter series, where a witch or wizard teleports instantaneously from one location to another. By this the mind and body seem to come undone. Paradoxically, by the erotic approach, the first step forward is also a step backward.[14] The advance is a retreat. Boldness and humility, even if different from person to person, are opposite sides of the same coin.

Curating this first step opens the way to a second step that we are invited to curate in and through worship. An erotic liturgical theology demands that we curate *approaches* to liturgical phenomena that do not try to seize knowledge of God. Such establishes a state in which the worshiper approaches *liturgical elements* in order to abandon his, her, or their self in the very approach. In short, it does not aim to *take* knowledge, understanding, or spiritual enlightenment from liturgical elements.

In the second step, we learn to wait and to listen for God to present Godself to us in some way. This in no way binds God to show us anything. That's the risk we take in deciding to love. Here it is important to deconstruct another binary that further contributes to our feeling of vertiginous uncertainty: the God/neighbor binary.[15] Worship must not be oriented to love of God *rather than* neighbor; instead, in Christian worship we are summoned to draw near to human and non-human others inasmuch as we love God. Love of God and love of neighbor are of a piece.

As minister-curators, we may learn to see worship as a way to curate a kind of listening. This kind of listening in and through love opens us to

---

14.   See Jean-Luc Marion, *Reduction and Givenness: Investigations of Husserl, Heidegger, and Phenomenology*, Thomas A. Carlson, trans. (Evanston, IL: Northwestern University Press, 1998), 203–204: "The more that that which or the one who reduces reduces radically, the more things give themselves amply to it or him. But likewise, that which or the one who reduces lets itself or himself be measured by the dimension of what gives itself and be identified with and by the identity of that givenness in such a way that the amplitude of what gives (itself) always also anticipates the determination of that which or the one who reduces."

15.   Karl Barth, *The Epistle to the Romans*, 6th ed., Edwyn C. Hoskyns, trans. (London: Oxford University Press, 1933), 323: "To accompany [Jesus] along His road and become messengers on His behalf—that is to say, to allow the word of reconciliation to be spoken over them as a genuine condemnation against which they have no defense (1 Cor. v. 19, 20)—this is to love God."

another's pain and suffering, and in so doing it inverts the polarity of our engagement with the neighbor, so to speak. Such listening is not a mere hearing, but one that is bolstered by hope borne for the other. Such a hope emerges out of a loving engagement with the Word of God revealed in scripture, and it is henceforth made available for the neighbor whom we love in the world.

Listening toward life is a double listening. It is not a sequential listening, but a kind of listening that hears with both ears, discerning both the pains inherent in the struggles of many for life and to God's summons to be radically oriented to the neighbor's flourishing. This is what it means, at its most basic sense, to be a Christ-follower. This double listening is both theological and ethical, while exceeding both *in love*.

With the one ear we listen toward life in terms of the lived realities of others. With the other ear—again, not by another listening, but at the same time—one listens toward life by listening to God's life-giving and boundary-breaking Word in the world that places us in the path of others, that makes us neighbors to and for other people.[16]

The third step toward an erotic liturgical theology consists in a prayerful renunciation of the will to knowledge. Jean-Luc Marion writes, "Knowledge does not make love possible, because knowledge flows from love. The lover makes visible what she loves and, without this love, nothing would appear to her. Thus, strictly speaking, the lover does not know what she loves—except insofar as she loves it."[17] Another way to put this is that God is greater than our capacity to know God with any degree of certainty.

Curating an erotic approach to liturgical curation maintains a proper perspective vis-à-vis the God who has elected to reveal Godself in and through Christian worship. Neither liturgy nor liturgical theology can exploit this relation as a means of accessing knowledge of the Divine. The only true knowledge of God is revealed knowledge. Or as Orthodox liturgical theologian Alexander Schmemann puts it:

> "No one has seen God" (John 1:19). This is known to any genuine religious experience, which is always above all an experience of the *holy*, in the

---

16. See Gustavo Gutiérrez, *Essential Writings*, James B. Nickoloff, ed. (Maryknoll, NY: Orbis Books, 1993), 76.

17. Marion, *The Erotic Phenomenon*, 87.

original, primordial meaning of this word—"holy" as *absolutely other*, incomprehensible, unknowable, unfathomable and ultimately even frightful. Religion was born and is born simultaneously from attraction to the *holy*, from knowledge that the absolutely other *is*, and from incomprehension as to *what* it is.[18]

Here's how I put it in my book, *Making Love with Scripture*: Truth is not something we can possess. You can't carry it in your pocket like Chapstick. When scripture talks about truth it does so in terms of a way of being; it is not inert but alive in the thoughts and behaviors of men and women (e.g., Pss 25:5, 43:3). Furthermore, truth is always spoken of as something external to us (e.g., Gal 2:5; Jas 5:19).[19]

As we move toward the third step in the erotic approach to God's Word, we need to understand what we might actually receive from God. We must come to a deeper appreciation for what we receive as Word, as truth, because our Western mode of thinking has distorted this.

The Word of God given in and through [worship] cannot be handled; it can only be lived. The Word is like lava. Once it hardens it is no longer the Word, but becomes a witness to the Word. This is why deconstruction is the liturgical curator's friend; it saves us from the idolatry to which we are ever prone.[20] Such is the task of liturgical curation in a world of uncertainty.

---

18. Alexander Schmemann, *The Eucharist: Sacrament of the Kingdom*, Paul Kachur, trans. (Yonkers, NY: St. Vladimir's Seminary Press, 2003), 182.

19. Jacob D. Myers, *Making Love with Scripture: Why the Bible Doesn't Mean How You Think It Means* (Minneapolis: Fortress, 2015), 146.

20. "Not letting our beliefs and practices harden over into pure presence is a lot of what 'deconstruction' means." John D. Caputo, *Philosophy and Theology* (Nashville: Abingdon, 2006), 63.

Being Church after #BlackLivesMatter

The burden of being black and the burden of being white is so heavy that it is rare in our society to experience oneself as a human being.

—Howard Thurman[1]

America, along with every modern denomination, originated out of racism. The US Constitution and its supporting documents institutionalized the sovereignty of whiteness—and male whiteness, in particular. Our founding writs of independence are by no means universal. This is undebatable. Native Americans, women, the poor, and Americans of African descent remained subservient to white, land-holding men. To borrow a line from Michael Che's recent Netflix special, these documents were FUBU: for us, by us.

But why should this be the church's problem? Well, where do you think the founding fathers learned to think this way? In his illuminating text *Race: A Theological Account*, theologian J. Kameron Carter argues that the whole concept of race is a Christian invention that was "inside of, nurtured itself on, and even camouflaged itself within the discourse of theology." By striving to assert their difference from—and to assert dominance over—Jews and Judaism, white European Christians severed Christianity from its Jewish roots. These theologians *established* the Jew as the radicalized "other," and African

---

1. Howard Thurman, *The Luminous Darkness* (Richmond, IN: Friends United Press, 2014), 94.

Americans have been the unfortunate heirs of this "gulf."[2] To put this differently, it's not the case that there is this awareness of racial difference and that some people chose to be racist; rather, racism *produces* race as a construct of domination.

We as pastors and church leaders need to intervene at this point of confluence between race and theology. By curating liturgical spaces to disentangle Christian faith from racial prejudice, we will help our congregants and parishioners to imagine the world differently. But prudence is key. Because racialized fear and injustice are interwoven with our social imaginations in general, merely asserting this sinful coupling is unlikely to work. People will fight to protect their epistemological scaffolding. That is why the curative tasks of engagement can meet folks where we find them, and then move toward transformation. Christianity suffers from a "diseased and disfigured social imagination" in which ". . . the powerful, white, Western man, the image of self-sufficiency, social power, and social determination" has dominated our relational conceptualization.[3] It is imperative, therefore, that we do the hard work of interrogating our historical, theological, and cultural traditions: to *preserve* those aspects of our tradition that can chip away at the tradition's more insidious elements.

Theory Matters

The #BlackLivesMatter (#BLM) movement emerged as an eloquent protest following the acquittal of George Zimmerman, the man who murdered seventeen-year-old Trayvon Martin in cold blood. These three words first appeared on Oakland-based community organizer Alicia Garza's Facebook page. Garza wrote, "Black people. I love you. I love us. Our lives matter, Black Lives Matter." Garza's friend and fellow LA-based activist Patrisse Cullors replied to Garza's post with the hashtag #BlackLivesMatter, launching a national movement.

---

2. J. Kameron Carter, *Race: A Theological Account* (Oxford: Oxford University Press, 2008), 12.

3. Willie James Jennings, *The Christian Imagination: Theology and the Origins of Race* (New Haven, CT: Yale University Press, 2010) 6, 286.

In an essay entitled "A Herstory of the #BlackLivesMatter Movement," Garza explains that #BLM is not merely about consciousness raising; it is a call to action. Garza writes, "Black Lives Matter is an ideological and political intervention in a world where Black lives are systematically and intentionally targeted for demise. It is an affirmation of Black folks' contributions to this society, our humanity, and our resilience in the face of deadly oppression."[4] Such an intervention is close to the curator's twin occupations of *care* and *cure;* in fact, it is not difficult to conceptualize #BLM as curated exhibition on a national scale.

#BLM is instructive for pastors and church leaders both for its content as well as its method. In other words, it paints a vivid and multilayered picture of the injustices pervading African-American communities, *and* it instructs our curatorial imaginations in advancing a new way of conceiving leadership, engaging with digital technologies, and challenging the dominant cultural and epistemological structures in the United States. Let us examine each of these in turn.

Decentering Ecclesial and Political Leadership

One of the hallmarks of the #BLM movement is its diffuse and decentralized nature. This feature would be unthinkable, if not impossible, without the social media technologies that support it. This marks a huge shift in civil rights protests of the previous century, which were centered around a prominent personality: for example, King, Lewis, Jackson, Sharpton. Now, anyone with a cellphone and a Twitter or Instagram account may lend her/his/their voice to the conversation.

This structural shift has not gone unchallenged. When the Reverend Al Sharpton journeyed to Ferguson in an effort to become the mouthpiece for the movement, we witnessed the disillusionment promulgated by his attempt to take control. As a representative of the Black political establishment, Sharpton became acerbic about the young people on the ground in

---

4. Alicia Garza, "A Herstory of the #BlackLivesMatter Movement," The Feminist Wire, October 7, 2014, http://www.thefeministwire.com/2014/10/blacklivesmatter-2/.

Ferguson. In his eulogy at Mike Brown's funeral, Sharpton criticized those in Ferguson "being a gangster or a thug," arguing that violence of any kind was antithetical to Sharpton's narrow sense of "Blackness." In response to Sharpton's eulogy, Princeton University professor Keeanga-Yamahtta Taylor writes,

> In one fell swoop, Sharpton not only condemned the young people of Ferguson but invoked stereotypes to do so. It confirmed a sense among the new activists that Sharpton and those like him were out of step. There was a lingering, if unspoken question: What gave Sharpton or Jackson or the NAACP or the Justice Department the authority to tell protestors how they should respond to the violence of the Ferguson police?[5]

Darnell Moore explains that #BLM signifies a shift from a "singular political organizing centered on racial justice to an intersectional agenda." Thus, at work within the #BLM movement are organizers advocating for a more expansive view of justice beyond the sole effort to end anti-black racism. Moore continues, "Visions of true justice must include freedom for black people who are queer, transgender, formerly or presently incarcerated, undocumented or facing any number of other challenges."[6] By analogy, if the leadership structure of the Civil Rights Movement were a tree, then #BLM is better likened to kudzu.

Princeton professor Eddie Glaude Jr. talks about this in his book *Democracy in Black*. Leadership has decentralized beyond what he labels the HNIC model, the "Head Negro in Charge." Glaude writes,

> The idea of politics I'm suggesting here assumes a different kind of leadership. It insists on the capacities and responsibilities of everyday, ordinary black people and urges them to reach for a higher self even in opportunity deserts. Those deserts are fertile ground to be politically creative. They are the places in which we can think, reflect, and act anew. . . . Doing so, we

5. Keeanga-Yamahtta Taylor, *From #BlackLivesMatter to Black Liberation* (Chicago: Haymarket Books, 2016), 161.

6. Darnell Moore, "Two Years Later, Black Lives Matter Faces Critiques, But It Won't Be Stopped," The Mic, August 10, 2015, https://mic.com/articles/123666/two-years-later-black-lives-matter-faces-critiques-but-it-won-t-be-stopped#.wvukZB4lu.

say, loud and clear, that black lives matter and that we don't need HNICs. We simply need each other.[7]

This insight has ecclesial implications as well. As with leadership, #BLM has shown us a way of being church that does not capitulate to one-sided, myopic treatments of race. The critique runs deeper and broader, cutting across class, gender, social, and sexual lines of inquiry.

Consider the work of Michelle Alexander. In her eye-opening book *The New Jim Crow*, she exposes the ways in which racism is hardwired into economic, cultural, and political institutions to structure not just class differentiation, but a modern American caste system that structurally prohibits or at least limits economic opportunities for millions of Americans by bastardizing the very principles that shape contemporary American consciousness. She writes,

> The genius of the current caste system, and what most distinguishes it from its predecessors, is that it appears voluntary. People choose to commit crimes, and that's why they are locked up or locked out, we are told. This feature makes the politics of responsibility particularly tempting, as it appears the system can be avoided with good behavior. But herein lies the trap. All people make mistakes. All of us are sinners. All of us are criminals. All of us violate the law at some point in our lives. In fact, if the worst thing you have ever done is speed ten miles over the speed limit on the freeway, you have put yourself and others at more risk of harm than someone smoking marijuana in the privacy of his or her living room. Yet there are people in the United States serving life sentences for first-time drug offenses, something virtually unheard of anywhere else in the world.[8]

Drawing congregants and parishioners to the horrid realities facing African Americans can foster the decoding and recoding of the worshipping life of the church from the inside of its institutionalization. What #BlackLivesMatter has done, at least in my church, is resituate worship as a mode of resistance, challenging theological assertions that fail to address the pervasive suffering

---

7. Eddie S. Glaude Jr., *Democracy in Black: How Race Still Enslaves the American Soul* (New York: Crown, 2016), 227–28.

8. Michelle Alexander, *The New Jim Crow: Mass Incarceration in the Age of Colorblindness* (New York: New Press, 2012), 215.

of members of our church and society. This, I believe, is good news for the church.

Digitizing Experience

State-sanctioned violence against African Americans is nothing new. In 1979, singer-songwriter Gil Scott-Heron presented his groundbreaking song "The Revolution Will Not Be Televised." In that song, we hear this haunting refrain: "No pictures of pigs shooting down brothers on the instant replay." Scott-Heron could not have imagined the ubiquity of cellphones, the ease with which community members can now record police brutality, nor the global reach of Twitter, Facebook, and Instagram.

Just over thirty years later, Patrisse Cullors would credit social media as instrumental in revealing state violence against African Americans, saying that "On a daily basis, every moment, black folks are being bombarded with images of our death. . . . It's literally saying, 'Black people, you might be next. You will be next.'" Cullors continues, "There's sort of like this instinctual act where we have to protect ourselves— we have to protect each other. It forces black folks to really deal with the reality of how oftentimes painful it is to just say out loud, 'We might die.' But it also forces other groups, it forces other groups of color, it forces white people to really be like, 'Wait, black people really weren't exaggerating.'"[9]

#BlackLivesMatter shows us how digital technologies can serve the work of the church as it follows Jesus's charge to ensure that people have equal access to the abundant life he inaugurated (John 10:10b). It has emerged as a powerful rejoinder to the dehumanization and criminalization that made Trayvon Martin appear suspicious in the first place. His black skin and partially concealed face were sufficient for Zimmerman to pursue the vigilante course of actions that would leave another mother wailing for justice.

Smartphone recording devices coupled with social media technologies allow ordinary citizens the means to public dissent. Now victims' families may bypass mainstream media channels that have historically suppressed news

---

9.   Rahel Gebreyes, "Patrisse Cullors Explains How Social Media Images of Black Death Propel Social Change," *Huffington Post*, October 9, 2015, http://www.huffingtonpost .com/2014/10/09/patrisse-cullors-social-media-black-death_n_5956906.html.

that would denigrate the American criminal justice system, a system that President Obama has left almost entirely intact. As Taylor notes, "The Black political establishment, led by President Obama, had shown over and over again that it was not capable for the most basic task: keeping Black children alive. The young people would have to do it for themselves."[10] So, in many ways, media technologies summon Black political thought from the shadows and into the light; it provides a platform and makes these ideas more accessible—maybe even a little less subaltern and counter in character.[11]

Digital technologies, while ineffective against bullets, can provoke social action. Consider a recent horrifying event. On Wednesday, July 6, 2016, Philando Castile was pulled over by a police officer outside of St. Paul, Minnesota. Castile was driving a car with his girlfriend, Diamond Reynolds, and her four-year-old daughter. According to Reynolds, after being asked for his license and registration, Castile told the officer he was licensed to carry a concealed weapon and had one in the car. Reynolds stated, "The officer said don't move. As he was putting his hands back up, the officer shot him in the arm four or five times."

This unconscionable act of violence prompted Diamond Reynolds to record what happened next through Facebook Live, a video interface that allows users to livestream content from their smartphones. Followers can receive notifications when you go live so they know to tune in to your broadcasts at just the right time. Facebook Live automatically records live streams and lets people re-watch them later. Reynolds's video was spotted quickly and shared by Black Lives Matter activists. By the end of the night, other live streams showed mourners and protesters gathering outside the Minnesota governor's mansion.

By noon on the following day, according to Facebook's measurement tool, the video had been viewed 3.2 million times on Reynolds's page. And it has been seen millions more times on television.

The veil of social disparity, along with the truth about state-sanctioned racism and police brutality, has been lifted through online technologies. Social media has also become a powerful tool for community organizing. The

---

10. Taylor, *From #BlackLivesMatter to Black Liberation*, 152.

11. On subalterity, see Gayatri Chakravorty Spivak, "Can the Subaltern Speak?" in *Marxism and the Interpretation of Culture*, ed. Cary Nelson and Lawrence Grossberg (Champaign: University of Illinois Press, 1988), 271–313.

most prominent example of this began in late August 2014, when Darnell Moore and Patrisse Cullors organized a "freedom ride" to Ferguson, Missouri, in response to the murder of Mike Brown by white police officer Darren Wilson. Over five hundred protestors joined those already taking to the streets of Ferguson in peaceful protest against Brown's murder.

Denigrating Justice: The Palinode

Something more than leadership restructuring and technological savvy is happening within the #BLM movement. As we will examine much more closely in the following chapter, technology is both object and objectifying, masterable and mastering; technology can stimulate agency *and* passivity. With this in mind, I wish to move us beyond the technological function of #BLM to interrogate the epistemological and sociopolitical effects the movement fosters.

What I see going on in the #BLM movement is a subversion of Western ways of thinking that finds corollaries in the realms of psychoanalytic philosophy and literary theory. These corollaries find expression in the concept of *denegation* and the *palinode*. Let me explain.

The word *denegation* (*dénégation* in French; *verneinung* in German) has been put to great use by several influential figures in the history of Western thought. Most notable are the psychoanalyst Sigmund Freud, the social theorist Louis Althusser, and philosopher/literary critic Jacques Derrida.[12] In brief, *denegation* signifies a kind of denial. As such it shares a Latin root (*negare*) with the English words *negate, abnegate,* and *renegade*. But to equate the word *denegation* with *denial* is not quite right. You see, the prefix *de* already signals a negation: *de*escalate, *de*mystify, *de*couple. So, it's a bit like how multiplying two negative numbers produces a positive number in math, except that when you *de-negate* something, you simultaneously affirm and deny it.

Consider a few examples. If I tell you that I have a secret that I can't tell you, I am participating in the counter logic of denegation. A secret as such *already* signifies a certain negation, a certain refusal to speak. By definition.

---

12. Within psychoanalysis and in particular in Freud, the term *verneinung* implies that when the patient denies a desire or wish, he or she has indicated to the analyst precisely what he or she unconsciously desires or wishes. The denial then functions as a sort of disguised confirmation of the analyst's interpretation of the patient's symptoms or problem.

Furthermore, if I *have* a secret, it isn't totally a secret because I have already told said secret to someone: myself. And if I tell you that I have a secret, I am, in effect, saying the unsayability of the secret, which is always already unsayable. It is negation that denies or de-negates itself. This is paradoxical, I know. If the secrecy of the secret is affirmed at the same time it is being negated, ought we speak about it or remain silent?

Or think about it this way. What happens when I assert, as an increasing number of pastors do, that gay and lesbian-identifying persons should be allowed to marry? Were I to make such a declaration, I would be *denying* the social convention that excludes same-loving partners from the religious and legal recognition of marriage. But at the same time, I would be *affirming* the right to regulate covenantal fidelity in the first place. My statement would therefore designate a conscious acceptance masked by an unconscious denial. It is a kind of *denegation*.

Here's where this concept of denegation informs my understanding of #BLM in the US political context. To assert that the lives of Black people matter is first an affirmation of the core value at the heart of America's founding and its constitutional democracy, namely, that all people are created equal and are endowed by their creator with certain inalienable rights: life, liberty, and the pursuit of happiness. To deny that Black lives matter is to deny America's central and most sacrosanct affirmation.

At the same time, asserting that Black lives matter is a denunciation. It says "no" to American policies and practices that bear witness disproportionately against Black bodies. In the words of Ta-Nehisi Coates, "It is not necessary that you believe that the officer who choked Eric Garner set out that day to destroy a body. All you need to understand is that the officer carries with him the power of the American state and the weight of an American legacy, and they necessitate that of the bodies destroyed every year, some wild and disproportionate number of them will be black."[13] Affirming the unconditional value of Black lives in America simultaneously indicts American policies and practices, which, by this very (racialized) conditioning, goes against America itself.

---

13. Ta-Nehisi Coates, *Between the World and Me* (New York: Spiegel and Grau, 2015), 103.

We might also flip the whole argument around and get the same result. Black activists and their allies affirm the sanctity of life, less as a uniquely American ideal than a fundamental, supranational virtue. When these same people also name actions and policies that profane Black lives through surveillance, physical and psychological manipulation, economic exploitation, violence, and even murder, they are highlighting exceptions that prove the existence of the rule. In other words, one cannot assert that *all* lives matter, that *every* human life is sacred, while at the same time ignoring the fact that Black lives are disproportionately devalued and desacralized in American society.[14]

The second way that #BLM works to subvert the US system of thinking is its participation with the order of a palinode. A *palinode* is a gesture of retraction. A literary term, the *palinode* is often employed by poets to formally retract something they said in an earlier poem. For instance, Geoffrey Chaucer's *The Canterbury Tales* ends with a famous retraction, in which he apologizes for his work's "worldly vanities" and sinful contents. This gesture performs a certain undoing of all that has been done while maintaining the legibility of the doing.

Traditionally, Western logic would stipulate a particular response to injustice: negation. In response to systematic injustice and oppression, it is natural to expect a denunciation: this is wrong; this is unjust. However, by saying "no," the protestor is also unwittingly saying "yes." Paradoxically, even a denunciation affirms the conditions of possibility for affirmation/denunciation. In other words, if I say "no" to the cold-blooded murder of men and women of color and the system that allows police to gun down these citizens with impunity, I am doing nothing to challenge the underlying conditions, structures, and premises that make it possible for me to denounce such acts of injustice in the first place.

#BLM is different. It refuses to play by the rules of traditional Western logic. The "no" of #BLM is not just a no; it *performs* a negation that destabilizes the conditions of possibility of injustice. Such speech is a servant of

---

14. See George Yancy, *Black Bodies, White Gazes: The Continuing Significance of Race in America*, 2nd ed. (Lanham, MD: Rowman & Littlefield, 2017); Charles W. Mills, *Black Rights/ White Wrongs: The Critique of Racial Liberalism* (Oxford: Oxford University Press, 2017); and Carol Anderson, *White Rage: The Unspoken Truth of our Racial Divide* (New York: Bloomsbury, 2016).

truth inasmuch as it poetically aims beyond a dialectical synthesis by merely negating what came before. Such syntheses remain non-synthetic by forcing the system and its excess to sit beside one another. This is the genius of the palinode.

In particular, hashtag campaigns like #SayHerName, #StayWoke, #toxicfuller, and #SeminaryWhileBlack function according to the un-logic of the palinode: affirming an ideal at the heart of the system of justice while, at the same time, denying the reality of that justice in the name of a Black citizen who has experienced injustice. Especially with #SayHerName, the name of the victim is invoked and set on repeat through the technology of the hashtag. It is at once a call and its echo, yearning for a response that will not come and cannot come until our systems of injustice are remedied.

Observations and Innovations

There are (at least) four observations relevant for the curating church in the wake of #BLM.

1. #BLM reveals the extent to which social media connections can foster solidarity across difference.

The church in North America is notoriously segregated. Social media activism is a harbinger of real social change on this front. In the words of one Ferguson protestor, Johnetta Elzie, "Thanks to Twitter, I had been able to see photos of Gaza weeks before, and feel connected to the people there on an emotional level. I never thought the small county of Ferguson, this little part of Greater St. Louis, would become Gaza."[15] Or consider the statement released by Ferguson Action, the umbrella organization supporting the various activist movements taking shape post-Ferguson:

> This is a movement of and for ALL. Black lives—women, men, transgender and queer. We are made up of both youth AND elders aligned through the possibilities that new tactics and fresh strategies offer our movement. . . . We are decentralized, but coordinated. Most importantly, we are organized. Yet we are likely not respectable Negroes. We stand beside each other, not

---

15. Taylor, *From #BlackLivesMatter to Black Liberation*, 162.

in front of one another. We do not cast any one of ours to the side in order to gain proximity to perceived power. Because this is the only way we will win. We can't breathe. And we won't stop until Freedom.[16]

Learning from these testimonies, the curating church would do well to employ social media technologies much as my friend and Columbia Seminary colleague Ralph Basui Watkins has. In 2017, Watkins was installed as the pastor of Wheat Street Baptist Church. Wheat Street Baptist has a long and esteemed history, serving residents of the Sweet Auburn neighborhood (where Rev. Dr. Martin Luther King Jr. was reared and later pastored) and beyond. Under Watkins's leadership, Wheat Street has developed a robust social media ministry, that has connected folks from across Atlanta to a degree that would've been inconceivable apart from these technologies.

2. #BLM produces curatorial space.

To employ Homi Bhabha's term, social media constructs a "third space" that places cultural signs up for negotiation. It is an "inter" space where pseudo-cultural diversity can be ruptured. Curator Youngchul Lee (whose work we examined in Gallery II) talks about the role of space in artistic curation. He explains that in premodern space, things within it were assigned a place along a predominantly vertical axis. Modern space, on the contrary is "Euclidean, horizontal, infinitely extensible, and therefore, in principle, boundless." Now we understand that space is not politically a neutral container or (simple context) within which social activities take place. Lee concludes, "In regard to its use, rights, or intervention, space goes beyond treating the subordinates as passive recipients of 'occupying.' Curators observe and experience the plurality of space through contestation and negotiation in the curatorial process."[17] By extension, liturgical curators listening to and learning from the #BLM movement may cultivate *boundless* spaces for contestation and negotiation, thereby extending worship.

---

16. "About This Movement," Ferguson Action, Dec 9, 2014, http://fergusonaction.com /movement/.

17. Youngchul Lee, "Curating in a Global Age," in *Curating Now: Imaginative Practice, Public Responsibility*, ed. Paula Marincola and Robert Storr (Philadelphia: Philadelphia Exhibitions Initiative, 2002), 100.

In the 2016 General Conference of the United Methodist Church, we witnessed a hashtag campaign lifted straight out of the #BLM playbook. Clergypersons and delegates employed the hashtag #ItsTime to coordinate a protest against the United Methodist Church's *Book of Discipline* that forbids LGBTQ-identifying persons to be certified and appointed as clergy within UMC. These committed Methodists evoked a kind of "infinitely extensible" and non-Euclidean space for debate and affirmation. This space the ItsTime hashtag curated became at once coextensive with that of the General Conference while exceeding it spatially and temporally.

3. #BLM shows the church the way to organize for social change.

Gary Hamel is a modern management theorist. He argues that what is happing on the web today has the power to "totally transform" how we think about organizations. Hamel argues that throughout history there have been only two ways to "aggregate and amplify human capabilities." These were bureaucracy and markets. The web has added a third: networks. He avers that such networks help us work together on complex tasks while blocking the powerful elite from determining who gets heard."[18] Hamel's observation proved prescient with the #BLM movement.

Taylor argues that the social and political successes of the #BLM movement arose out of the cross-pollination of traditional modes of Black social protest and the Occupy Wall Street movement. This connection was forged by accident—or providence, as you will. In September 2011, thousands were protesting the impending execution of Troy Davis, who was on Georgia's death row. The circumstances leading to Davis's arrest and conviction were dubious, to say the least, and it became clear to many that Davis was about to die for a crime he did not commit. The day following Davis's execution, which garnered no comment from President Obama, more than a thousand people took to the streets in New York City as a part of Amnesty International's "Day of Outrage" in opposition to the death penalty. It just so happened that the protesters marched directly into the small encampment on Wall Street that had arisen just one week prior to Davis's execution in protest to the economic disparity brought to light by the economic recession of 2008.

---

18. David Kirkpatrick, *The Facebook Effect: The Inside Story of the Company That is Connecting the World* (New York: Simon and Schuster, 2011), 298.

Following the events that transpired in Ferguson, two relatively novice activists employed Twitter and Facebook to organize a march in New York City. Within hours, thousands of people had "liked" this announcement, and eventually over fifty thousand people showed up to the rally. Organizations aiming at dissent have always employed creative means of alerting their members about how and when to take public action; but social media has fueled these traditional means of organizing like gasoline on a match.

Taylor observes, "Protests to save the life of death-row inmate Troy Davis and the electrifying Occupy Wall Street protests in 2011 seemed to signify the beginning of the 'American Spring.'"[19] The Occupy movement rallied around the slogan "We are the 99 percent." After the fortuitous comingling of protests, the Davis campaign began to chant "We are all Troy Davis," spurring a new mode of solidarity.

4. #BLM participates in the democratizing nature of curation, lending value beyond traditional structures of "authority."

Chris Cox, Facebook's chief product officer, said in an interview, "We want to give everyone that same power that mass media has to beam out a message."[20] Social media gives a "voice" to each of its users. It offers everyone with Internet access a means to tell his/her/their own story. In an article published in *The Atlantic* entitled "Hashtag Activism Isn't a Cop-Out," Noah Berlatsky interviewed DeRay Mckesson, a social rights activist, #BLM organizer, and leading signatory for "Campaign Zero," a policy platform to end police violence. In the wake of the death of Freddie Gray, who died in police custody as a result of neglect and excessive use of force, Mckesson spoke about the nontraditional authority structure of #BLM.

"The history of blackness is a history of erasure," argues Mckesson. He attributes social media for the success of the Ferguson protests, without which the powers that militate against Black bodies and silence Black voices would have squelched the protest. It was largely the power to record what was actually happening on the ground and to share that information live that spurred thousands to join the protest.

---

19. Taylor, *From #BlackLivesMatter to Black Liberation*, 145.

20. Kirkpatrick, *The Facebook Effect*, 296.

Twitter, in particular, facilitates what Mckesson labels "a democracy of feedback." Through the Twitter interface, accountability is maintained through immediate feedback, and voices on the periphery of protests are given the same opportunity to be heard as those enjoying some degree of prominence or power. Mckesson is a prime example. When he got in his car in Minnesota to drive to Ferguson, he had eight hundred Twitter followers. By documenting what was happening in Missouri and adding his voice to the #BLM conversation, Mckesson now has over 360,000 Twitter followers. Taylor warns, however, that "at a time when many people are trying to find an entry point into anti-police activism and desire to be involved, this particular method of organizing can be difficult to penetrate. In some ways, this decentralized organizing can actually narrow opportunities for the democratic involvement of many in favor of the tightly knit workings of those already in the know."[21]

Mckesson goes on to highlight the opportunities and challenges of Twitter: "Individual people can come together around things that they know are unjust. And they can spark change. Your body can be part of the protest; you don't need a VIP pass to protest. And Twitter allowed that to happen." But, at the same time, Twitter exposes users to hatred and even violence (someone posted Mckesson's home address on Twitter). At day's end, Mckesson contends, "The harassment is never a good thing. But there's something valuable in making sure you're not surrounded by people who think like you. It helps you understand what you think better. And I appreciate that about Twitter. It's a cacophony of voices. Even when you don't agree, you at least understand different perspectives. The medium itself sets that up."[22]

Moving Forward: Liturgical Possibilities

The #BlackLivesMatter movement challenges much. It forces us to grapple with the *content* of our worship, testing what we say we believe about

---

21. Taylor, *From #BlackLivesMatter to Black Liberation*, 176. I should also note that Mckesson seems to share a troubled relationship with many #BLM activists. Some have leveled critiques against him for his seeming opportunism and efforts to resurrect what those of the "old guard" of the Civil Rights Movement tried to establish for themselves.

22. Noah Berlatsky, "Hashtag Activism Isn't a Cop-Out," *The Atlantic*, Jan 7, 2015, http://www.theatlantic.com/politics/archive/2015/01/not-just-hashtag-activism-why-social-media-matters-to-protestors/384215/.

loving our neighbors as ourselves against what we actually say from the pulpit and from the choir loft. #BLM also challenges our worship gatherings at the level of *praxis*. How can a church declare that Black lives matter when the entire church staff is white (or Asian or Latino)? How we worship often speaks louder than what we do when we worship.

This is why my family and I worship at Park Avenue Baptist Church. Our leadership structure and how we model less-hierarchical, decentered leadership opens possibilities for worship that are rare when you have one person dictating what happens in worship. Park Ave is a diverse fellowship along multiple axes (e.g., race, sexuality, economic status, education level, ability). There's something about the diversity of the congregation that pushes us to curate worship that is intersectional. Segregated worship services don't demand that. Because on any given Sunday I may sit next to a Black person, a differently abled person, a queer person, etc., I am drawn face to face with folks who are different from me on a weekly basis. Indeed, the presence of these others makes viral videos of Black wo/men getting shot all the more real because next Sunday I'll see Brandon, or Adriel, or Leah and I'll know that, for *my* neighbor, the struggle is real. This prevents me from "crossing to the other side" but instead "to draw near" and to allow myself "to be moved with compassion" (Luke 10:25-37).

Another liturgical possibility emerging out of this consideration of #BLM is the way it challenges liturgical production. In his book *Remix: Making Art and Commerce Thrive in the Hybrid Economy*, Lawrence Lessig distinguishes between "Read/Only" (RO) cultures and "Read/Write" (RW) cultures. From computer parlance, RO cultures are content with simple consumption. Lessig shows that the twentieth century was a "time of happy competition among RO technologies."[23] Better and better technologies emerged supplanting what came before (e.g., VCRs, DVDs, Blu-ray, video streaming). But each of these technological innovations continued to participate in the same culture that rendered consumers passive.

RW cultures are different. Lessig argues that the twenty-first century witnessed the expansion of "amateur creativity" that allowed consumers to become producers. Technologies emerged that allowed everyone to become

---

23. Lawrence Lessig, *Remix: Making Art and Commerce Thrive in the Hybrid Economy* (New York: Penguin, 2009), 30.

active creators of new content. WordPress. YouTube. MySpace. Twitter. Instagram. These services facilitated ingenuity, which has now transformed cultures all over the world. I would argue that without these technological and cultural shifts we could not have a movement like #BLM. Unfortunately, the church has been slow to embrace RW culture in worship. The majority of American worshipers are passive consumers of religious goods and services.[24] I believe that this passivity that pervades the church's worship life is one of the major reasons that millennials experience such dissonance with ecclesial cultures.

In her seminal essay "One Place after Another," art historian and curator Miwon Kwon shows how attention to *specificity* in art began to "decode and/or recode the institutional conventions so as to expose their hidden yet motivated operations." By this she names a process of discernment, whereby people begin to see the ways in which "institutions mold art's meaning to modulate its cultural and economic value, and to [make] apparent its imbricated relationship to the broader socioeconomic and political processes of the day."[25] This is equally true for many church participants. Moving forward in the wake of #BLM, we pastors and church leaders will need to fess up to and trouble the politics that motivate our liturgical practices. We will need to embrace a curatorial imagination that values difference, participation, and pursues transformation in search of justice.

Conclusion

I believe that the key to helping congregants and parishioners connect with the plight of African Americans and to stand up against these injustices requires more than understanding or even sympathy. Transformation demands empathy. As Michael Eric Dyson puts it in his powerful book *Tears We Cannot Stop: A Sermon to White America*:

Empathy must be cultivated. The practice of empathy means taking a moment to imagine how you might behave if you were in our positions. Do

---

24. This trend works in the opposite direction as well, wherein Christian desires shape sociopolitical and economic practices. See William Cavanaugh, *Being Consumed: Economics and Christian Desire* (Grand Rapids, MI: Eerdmans, 2008).

25. Miwon Kwon, "One Place After Another: Notes on Site Specificity," *October* 80 (Spring 1997): 88.

not tell us how we should act if we were you; imagine how you would act if you were us. Imagine living in a society where your white skin marks you for disgust, hate, and fear. Imagine that for many moments. Only when you see black folks as we are, and imagine yourselves as we have to live our lives, only then will the suffering stop, the hurt cease, the pain go away.[26]

Empathy serves transformation by challenging apathy and callousness. When we are able to see the world differently, we are unable to dismiss the cries of our neighbor.

#BLM is an experiment in democracy—a performance of a "democracy to come" in Jacques Derrida's parlance. What it gives us are not doctrines or declarations or even operating instructions. The hashtag and all that ramifies under its auspices mark the flow of time with events. This is key. #BLM is instructive for Christian ministry in general, and for curatorial practices of ministry in particular, in all that it teaches us about the power of what I would label incarnational performativity.

#BLM leaves us with a certain "aura," to borrow Walter Benjamin's term. In other words, it passes on a certain affect, a certain orientation to the world of our and other's experience. In the wake of #BLM events, we are left with an aura rather than an object. What is preserved is the event's metadata—information about the here and now of its original inscription into the material flow: photos, videos, tweets. It is this aura that cannot be subdued or twisted to the machinations of white privilege and the state-sanctioned persecution, surveillance, and control of Black bodies.

By comparison, Dr. King's "I Have a Dream" speech is an artifact, an object readily available for appropriation and interpretation. The events of Ferguson and Baltimore and Chicago are far less appropriable. They are, to employ the words of Jean-Luc Marion, "saturated phenomena." Their objectivity exceeds objectification and appropriation. They lend themselves only to reenactment. We cannot go back in time to experience the singularity of King's 1963 oration from the steps of the Lincoln Memorial, nor his speech at Mason Temple in 1968. Time flows forward. With #BLM, however, aided as it is by the Internet, we receive the possibility of return.

---

26. Michael Eric Dyson, *Tears We Cannot Stop: A Sermon to White America* (New York: St. Martin's, 2017), 212.

Forging Connections across Digital Difference

> *These days, insecure in our relationships and anxious about intimacy,*
> *we look to technology for ways to be in relationships and protect*
> *ourselves from them at the same time.*
>
> —*Sherry Turkle*[1]

In her book *The Cyber Effect*, cyberpsychologist Mary Aiken writes, "Whenever technology comes in contact with an underlying predisposition, or tendency for a certain behavior, it can result in behavioral amplification or escalation."[2] She means that if one has stalker tendencies in life, cybertechnology will allow that person to stalk multiple people more of the time, and all of this without "real world" barriers. If you are prone to contentiousness, or gossip, or voyeurism, digital technologies can amplify these traits, making them harder to control. Attending to the digital lives of our congregants and parishioners, therefore, requires pastoral care on steroids.

This chapter examines the societal, personal, and relational effects of digital life. This requires examination of both hardware and software. Facebook and Instagram are nothing but lines of software code. However, when we have

---

1. Sherry Turkle, *Alone Together; Why We Expect More from Technology and Less from Each Other* (New York: Basic Books, 2011), xii.

2. Mary Aiken, *The Cyber Effect: An Expert in Cyberpsychology Explains How Technology Is Shaping Our Children, Our Behavior, and Our Values—and What We Can Do About It* (New York: Random House, 2016), 22.

access to that code through devices we can wear on our wrist or carry in our pockets and purses (i.e., hardware), those ones and zeroes can transform how we relate to one another and how we understand ourselves in community.

Theory Matters

We can't seriously grapple with our cultural and epistemological realities today without considering the role digital technologies are playing in how we relate to God, self, and others. Indeed, the proliferation of information spurred by the technological advances of the last thirty years plays a huge role in postmodernity, shaping our aesthetic and epistemological sensibilities. Nicolas Bourriaud rightly identifies that postmodernity and digital realities were brought up in the same nursery. He writes,

> If the postmodern aesthetic is born of the extinction of political radicalism, it should not be forgotten that it gathered force in the early 1980s, at the very moment when cultural and media production were entering a period of exponential expansion. It is the great cluttering of our era, which is reflected in the chaotic proliferation of cultural products, images, media, and commentaries, and which has destroyed the very possibility of a *tabula rasa*. Overloaded with signs, buried under a mass of works that is constantly expanding, we no longer have even a . . . concept with which to conceive of a new beginning, much less a rational alternative to the environments in which we live.[3]

The technological innovations of the past thirty years are much more than mere byproducts of our culture. They share in the production of postmodernity itself.

In this chapter, I want us to take a critical look at the challenges and opportunities for curating church in a digital age. We'll focus primarily upon Web 3.0, social media, and search technologies (like Google). We'll talk about the social and existential significance of these technologies, focusing on how these new modes of interaction and self-presentation can foster community *and* isolation. Throughout we'll be questioning the theological significance of these burgeoning technologies and their significance for curating church.

---

3. Nicolas Bourriaud, *The Radicant* (New York: Lukas & Sternberg, 2009), 48.

Media Matters

Let's begin with a word about media in general. Media theorist extraordinaire Marshall McLuhan has argued convincingly that all technologies are "extensions" of our humanity. For instance, the automobile is an extension of our feet and legs, enabling us to cover more ground in less time; the telephone is an extension of our voice and ears, allowing us to communicate over distances that would be impossible with our innate speaking and hearing capacities alone. At this point, McLuhan is merely describing the effects of technology on humanity.

Moving deeper in his analysis, McLuhan observes that we handle technologies as if we are in control. *We* pick up the telephone receiver. *We* turn on the TV. We remain the subject of our verbs and our technologies remain objects of our actions. And yet, McLuhan warns that "any medium has the power of imposing its own assumption on the unwary."[4] What he means is that technologies have the capacity to exert their will upon their user—to cast a spell, so to speak. And you've been there yourself. Netflix is a perfect example. You watch an episode of *Orange is the New Black* or *House of Cards* or *Dear White People,* and as soon as it's over, another automatically loads in the queue. "Just one more," you tell yourself. You are rendered passive.

"The medium is the message." This is McLuhan's most famous and incisive insight. What he means by this is that the social and personal consequences of any medium—that is, of any extension of ourselves—result from the new scale that is introduced into our affairs by each new technology. Scale is key here. Texting is not just another way of communicating; rather, it transforms the communication process itself. The medium of texting is not simply another way of saying the same thing that could be said in person; it fundamentally alters the message.

When humans encounter a new technology, it is imperative that we interrogate its detriments along with its benefits. Twitter allows us to share our thoughts on any topic through the medium of its public interface and hashtag algorithms. On the one hand, Twitter epitomizes democracy, submitting world affairs to the court of public opinion. In this sense, Twitter is an

---

4. Marshall McLuhan, "The Medium is the Message," in *Understanding Media: The Extensions of Man* (Cambridge, MA: MIT Press, 1994), 15.

extension of the Greek agora or Roman forum, a *place* for sharing informa-tion, engaging in public debate, and hosting conversations that affect both population and polis.

On the other hand, however, Twitter introduces a new *ratio*, a new scale, to the medium of public discourse. Twitter alters the human sensorium, the faculties by which we perceive reality. Twitter floods the channels of discourse, at once delivering more and diverse opinions while also exceeding human ca-pacities to organize and synthesize information. The spin becomes a snare.

Consider a historical example. Christian monks in the Middle Ages sought a more precise way of ordering time to better structure their prayer lives. The Cistercians, in particular, spurred a quest for temporal exactitude that led to the development of the first mechanical clocks. Employing swing-ing weights to strike bells at regular intervals, these monks actively ordered their days in accordance with these sounds.

Fast-forward a few hundred years and clocks are everywhere. They be-came smaller and cheaper, allowing more and more people to regulate their days according the metrics established by the monks of old. But here's the thing: *the very technology designed to help us control time ended up allowing time to control us.* As research journalist Nicholas Carr reports, "Once the clock had redefined time as a series of units of equal duration, our minds began to stress the methodical mental work of division and measurement. We began to see, in all things and phenomena, the pieces that composed the whole, and then we began to see the pieces of which the pieces were made."[5] Thus, the clock's methodical ticking was not merely a way of helping us keep track of time; it helped to produce the scientific mental framework that now orients much contemporary thinking. Clocks changed our brains. The medium is the message.

McLuhan writes that "[a] theory of cultural change is impossible without knowledge of the changing sense ratios effected by various externalizations of our senses."[6] That's the focus of this chapter, to help us take a closer look at

5. Nicolas Carr, *The Shallows: What the Internet is Doing to Our Brains* (New York: Nor-ton, 2011), 43, 44.

6. Marshall McLuhan, *The Gutenberg Galaxy* (Toronto: University of Toronto Press, 2011), 49.

several aspects of our trending digital technologies and interrogate how these extensions of ourselves are shaping our (liturgical) perceptions.

The Platform

Web 2.0 emerged on the US scene in the mid 2000s, transforming us from content *consumers* to content *generators*. Blogs proliferated at a mind-blowing rate, providing users with a platform to share their thoughts with the world—or at least those with Internet access. A 2016 report documented that 23 percent of all online activity is dedicated to reading user-generated content on blogs and social media sites. There are currently over 6.7 million people blogging in the world today, and an additional twelve million people blog through social media platforms. But this is not the most alarming statistic from the study. The researchers projected that by 2020, humans are predicted to manage 85 percent of their relationships without actually talking to a human.[7]

Upon the heels of the information explosion on the web came the "semantic web" or Web 3.0, which provides a common framework for users to share data and reuse it across applications, enterprises, and community boundaries. Web 3.0 is an extension of the current web, but what sets it apart are the tools it provides us to find, share, reuse, and combine information more easily. Web 3.0 is based on machine-readable information and builds on XML technology's capability to define customized tagging schemes and RDF's (Resource Description Framework's) flexible approach to representing data. The semantic web provides common formats for the interchange of *data* (where on the web there is only an interchange of *documents*).

Web 3.0 also provides a common language for recording how data relates to real world objects, allowing a person or a machine to start off in one database and then move through an unending set of databases that are connected not by wires but by being about the same thing. Hashtags are the primary example of the semantic web's functional capacities. They allow us to join conversations without having to go to a particular webpage or blog and post

---

7. Zac Johnson, "A Look at Blogging Industry Stats from 2016," Tech.Co., February 10, 2017, https://tech.co/look-blogging-industry-stats-2017-02.

our thoughts. Hashtags allow us to join conversations without first having to know where such conversations are taking place.

Digital Devices

Let's talk now about digital devices. Mobile devices don't just change what we do, but who we are. As psychologist Sherry Turkle observes, "Our new devices provide space for the emergence of a new state of the self, itself split between the screen and the physical real, wired into existence through technology."[8] This is key for pastors and church leaders to understand. These devices, while affording us the opportunity to remain in contact with our friends and family, can also subvert our contact with the people we profess to love the most.

Digital devices both connect and disconnect us from others and from ourselves. Digital devices shape us in several ways.

1. Digital devices intensify our status as consumers.

As people spend more time and do more things online, we see more ads and we disclose more information about ourselves. Macro media engines like Facebook and Google use this information to rake in more money. Through the use of Accelerated Mobile Pages (AMP) and Mobile-first indexing, companies are finding more efficient ways to connect users of digital devices with consumer options. And though it may sound cute and cuddly, Google's new Penguin 4.0 algorithm is more akin to a digital, spam-slaying ninja with the sole intention of delivering you to websites *in real time.*

Furthermore, as additional products and services have come to be delivered digitally over computer networks—entertainment, news, software applications, financial transactions, phone calls—companies that traffic in this information have expanded their range of complements into ever more industries.[9] The recent acquisitions of Whole Foods by Amazon and the merger of Time Warner with AT&T are prime examples of this. Researchers working at the intersection of digital media and consumer practices report in a 2017

---

8. Turkle, *Alone Together*, 16.

9. Carr, *The Shallows*, 160.

study that consumers' cognitive abilities are being *extended* by and *externalized* to digital technologies, which is revolutionizing how we learn about and purchase products and services.[10]

All of this points to the issue of scale I mentioned earlier. It's not new to end up on a company's mailing list or e-mail distribution list. What is new are the metrics and technologies that are shifting our relations to companies: They know what we want before they begin to advertise it to us. Digital devices facilitate greater amounts of input to the web of information, providing retailers with better and more ingenious ways of shaping our buying habits, as well as our politics.

2. Digital devices impact our productivity and cognitive performance.

Digital devices keep us connected to the world beyond our immediate sense experience. They *extend* nearly all our senses. This has produced a pervasive and rarely questioned espousal of the virtues of multitasking. In his 2014 book *The Organized Mind*, neuroscientist Daniel Levitin attends to the cognitive effects of what he labels "infomania," the inundation of data beyond our neural capacities. Drawing from multiple studies, he notes that even an awareness that you have an unread e-mail in your inbox can reduce your effective IQ by ten points. Levitin contends that "the cognitive losses from multitasking are even greater than the cognitive losses from pot smoking."[11] Few would deny the deleterious effects of marijuana use for our productivity; it is staggering to consider that that Apple watch on your wrist could have an even greater effect on your brain.

In a 2017 study, researchers instructed a group of students to attend to two simultaneous sources of information: a text article and a documentary video. The test was to see how well they could attend to the information presented in the text while ignoring the video. Unsurprisingly, the results revealed that students who attended to two sources during study showed poorer

---

10.   See Rebecca Jenkins and Janice Denegri-Knott, "Extending the Mind: Digital Devices and the Transformation of Consumer Practices," in *Digitalizing Consumption: How Devices Shape Consumer Culture*, Franck Cochoy, ed. (London: Routledge, 2017), 85–102.

11.   Daniel Levitin, *The Organized Mind: Thinking Straight in the Age of Information Overload* (New York: Random House, 2014), 97. See also Faria Sana, Tina Weston, and Nicholas J. Cepeda, "Laptop Multitasking Hinders Classroom Learning for Both Users and Nearby Peers," *Computers and Education* 62 (March 2013), 24–31.

retention of material from both. Accounting for data discrepancies, the researchers added that a student's working memory, level of interest in the material being presented, and confidence are what separated the good multitaskers from the rest.[12] We need not strain to think about how these and similar studies inform congregational awareness and retention during corporate worship.

3. Digital devices facilitate our ability to outsource our thinking—even when we don't realize it.

In his fascinating book *The Shallows: What the Internet is Doing to Our Brains*, Carr explains the effects of digital technologies on cognitive processes. He writes,

> When we go online, we . . . are following scripts written by others—algorithmic instructions that few of us would be able to understand even if the hidden codes were revealed to us. When we search for information through Google or other search engines, we're following a script. When we look at a product recommended to us by Amazon or Netflix, we're following a script. When we chose from a list of categories to describe ourselves or our relationships on Facebook, we're following a script. These scripts can be ingenious and extraordinarily useful . . . but they also mechanize the messy processes of intellectual exploration and even social attachment.[13]

If Carr is right, then the applications many of us house on our iPhones or Androids are doing far more than providing us momentary respites from boredom or connecting us with information. To a certain extent, they are doing the thinking for us and thereby curbing our minds to a code designed by companies that have a vested financial interest in leading us to think in the ways they want us to.

4. Digital devices have transformed how we interact with others.

Neuroscientific researchers have revealed beyond a doubt that constant contact technologies like texting, Snapchat, and Instant Messenger chemically rewire our brains to lose patience with people, lower our capacity to refrain from sharing hurtful comments, and decrease our capacity for empa-

---

12. Megan A. Pollard and Mary L. Courage, "Working Memory Capacity Predicts Effective Multitasking," *Computers in Human Behavior* 76 (Nov. 2017), 450–62.

13. Carr, *The Shallows*, 218.

thy.[14] Digital devices also discourage thoughtful discussion. Turkle labels this the "flight from conversation." In her research with college students, she reports that the presence of smartphones produces fewer and more fragmented conversations with fellow students. She shares what her students call "the rule of three." Such is a matter of decorum: if you are with a group at dinner, etiquette dictates that you ought to check that at least three people have their heads up from their phones before you give yourself permission to check your phone. This results in shallower conversations, Turkle reports.[15]

The relational impact of digital devices is not just for children. In a recent in-depth observational study of coffee shop patrons, researchers found that, on average, many individuals in pairs or small groups checked their phones every three to five minutes, regardless of whether it rang or buzzed. They also note how often their research subject held their phones or placed them on the table in front of them.[16] What does this communicate to our friends and family members? We are, in effect, communicating that whatever they are saying to us right now, in person, is less important that what someone else might be saying somewhere else.

5. In addition to shaping a person's intellectual and emotional experiences, digital devices also impact one's physical experience.

In a recent study, researchers found that a large percentage of individuals experience what has been termed by neuropsychologists as the "phantom vibration syndrome." These are perceived vibrations from a device that is not

---

14. See Yalda T. Uhls et al., "Five Days at Outdoor Education Camp Without Screens Improves Preteen Skills with Nonverbal Emotional Cues," *Computers in Human Behavior* 39 (Oct. 2014): 387–92; John Suler, "The Online Disinhibition Effect," *CyberPsychology & Behavior* 7, no. 3 (2004): 321–26; Stephanie M. Reich, Kaveri Subrahmanyam, and Guadalupe Espinoza, "Friending, IMing, and Hanging out Face-to-Race: Overlap in Adolescents' Online and Offline Social Networks," *Developmental Psychology* 48 (2012): 356–68; Leslie J. Seltzer, et al., "Instant Messages Versus Human Speech: Hormones and Why We Still Need to Hear Each Other," *Evolution and Human Behavior* 33 (2012): 42–45; and Lisette Mol, et al., "Seeing and Being Seen: The Effects on Gesture Production," *Journal of Computer-Mediated Communication* 17 (2011): 77–100.

15. Sherry Turkle, *Reclaiming Conversation: The Power of Talk in a Digital Age* (New York: Penguin Books, 2015): 20.

16. S. Misra and J. Genevie, "The Experience of Place: How Digital Technologies are Restructuring Public Places" (paper, Environmental Design Research Association, Providence, RI, May 2013).

really vibrating.[17] Such psychosomatic experiences are shared by people suffering from nicotine withdrawal, along with other forms of drug addiction. What does it say about us that our bodies have begun to receive signals from our brains that put us in the same categories as heroin addicts? The ironic part of all of this is that nobody bats an eyelash if someone pulls his phone from his pocket during worship or Bible study; I wonder if producing a rubber hose and syringe would have the same effect.

In their 2016 book *The Distracted Mind: Ancient Brains in a High-Tech World*, researchers Adam Gazzaley and Larry D. Rosen shared what happened to a person's anxiety level by taking away his/her/their phone. They discovered from their study that a person's separation anxiety from his/her/their smartphone was in direct proportion to that person's level of use. Folks who check their phone here and there throughout the day showed no anxiety across the hour-long investigation. Moderately heavy users displayed an initial increase in anxiety that leveled off to a moderate level as the time passed. Heavy smartphone users, however, demonstrated high levels of anxiety right away, which "increased by leaps and bounds over the rest of the testing time."[18] From this and similar studies they conclude, "As a population, it would seem that we feel an increasing need to stay connected, and this 'obsession' compels us to check in with our technology often—to the detriment of our ability to stay focused on what we are doing in the moment." They continue, noting that "when we cannot check in as often as we like (or are driven to), we feel anxious."[19]

Social Media

Social media flows from the logic of Web 3.0. Through the built-in filters and algorithms behind technologies like Facebook, Twitter, Periscope, and

---

17.　Michelle Drouin, Daren H. Kaiser, and Daniel A. Miller, "Phantom Vibrations Among Undergraduates: Prevalence and Associated Psychological Characteristics," *Computers in Human Behavior* 28, no. 4 (July 2012): 1490–96; Yu-Hsuan Lin, et al., "Prevalent Hallucinations During Medical Internships: Phantom Vibration and Ringing Syndromes," *PloS One* 8, no. 6 (June 2013): 1–6; and Daniel J. Kruger and Jaikob M. Djerf, "Bad Vibrations? Cell Phone Dependency Predicts Phantom Communication Experiences," *Computers in Human Behavior* 70 (May 2017): 360–64.

18.　Adam Gazzaley and Larry D. Rosen, *The Distracted Mind: Ancient Brains in a High-Tech World* (Cambridge, MA: MIT Press, 2016), 173.

19.　Ibid., 174.

Snapchat, we build a world of discourse for ourselves. These technologies enable us to shape the world we want to live in by regulating the people we "friend" and the voices we "follow," and eventually, if we use it enough, these technologies alter who we are—individually and communally.

It may not be immediately obvious how social media is able to exert this much control over us. One of the defining features of social media is the power it seems to lend to its user to bend the technology to her will. If your social media feed looks anything like mine, you can't have missed the fact that everyone uses it differently. For some it functions as a diary. For others, it's a political or religious "stump." For others, it is a photo album. For others still, it is a billboard. How can you play a game when everyone is playing by a different set of rules? You've seen this when a parent or wily aunt starts using Facebook. Lord, have mercy.

As with all media, as McLuhan observed long ago, the technological subject often becomes the technological object; the things we use end up using us. Even if many people do not articulate this phenomenon in as many words, they know it to be true. How many of your friends (or perhaps you yourself) have given up social media for Lent? This communicates something that pastors and church leaders ought to pay attention to. As Levitin writes, "Make no mistake: E-mail, Facebook, and Twitter checking constitute a neural addiction."[20] The church has done a pretty good job providing help for those suffering from addictions of all kinds—many churches host AA and NA support group meetings. We help people who are addicted to gambling, pornography, hoarding, and even shopping. I have never heard of a church advertising a Facebook Anonymous support group.

In March 2009, the Nielsen Company reported that time spent on social media networks surpassed, for the first time in history, time spent on e-mail. In that same report, Nielsen reported that time spent on Facebook had increased 566 percent in a year, to 20.5 billion minutes. The medium of Facebook and Twitter facilitate their success. As David Kirkpatrick observes in his book *The Facebook Effect*, "Zuckerberg kept Facebook's interface simple, clean, and uncluttered. Like Google, an elementary look successfully masked an enormously complex set of technologies behind the

---

20. Levitin, *The Organized Mind*, 97.

curtain and made a wide variety of people feel welcome."[21] This aesthetic facilitates adoption.

Pastor, speaker, and social media guru Bruce Reyes-Chow argues that the church should proceed in social media with a posture of "deliberate urgency." In other words, he wants us to be open to novelty and experimentation while clinging to our "core understanding of faith and community." He concludes, "It is only by risking the openness and the usage that we will discover the new ways of being the church that can be unleashed and enabled by social media."[22] Reyes-Chow is a big proponent of social media in the church, but we don't need to search far to find a dark side to social media's desultory effects.

Social media is an *other* milieu that works alongside, or on top of, the "real world" of technology-free interactions. It is not an alternative; that would suggest that one might step out of or abandon the "real world" for a wholly digital existence. Social media is *other* precisely in its relation to norms and practices dominant within one's biological milieu. If the medium is the message, we need to think critically with our faith communities about how the messages we send to one another are being shaped by social media technologies. Here are some matters for us to consider.

1. Social media allows us to curate knowledge before we even encounter it.

Social media allows us to filter whom we follow and whom we friend. This in turn filters the information we receive from said friends. Sean Parker, the inventor of Napster and an early advisor to Mark Zuckerberg, is passionate about Facebook's role in altering the landscape of media. He likens the work of social media users to an editor at a newspaper. Facebook permits your friends to, in effect, construct for you a personalized news portal. Parker calls these "networks of people acting as decentralized relevancy filters."[23] In the

---

21.   David Kirkpatrick, *The Facebook Effect: The Inside Story of the Company That is Connecting the World* (New York: Simon and Schuster, 2011), 276.

22.   Bruce Reyes-Chow, *The Definitive-ish Guide to Using Social Media in the Church* (Shook Foil Books, 2012), Kindle edition.

23.   Kirkpatrick, *The Facebook Effect*, 296.

months leading up to and following the 2016 US presidential election, the same "relevancy filters" that helped us tap into conversations about Appalachian Trail thru-hiking or cake baking or Lord of the Rings user-groups also facilitated our national polarization and estrangement from those "others" who failed to think and communicate from "our" political perspective.

In June 2017, Zuckerberg changed Facebook's mission statement: "To give people the power to *build community* and *bring the world closer together*." This marks the first time the company has revised its mission since its founding. Facebook's previous mission statement had been "to give people the *power to share* and *make the world more open and connected*." Note the shifts. The power to share is not the same as community building. Openness and connectedness are not equivalent to relational proximity.

In an interview with CNN Tech's Laurie Segall, Facebook's CEO reflected on the role of social media in fostering discord and disinformation: aka "fake news." Segall shared a recent report from the Pew Research Center, reporting that roughly nine-in-ten US adults (93 percent) get their news online, and 47 percent of those users report that Facebook provides *all* or *most* of the news they receive.[24] In light of these statistics, Zuckerberg pledged that Facebook would begin using artificial intelligence technologies to recommend groups to its users that foster civil discourse directed to the betterment of society. The company is also adding tools to help group leaders screen new members, block people, schedule posts, and link groups together. In other words, "sharing" and "connecting" are no longer ends in themselves. Rather, Zuckerberg and his team are working to facilitate *community*.

2. Social media allows us to curate selfhood.

In his book *Curation Nation*, Steven Rosenbaum writes, "In a manner of speaking, you are what you tweet. The trend of wearing Nike logos and other symbols of your tribe on your clothing has now entered the digital realm."[25] In

---

24. "Digital News Fact Sheet," Pew Research Center, August 7, 2017, http://www.jour nalism.org/fact-sheet/digital-news/. See also Amy Mitchell et al., "The Role of News on Facebook," Pew Research Center, October 24, 2014, http://www.journalism.org/2013/10/24/the -role-of-news-on-facebook/.

25. Steven Rosenbaum, *Curation Nation: How to Win in a World Where Consumers are Creators* (New York: McGraw-Hill, 2011), 205.

other words, when we use social media we are painting a picture of ourselves for all the world (or at least our friends/followers) to see. To illustrate, I have a friend who is the "mayor" of Pizzeria Lola in Edina, Minnesota, through Foursquare, a social media app that allows users to "check in" at specific locations. On the one hand, Foursquare is a commercial tool, crowd-sourcing user experiences. On the other hand, Foursquare curates a person's selfhood to other users. Sure, my friend patronized his favorite local pizza joint before he created a Foursquare account; but the technology he carries in his pocket has allowed him to identify himself to others, to proclaim that he is the kind of person who frequents Pizzeria Lola (rather than Pizza Hut or Dominoes).

Another ubiquitous feature of social media along these lines is the selfie. In a project called *Selficity*, computer scientist and media expert Lev Manovich and his team ran computer analysis on over 650,000 Instagram selfies.[26] The selfie is not only a photographic image that we recognize as a self-portrait and which bears a formal resemblance to numerous canonical photographic self-portraits from the nineteenth and twentieth centuries. A selfie is a product of a networked camera. The essential attributes of a selfie include its instantaneous distribution via Instagram or similar social networks as well as the related metadata (generated automatically such as geo-tags, added by the user such as hashtags, or appearing subsequently such as the comments, "likes," and re-sharing by other users). From this study, Manovich observed that the very *raison d'être* of a selfie is to be shared in social media; it is not made for the maker's own personal consumption and contemplation. By sharing their selfies, Instagram users construct their identities and simultaneously profess their belonging to certain communities.

3. Social media allows us to curate relationships while shaping our relationality.

Our relationships can be life-giving, to be sure. But Turkle reminds that they are also "messy and demanding." In her most recent book, *Reclaiming Conversation*, she writes, "We have learned the habit of cleaning them [relationships] up with technology. And the move from conversation to connection is

---

26.   Lev Manovich and Alise Tifentale, "Selfiecity: Exploring Photography and Self-Fashioning in Social Media," in *Postdigital Aesthetics: Art, Computation and Design*, David M. Berry and Michael Dieter, eds. (New York: Palgrave Macmillan, 2015), 109–22.

part of this."[27] She goes on to document the desultory effects of social media to block empathic connections and, ironically, *disconnect* us from those around us.

This disconnect manifests both socially and theologically. Because I am able to follow particular (kinds of) people on Twitter and Instagram, and because I can "friend" or "defriend" people on Facebook, I hold the power to draw close or pull away from other people. Just because this takes place on a digital rather than material plane does not make it any more impactful for my relationality. Particularly leading up to the 2016 presidential election, many used their social media feeds to rain hellfire upon their political opponents. We created silos in the Cloud, where we comforted ourselves with voices that sounded much like our own. Writing for *Rolling Stone*, after the election ended Matt Taibbi ushered a critique against those on the political left for refusing to listen to what was taking place within the rhetoric of our more politically conservative friends and family members. "The People [who elected Trump] didn't speak our language, true. But that also meant we didn't speak theirs."[28] Social media made it easy for many of us to curate our relationality, which in turn shaped our relationships.

From a theological frame, the relational significance of social media is also troubling. Consider the amount of editing or Photoshopping that we do to the things we post—both pictures and texts. What type of relationship/community are we inviting people into? One that is highlighted and as close to perfect as we can make it? How might worship turn this on its head? Here I'm thinking about the Eucharist, about the messy brokenness at the center of our faith. If not for pragmatic reasons, it ought to trouble us theologically to proclaim the beauty that comes from that brokenness when we exert so much effort to hide these aspects of ourselves from public view.

Search Technologies

Lastly, let's talk about search technologies. Researcher Nicholas Carr writes about the "cybernetic blurring of mind and machine" marked by the

---

27. Turkle, *Reclaiming Conversation*, 21.

28. Matt Taibbi, "President Trump: How America Got It So Wrong," *Rolling Stone*, http://www.rollingstone.com/politics/features/president-trump-how-america-got-it-so -wrong-w449783.

digital age. He notes that while this union "may allow us to carry out certain cognitive tasks far more efficiently, it poses a threat to our integrity as human beings. Even as the larger system into which our minds so readily meld is lending us its powers, it is also imposing on us its limitations. . . . we program our computers and thereafter they program us."[29]

This has huge implications for preaching, worship, and spiritual formation. When we spend the bulk of our lives in an ecosystem of content discovery, we lose patience for modes of communication that force us to dwell with uncertainty or mystery. We have a growing expectation as a nation that information ought to manifest itself in .56 seconds, or however long it takes Google to deliver our content. These expectations, with their immediate gratification, are having huge impacts on university and seminary education, and also religious education.

Returning to McLuhan: "Our conventional response to all media, namely that it is how they are used that counts, is the stance of the technological idiot. For the 'content' of a medium is like a juicy piece of meat carried by the burglar to distract the watchdog of the mind."[30] What this means for our relationship to search technologies is that using them without recognizing how they are shaping our cognitive processes marks us as "technological idiots."

Every medium—technological or otherwise—develops some cognitive skills at the expense of others. Our growing use of the Internet has expanded our capacity for visual-spatial understanding. We can, for example, rotate objects in our minds better than we used to be able to. But, as Carr observes, our "new strengths in visual-spatial intelligence" go hand in hand with a weakening of our capacities for the kind of "deep processing" that underpins "mindful knowledge acquisition, inductive analysis, critical thinking, imagination, and reflection." Carr continues, "What the Net seems to be doing is chipping away my capacity for concentration and contemplation. Whether I'm online or not, my mind now expects to take in information the way the Net distributes it: in a swiftly moving stream of particles. Once I was a scuba diver in the sea of words. Now I zip along the surface like a guy on a Jet Ski."[31]

---

29. Carr, *The Shallows*, 214.

30. McLuhan, "The Medium is the Message," 18.

31. Carr, *The Shallows*, 7.

What is more, our immediate access to information through search engines like Google or Bing has weakened our capacity to store long-term memories and access deeply integrated understandings. Carr writes,

> As the time we spend scanning Web pages crowds out the time we spend reading books, as the time we spend engaging bite-sized text messages crowds out the time we spend composing sentences and paragraphs, as the time we spend hopping across links crowds out the time we devote to quiet reflection and contemplation, the circuits that support those old intellectual functions and pursuits weaken and begin to break apart. The brain recycles the disused neurons and synapses for other, more pressing work. We gain new skills and perspectives but lose old ones.[32]

In other words, the algorithms that enable us to search for and locate information in fractions of a second are also restructuring our brains' ability to perform other tasks—like thinking. This should give pastors and church leaders pause, at least.

Moving Forward: Liturgical Possibilities

The information I have curated above offers several possibilities for conceiving worship in our contemporary ecclesial contexts.

1. Imagine a liturgy that helps people see how digital technologies enable us to transcend our cultural differences.

Digital technologies level the political playing field—to an extent. In their book *Occupy Religion*, Joerg Rieger and Kwok Pui-lan offer us a helpful analytic for interrogating the impact of digital technologies on our relationships. They employ the term *multitude* in their book to reflect on unity and difference. This term, made prominent by political scientists and philosophers Michael Hardt and Antonio Negri, has deep roots in our theological traditions.

Several decades ago, exponents of Korean Minjung theology noted the prominence of the notion of the multitude (this is how the term *minjung* can be translated into English) in the Bible. In the Gospels, the so-called *ochlos* (the Greek term for the masses or the common people) does not describe only

---

32. Ibid., 120.

the ones who are the recipients of Jesus's transformative ministry; the ochlos also describes the participants in it and the agents of change. In addition, Latin American liberation theologians have highlighted the importance of the Greek term *laos* in the biblical traditions, which is also used to designate the common people rather than the elites.

Rieger and Pui-lan help us think more critically about the democratizing potential of the Internet. There is a distinct difference, they suggest, between the Greek notions of democracy and laocracy/ochlocracy. Democracy describes the rule of the *demos*, which is constituted by the elite citizens of a city-state. Lower-class citizens, women, and slaves are not part of this rule. Laocracy and ochlocracy, on the other hand, describe the rule of the common people, including the proverbial "least of these" of whom Jesus frequently speaks.

These common people include all those who have been and are being marginalized on the basis of their gender, sexuality, race, ethnicity, ability, and class. In the ministry of Jesus, which is informed by the ministries of Moses, Miriam, Hannah, and the prophets, the common people are organized and become agents. God values their diverse contributions to life. In the world of laocracy and ochlocracy, there are different ways of being productive in the community, and all of them are acknowledged and needed. As Hardt and Negri remind us, the multitude is not the uniform entity of what has often been called "the people" in various nationalisms or fascisms. Neither is the multitude the undifferentiated mass or the mob.

What brings the various liberation movements together, therefore, is not uniformity or a request to surrender difference. What brings us together is something Rieger and Pui-lan term "deep solidarity."[33] This is the recognition that we are all in the same boat under the conditions of global capitalism. This insight is related to the topic of class, which has consistently been pushed underground in the United States, but which has reemerged in the context of the Occupy Wall Street movement and more recently in the #BlackLivesMatter movement.

The now-familiar notion of the 99 percent versus the 1 percent is a reminder that the majority of people are benefitting less and less from the neo-

---

33. See Joerg Rieger and Kwok Pui-lan, *Occupy Religion: Theology of the Multitude* (Lanham, MD: Rowan and Littlefield, 2012).

liberal market economy. This includes members of the middle class—and even more middle-class African Americans—as they have seen their retirement accounts dwindle, their job security take ever-more severe hits, their benefits erode, and their political power fade.

Furthermore, the aspects of gender, sexuality, race, ability, and ethnicity are closely linked to class, as they all increase the disadvantages of people in the neoliberal market economy, thus boosting the reality of deep solidarity. Deep solidarity ties together members of the 99 percent across the lines of gender, sexuality, race, and ethnicity, and it thrives on difference—as they can now work together and make use of their various opportunities and gifts.

Deep solidarity differs from conventional ideas of solidarity that were often based on the idea that those who are privileged place themselves on the side of those without privilege. While it is still possible for members of the 1 percent to place themselves on the side of the 99 percent, the majority of us are now part of the 99 percent, and thus belong to classes that have something to gain from liberation.

To service this, Rieger and Pui-Lan argue that we need a "Church of the Multitude," which is a People of God that assembles "not just for Sunday morning worship services but also to discuss common affairs of the community and to take faithful action for justice."[34] It is a community of human togetherness, mutuality, and openness. It is a community of radical egalitarianism and democracy, a community that teaches polydoxy, "rooted in the encounter of plurality of the divine and the cosmos all around us."[35] This is a beautiful vision, one that might help the church—the segregated church, the divided-by-denomination church—enter into solidarity with those who are not sharing pews with us. Social media may help us here.

2. Imagine a liturgy that creates space for participants to reflect on social media and social isolation and inequity.

In a now famous 2006 study, researchers found that the number of Americans who perceive that they have no one with whom to discuss important matters tripled between 1985 to 2004. This study lent sociological

---

34. Ibid., 117.

35. Ibid., 129.

rigor to Robert Putnam's incisive investigation into the social disparities that technology can exacerbate. Even as digital technologies increase access to knowledge, in his 2015 book *Our Kids: The American Dream in Crisis*, Robert Putnam shows how access and use of these systems are actually widening the gap between poor and wealthy children. He writes, "Kids from more educated homes learn more sophisticated digital-literacy skills—knowing how to search for information on the Internet and how to evaluate it—and have more social support in deploying those skills. Such children are using the Internet in ways that will help them reap the rewards of an increasingly digital economy and society." Putnam continues with this disturbing observation. "Even though lower-class kids are coming to have virtually equal physical access to the Internet, they lack the digital savvy to exploit that access in ways that enhance their opportunities."[36] How might this discomfort empower congregants and parishioners to broaden the scope of their digital influence?

Or consider this liturgical possibility. Text messages magically appear on the screen of our phones and demand immediate attention from us. Add to that the social expectation that an unanswered text feels insulting to the sender, and we've got a recipe for addiction. As I shared above, the simple act of receiving a text activates our novelty centers in our brains. We respond and feel rewarded for having completed a task (even though that task was entirely unknown to us fifteen seconds earlier). Each of those delivers a shot of dopamine to our limbic systems, which causes them to cry out, "More! More! Give me more!"

I'm imagining a liturgical experience that forces us to sit with these sensations. Perhaps we could arrange ourselves into pairs or small groups and, setting our phones on vibrate, we could experience how the giving and receiving of text messages breaks our face-to-face interactions. I might situate such an encounter within a Taizé context. What better way to illustrate the ruptures in our community than to apply digital nails to our liturgical chalkboards?

3. Imagine a liturgy that helps congregants and parishioners to reflect on their capacities for empathy in light of Jesus's ministry.

One of the negative effects of digital technologies is their capacity to numb us to the pain of others. Even as we now possess great facility to access

36. Robert Putnam, *Our Kids: The American Dream in Crisis* (New York: Simon and Schuster, 2015), 212.

the pain of others, thanks to the ubiquity of smartphones and easy means of sharing lived experiences with others, the inundation of human suffering can become paralyzing for some. What happens when we witness a proliferation of violent crimes against black/brown people and/or gender non-conforming/ trans people? On the one hand, our digital technologies allow us to know about such horrendous occurrences and to act. On the other hand, it becomes far too easy for us to post an angry- or sad-face emoji and move on to the next news article. If the only place we have to encounter the other, to be in solidarity with the other, is in the online "third space," how much does that encounter fill us with empathy that drives us to act?

I could imagine a liturgy curated to force congregants and parishioners to abide at the nexus of human suffering and material response. Consider how your congregation or parish might respond if you presented two screens in the worship space. On one screen, you could play movie clips from a variety of films that depict Jesus responding to the real-world pains and material needs of those marginalized by his society. On the second screen, you could loop the names and faces of African-American men who have been murdered by police in recent years. How would your church respond? How might this solicit empathy and perhaps action?

Conclusion: The Power (to) Filter

We must pay careful attention to the power of digital technologies to render us passive while at the same time structuring our active engagement. McLuhan writes that in using technology, humanity enters a process of "perpetual modification." Technologies modify us, but we modify technologies through how we chose to use said technologies. It is this active process that I wish to underscore. Again, quoting McLuhan, "Our need today is, culturally, the same as the scientists who seeks to become aware of the bias of the instruments of research in order to correct that bias."[37] We need to lead our churches in thinking critically about our digital technologies.

The most significant point to all of this, from my perspective, is to curate spaces to help people consider the human and spiritual costs of digital

---

37. McLuhan, *The Gutenberg Galaxy*, 36.

technologies. As Turkle reminds us, "This isn't a game in which we can cross our fingers and hope that the good will outweigh the bad. We want to take the good and also make the changes necessary so that we don't pay a price that no technology is worth."[38] But what alarms me even more is the effect that digital technologies have on our relationships. This interpersonal dynamic that digital technologies simultaneously nurture and frustrate is something we must consider as we curate spaces in church for meaningful and even transformative connections.

In his book *The Filter Bubble*, Eli Pariser argues that one of the best ways to understand how filters shape our individual experiences is to think in terms of our "information diet." Here, Pariser draws upon the work of sociologist danah boyd, who reminds us that our bodies are genetically designed to consume fat and sugars because they're rare in nature. "In the same way," boyd explains, "we're biologically programmed to be attentive to things that stimulate: content that is gross, violent, or sexual and that gossip which is humiliating, embarrassing, or offensive. If we're not careful, we're going to develop the psychological equivalent of obesity. We'll find ourselves consuming content that is least beneficial for ourselves or society as a whole."[39] By curating worship experiences that force congregants and parishioners to assess and reflect critically on their "information diets," we will begin to move them toward spiritual and relational health.

---

38. Turkle, *Reclaiming Conversation*, 12.

39. Eli Pariser, *The Filter Bubble: How the New Personalized Web is Changing What We Read and How We Think* (New York: Penguin Books, 2011), 13–14.

Life Imitates Art

*In order to entertain certain ideas, we may be obliged
to abandon others upon which we have come to depend.*

—*Harald Szeemann*[1]

To what, then, are we called? If we are called out (*ek-klesia*) to serve a community that is also being called out of lethargy, apathy, and selfishness by God in the name of Jesus Christ, then this summons ought to condition our work as pastors and church leaders. I've argued throughout this book that a *curatorial* imagination supports our liturgical efforts in response to God's calling of and upon the church. Curation is by no means the *only* way toward ecclesial faithfulness, but its focus upon *engagement, conservation*, and *transformation* structure *a* way that I believe is helpful for the work of Christian ministry.

Curating church is at once nominative and accusative—indeed, it celebrates the undecidability at work within these dual trajectories of demarcation. In its nominative or subject sense, I hope we will embrace curation as a modifier that names who we are. By leaning into our identity as a church that is defined at its core by the calling to provide *care* and *cure* to the world God loves, we receive a framework for assessing our way of being and belonging in the world by embracing our uniqueness as those called of God. Who are we? *We are a curating church.*

---

1. Harald Szeemann, *Live in Your Head: When Attitudes Become Form—Works, Concepts, Processes, Situations, Information* (London: Institute of Contemporary Art, 1969).

Curating church also places us in the accusative case. By this I mean that the church is an object of curation—a people who are being engaged, conserved, and transformed at the nexus of culture and calling. It is here that our way of behaving in the world is sharpened by a curatorial imagination. This is the reason that the work of artistic curators guided our thinking in Gallery II. The curatorial disposition and its concomitant tasks provide clarity and insight that can inform our work as pastors and church leaders. What are we to do? *We ought to be curating church.*

I leave you with several additional theoretical and practical strategies for conceiving worship in these polarizing times.

1. Curating church calls for historical bricolage.

In the world of fine arts, *bricolage* denotes the construction or creation of a work from a diverse—even disparate—range of things that happen to be available, or a work created by such a process. The word has French roots and is derived from references to a *bricoleur*, a repairmen or jack-of-all-trades adept at the art of 'making do' with what's on hand. Bricolage helps us relate to our heritage in a particular way. It teaches us to recognize the rifts and worn places in our history. To be sure, bricolage can, as Vincent Miller astutely notes in his book *Consuming Religion*, lead to a passive alienation between the faithful turned passive consumers; however, bricolage that works with "complex building blocks," that is, cultural objects tethered to their symbolic and historical significance, can foster a more robust faith that defies the status quo and subverts commodified Christianity.[2]

The irony here is that even the most rigid ecclesial historicism is unwittingly bricolage. As one philosopher puts it, "If one calls *bricolage* the necessity of borrowing one's concept from the text of a heritage which is more or less coherent or ruined, it must be said that every discourse is *bricoleur*."[3] Texts arise out of a necessary intertextuality and an unmooring that simultaneously structures a text's foundation and the trembling of that very foundation.

---

2. Vincent J. Miller, *Consuming Religion: Christian Faith and Practice in a Consumer Culture* (New York: Bloomsbury Academic, 2003), 162–63.

3. Jacques Derrida, "Structure, Sign, and Play in the Discourse of the Human Sciences," in *Writing and Difference*, trans. Alan Bass (Chicago: University of Chicago Press, 1978), 285.

Getting very practical, I'm urging us to think of church and our task as ministers and church leaders as akin to the work of MacGyver or the A-Team, solving problems by making use of that which is *ready-to-hand*.[4] By way of illustration, we might ask how the Barmen Declaration speaks to our current political context or how your church's founding documents can be made to sing with the works of Augustine, Eckhart, or Teresa of Avila. Don't be afraid to "putter about," to make something new from something old, to make a mess.

2. Curating church calls for theological mashup.

For too long, church has functioned according to a *colonial* epistemology. By this I mean that we establish our sense of place and prominence by *othering*, by arresting political power from those others whom we have created to establish our own prominence. We don our denominational pith helmets and claim this land for Wesley, Luther, or Calvin. Some traditions even have flags.

The antidote to denominational imperialism is theological mashup. *Mashup* refers to a form of production that overtly draws upon previously published material to produce something new. Mashup takes many forms across genres. Think of films like *Abraham Lincoln: Vampire Hunter* or novels such as *Pride and Prejudice and Zombies*, which combines Austen's classic with elements of modern zombie fiction. Or the mashups produced by hip-hop artists, sampling riffs, beats, or lyrics from earlier songs. Consider *The Grey Album*, a mashup album by Danger Mouse, released in 2004. It mixes an a cappella version of rapper Jay-Z's *The Black Album* with samples from The Beatles' LP commonly known as *The White Album*.

A great resource here is found in the work of homiletician John McClure. In his book *Mashup Religion*, McClure contends that lived religion resembles a mashup: a song consisting entirely of parts of other songs, and thus his project is to help his readers "learn to invent messages that engage the textuality of cultural life more deeply."[5] Chapters two and three are particularly

---

4. "Ready-to-hand" was a neologism emphasized by twentieth century German philosopher Martin Heidegger to refer to our involvement with things in an ordinary way, without theorizing. In other words, *ready-to-hand* is our reach for what is primordial, not primitive, but rather things close to us.

5. John S. McClure, *Mashup Religion: Pop Music and Theological Invention* (Waco, TX: Baylor University Press, 2011), 10–11.

helpful. Chapter two introduces the reader to the complex world of multi-track composition, whereby music producers work with recording engineers to mix the song's rhythm, melody, backing, and fill-tracks to give songs their distinctive sound. By extension, McClure invites us to think of sermons as multilayered—consisting of scripture, culture, theology, and message tracks. Sampling, remixing, and mashup occupy chapter three. Here McClure encourages his readers to embrace the logic of textuality and file-sharing, recognizing that there is no original or pure doctrine to be communicated. We need not strain to detect the overlaps between musical mashup and artistic curation, each facilitating the important work of engagement, conservation and transformation.

3. Curating church calls for ideological deconstruction.

Our contemporary ecclesial landscapes call for more than a generic covering of one's proverbial bases so as not to offend the-powers-that-may-or-may-not-be. Instead, it calls for an interrogation of the underlying assumptions that structure our current beliefs and practices.

An excellent example of ideological deconstruction is found in *Justice beyond "Just Us": Dilemmas of Time, Place, and Difference in American Politics* by Gregory W. Streich. Streich points to a tension at work in the slogan "justice for all" that is originary for American democracy. He observes that this ideal co-exists with beliefs and practices that defend justice for members of particular in-groups ("us") while remaining somewhat or altogether indifferent or ignorant about justice for non-members ("them"). This "principles-practices gap," though attenuated by legislation and political action in recent years, still pervades the popular imagination—especially the popular white imagination. Accordingly, Streich examines the fallout produced by notions of justice that ignore time, geographic place, and sociodemographic difference. He argues for diachronic as well as synchronic assessments of "us," arguing that while we cannot undo injustices committed in the past, we can strive to ensure that those legacies of injustice do not adversely affect people today and in the future. And his attention to place sharpens our attention to special relations and the degree to which (if any) they shape our conceptions of justice and community.[6] When we understand ourselves as interconnected with all the "thems," and that *they* necessarily constitute our sense of "we," we can move toward a more expansive understand of justice beyond "just us."

Curating church exposes the church to its own innate deconstruction: reformed and always reforming (Calvin); simultaneously saints and sinners (Luther); God as mystery (orthodox); faith seeking understanding (Anselm); God of the Oppressed (Cone); God as radically other (Barth). The goal is to keep the theological and liturgical waters churning. That's why curation presents much for pastors and church leaders to consider. Curation's orientation toward engagement, conservation, and transformation present us with new ways of thinking about worship.

Conclusion

"Church" (*ekklesia* in Greek) is the collective name for those called out into fellowship for a particular purpose. Such a calling is not a calling to abandon one's culture; rather, we are called to be salt and light *in the midst* of culture. God's centripetal calling is at once a centrifugal sending. We have lost this—historically through the unholy alliance between church and state following Constantine's conversion, and we may see this being played out materially as the North American church genuflects to neoliberal economic practices that constitute globalization.

I don't need to tell you that engaging topics such as politics, race, and technology carry inherent risks. Change and growth can be difficult—scary even. Nevertheless, changing circumstances in the lives of individuals and the life of a community make it inevitable that changes should occur in worship. The mind is equipped to integrate change into the pattern of experience. At the same time, tradition serves our spiritual development by establishing a pattern into which changes may arise. Here is where the work of conservation becomes a crucial link between engagement and transformation.

Tradition carries the continuity of memory, which in turn recalls experiences on which we can build for our present well-being. Tradition allows us to participate in the corporate memory of our faith, which contributes a sense of

6. Gregory W. Streich, *Justice beyond "Just Us": Dilemmas of Time, Place, and Difference in American Politics* (New York: Routledge, 2016), 57–76, 77–98.

continuity. The emphasis on antiquity and much of the reform of the liturgy is an attempt to sync with a corporate memory.

Tradition should be seen as *protected* rather than *restricted*. Tradition protects the memory of the community, which is then applied to the new situations that we face in the present. A protected tradition has to be reshaped in response to the new circumstances without being abandoned. The memory will add new experiences as long as it retains links to previous experiences. When tradition is abandoned, the memory is left to fate and cannot assist in preparing the mind for new situations. When tradition becomes restricted, it isolates the memory of the past so that it cannot serve the present. Tradition is best conserved when it is amended before each new situation, and is not allowed to become fixed and fossilized. This is how the life of the church sustained by worship can learn to imitate art as we curate liturgical experiences in community.